ELVIS
THE SECRET FILES

ELVIS
THE SECRET FILES

JOHN PARKER

Anaya Publishers Limited
LONDON

First published in Great Britain in 1993 by
Anaya Publishers Limited
Strode House
3rd Floor
44–50 Osnaburgh Street
London NW1 3ND

The author and publishers would like to thank the following for their kind help with photographs:
The Elvis Presley Fan Club, P.O. Box 4, Leicester, and Elvisly Yours Ltd, P.O. Box 315,
London, NW10.

British Library Cataloguing in Publication Data
Parker, John 1938–
Elvis: Secret Files
I. Title
781.66092

ISBN 1-85470-039-1

Typeset in Monophoto Bembo
by Servis Filmsetting Ltd, Manchester
Printed and bound in Great Britain
by Butler & Tanner Ltd
Frome and London

Contents

Author's Sources

From time to time over the past decade, brief extracts from files and documents relating to Elvis Presley, locked away in various US government archives, have surfaced and their contents have been used to provide a backdrop of intrigue and continuing speculation concerning his death. This work is based largely upon an extensive search among those archives and every major item of quoted material herein is derived from original research, with sources that have provided a mass of detail – published here for the first time. A substantial amount of research centred around studies at the FBI headquarters, where I examined over 3000 pages of documents and reports. I have had issued to me under the Freedom of Information Act (FOI) 1031 pages of documents from the office and confidential files of J. Edgar Hoover, plus photocopies of 663 pages from the FBI general file on Elvis A. Presley and 196 pages from the FBI general file on John Lennon. To those, I added the complete, unedited text of letters and memos under the heading 'Presley, E.A.' from the papers of President Richard Nixon in the US national archives, in Washington.

The bulk of interviews with members of Elvis's personal entourage, most of whom have remained inaccessible to the media and television over the years, comes from a special source. The interviews were tape-recorded by Mr E.L. (Larry) Hutchinson, chief investigator to the district attorney-general for Memphis in 1980, when he led the investigation into the alleged over-prescribing of drugs to Elvis, in advance of a prosecution being brought against Elvis's physician, Dr George C. Nichopoulos. Those interviews were carried out with the weight of legal authority; each was asked to state that what they had said represented a true recollection.

In the event, few of those interviewed were called to give evidence at the subsequent trial, since it related to nine other patients, as well as Elvis himself, and thus the tapes made by Hutchinson were locked away in the archives of the attorney-general's office in Memphis. Some had never been heard since they were recorded. They remain unavailable for public scrutiny to anyone who resides outside the state of Tennessee. However, Larry Hutchinson, now retired and working as a court official, agreed to copy the tapes on my behalf and the district attorney-general's office told me it had no power to prevent Hutchinson from handing them to me for inclusion in this work. Those members of the entourage and others associated with Elvis Presley whom I have quoted from these tape recordings are as follows:

Colonel Tom Parker, who became Elvis's manager and promoter in the autumn of 1955, and continued to draw his commission even after Elvis died.

Joe Esposito, the most influential member of the Presley entourage. He met Elvis while they were serving together in the army, and was invited back to Memphis to become his foreman, road manager and closest friend. He has consistently refused to give any interviews regarding his association with Elvis.

Charlie Hodge, singer and guitarist, was another of Elvis's army buddies who remained by his side for the rest of his life. He was with Elvis the morning he died.

Sonny West, who was a schoolfriend and became his first bodyguard, joined by his cousin, Red West. When assassination threats on Elvis piled up, they became known for their heavy-handed methods. They co-wrote the book *Elvis: What Happened?* after he fired them following a six-million-dollar action for damages.

Jerry Schilling, another earlier associate of Elvis in post-army Memphis, joined Elvis for 'the movie years' in Hollywood. He was a personal aide who found it difficult to come to terms with Elvis's changing temperament and left twice. He was with Elvis on his famous visit to see President Nixon and later joined the management team in charge of Elvis's estate.

Linda Thompson, a Memphis beauty queen who became his lover in 1972, after Priscilla left, and stayed for four and a half years. She gives a frank and honest account of her life at Graceland.

Sam Thompson, Linda's brother, a former deputy sheriff who joined Elvis as a bodyguard after he had fired Red and Sonny West. Sam, today a respected member of the judiciary who sits as a judge in Memphis, worked alongside Elvis for the last eighteen months of his life; he was there, close at hand, on the night before Elvis's death.

James Caughley, the personal valet and aide for four years, who gave an often hair-raising account of his years in Elvis's employ.

John O'Grady, former sergeant with the Los Angeles police department, in charge of a drug-busting unit and an expert on drug enforcement; he became a friend to Elvis in 1969 and remained close until his death.

Alicia Kirwin, Elvis's secret girlfriend, who was visiting him at Graceland in the last months of his life when he was supposed to be engaged to marry Ginger Alden. She was a local girl, a bank teller, and he showed her the bright lights with tragic consequences.

★   ★   ★   ★   ★

These interviews were, in some cases, followed up with conversations in 1992. I have also relied upon extracts from hundreds of pages of legal documentation including: depositions and proceedings of the supreme court of Tennessee, ruling Tenn. 643, SW 2d 105; proceedings reports to the Memphis court of probate; depositions and proceedings from the criminal court, state of Tennessee versus George C. Nichopoulos; proceedings of the Tennessee board of medical examiners versus George C. Nichopoulos; the supreme court of California, statements of claim and counter-claim in Elvis A. Presley (deceased) versus Colonel Tom Parker; proceedings of the US district court, Memphis, Tennessee, concerning Elvis A. Presley, victim, fraud by wire; proceedings US district court, Louisville, Kentucky, concerning charges of racketeering and fraud; US district court, southern district of New York, proceedings indictments and proceedings of racketeering against numerous defendants, under reference 78 Cr.00688, 78 Cr.0809, 78 Cr.0610 and 78 Cr.0634 (Sept 28, 1978).

Additional sources for Hollywood-related interviews and previously unpublished statements by Elvis's first movie producer, Hal Wallis, I obtained from the DeGolyer Institute of American Studies at the Southern Methodist University, Dallas, Texas; based upon interviews made for the university oral history collection by its director, Professor Ronald Davis, and from the special collections department of the Doheny Facility at the University of Southern California, Los Angeles.

That, then, is the basis of the research. It forms a strange and disturbing story in which Elvis Presley will be seen as the ultimate victim who was prey to all comers, and who suffered at the sword wielded by many hands, not least of which was his own . . .

Prologue

Theories concerning the death of Elvis Presley have covered pretty well all of the options – natural causes, accidental drug overdose, suicide, and even the premise that he did not die at all, that his death was faked so that he could be spirited away into an FBI (Federal Bureau of Investigation) witness-protection programme to protect him from the Mafia. To these possibilities has been added another by his personal physician for nine years, Dr George C. Nichopoulos ('Dr Nick' to those who know him), who was at the death scene and attended the autopsy.

Elvis was murdered.

The very idea might easily be discarded as one more crackpot notion. After all, the jokes about Elvis being alive have become a cottage industry. In America, Johnny Carson lived off Elvis stories for years. Outlandish sightings have been reported from Niagara to Nairobi, and authors who claim to have had conversations with him, and say that he will reappear in 1993, hardly inspired serious study.

And yet, beneath the mirth, there was an underlying truth to it all. Jokes about him hiding from the Mafia were based upon rumours of documents suggesting he could have been the target for a hired killer. The rumours are correct in one respect. Elvis Presley was involved with Mafioso, and on the very day of his death, a federal grand jury was to have been convened in Memphis to consider indicting seven men for fraud. Elvis and his father were key witnesses in the case.

In the hours and days immediately after his son's death, Vernon Presley repeatedly posed the question, 'Could Elvis have been the victim of foul play?' The suggestion was never pursued in any official enquiry in Memphis. An autopsy report presented by Dr Jerry T.

Francisco, the county medical examiner and the same man who led the medical examination of Dr Martin Luther King following his assassination, announced to the world that Elvis Aaron Presley died of natural causes. Police made no real attempt at an enquiry into his death – even after it was revealed the body contained traces of at least eleven different prescription drugs – and the forty-four-page autopsy report was locked away in the vaults of the Memphis archives, never to be seen again.

So what possible reason could Vernon have had at that time that would have prompted him to enquire of those around the Presley home on the day of his death: had they seen anything unusual, people they did not recognise, entering the house?

The truth of the matter was that Vernon had very good reason to be suspicious and cautious. He was party to secret information not available to even the closest members of the Presley entourage: he and Elvis had unwittingly and innocently fallen into the centre of a major international investigation being conducted by scores of FBI agents worldwide. It was one of the largest criminal enquiries conducted by the bureau in the Seventies, involving a long and difficult undercover operation to discover the source of billions of dollars in worthless securities which were flooding the financial markets – first in America and then in major cities around the globe.

Banks in a dozen countries fell victim. The regulating fiscal authorities of America, the Bank of England, and authorities throughout Europe and the Far East were brought in to help. The investigation, reports of which run to a small mountain of paper-work, was littered with known figures in the world of organised crime, financial fraudsters and Mafia people. There was talk of proceeds being diverted to finance gambling operations in the Netherlands Antilles (in the Caribbean) and of connections with a drugs cartel linked to a high-profile Mafia family.

Ultimately, many people would be arrested across the United States and those prosecuted eventually faced jail sentences of up to twenty years. Back in Memphis, Elvis Presley was one of the victims of the fraud; in net terms he was out of pocket by almost a million dollars. The case involving him was the first in the whole FBI investigation – codenamed Operation Fountain Pen – to be brought to court. Document number ME-16994, for example, is a single sheet memo, buried in the middle of a mass of other FBI reports and documentation.

It reads as follows:

Concerning ELVIS A. PRESLEY, Victim: On August 1, 1977, Assistant US Attorney Glen Garland Reid, Jr, Memphis, Tennessee was contacted [by the FBI] relative to the prosecutive action in this case. He advised that he is prepared to present the facts to a Federal Grand Jury convening in Memphis on or about August 15, 1977.

Perhaps, naturally enough, when his son was found dead on 16 August, Vernon Presley began looking for clues that indicated foul play. The sequence of events was curious and to this day, never satisfactorily explained . . .

     ★   ★   ★   ★   ★

Just before two-thirty p.m., on the afternoon of 16 August 1977, an emergency alarm broke the routine calm of Memphis fire unit number twenty-nine, located at 2147 Elvis Presley Boulevard, and sent two paramedics, Charlie Crosby and Ulysses S. Jones, Jr, diving for their ambulance. With lights flashing and siren screaming, they swung out on to the highway and raced south, weaving in and out of the fairly heavy traffic. The address on their operations pad was familiar to them, and known to pretty well every other living soul in that city. It was where the image and aura of the world's most famous entertainer pervaded – the high and mighty son, the man who had for two decades lived his eccentric life behind the high walls surrounding the colonial mansion, Graceland, one and a half miles from the station, at 3764 Elvis Presley Boulevard. They had no idea then who they were to pick up. The message simply said that someone at the house was in difficulty, having trouble in breathing.

Within three minutes of leaving the station, the ambulance reached the famous music gates, so-called because of the motifs of the decorated ironwork, swerved to avoid the small contingent of ever-present 'gate persons', the fans who gathered daily in the hope of catching a glimpse of the star. On into the winding drive they went, grazing the metal as they raced by on their way to the huge and impressive canopied entrance, supported by four white columns.

They moved quickly inside, carrying their stretcher through the garishly decorated hall and up the stairs, padding along the colourful thick-pile carpet of the bedroom corridor to the suite of rooms of the master of the house. Inside the bedroom, with windows darkened like a casino hall to defeat the sun's attempts to distinguish night from day, they discovered a scene of chaos and drama.

The room was untidy, with clothes and papers strewn about. The eyes of the two men settled momentarily on objects and items, one after the other, that distractingly punctuated their rapid arrival into the mêlée – and between them they took in sufficient detail to be able to note, when they returned to this scene later that day to pick up their equipment, that it had been cleaned and tidied, looked spic and span.

The dominant feature of the bedroom was the nine-foot square bed, unmade and unkempt, and the platform of so many other Presley dramas, romantic and medical. Somewhere unseen, a child was crying, 'My daddy . . . my daddy . . . I think he's dead.' Lisa Marie had been ushered clear. A man was moaning, 'My baby . . . my baby.' Vernon Presley had slithered in a collapsed state to the floor and was propped up by the wall.

As they moved quickly into the bedroom, Crosby thought he caught sight of a gun, probably a Colt .45, lying on a bookcase, and what looked like a syringe close by. They were suspicious objects, but their presence could easily be explained. Elvis had a collection of guns and often left them lying around. The syringes were part of his daily routine. When the police saw them later, they accepted this explanation and left it at that.

The paramedics were led into the doorway of the bathroom, where a woman was attempting to give mouth-to-mouth resuscitation to the prostrate form of a man, lying back-down on the blood-red, shaggy-pile carpet. The room was in disarray. Jones noticed bottles and aerosols scattered about the tops of the bathroom furniture. There was a black bag, open on the floor, and pill bottles spilled out. There were papers and a book, which appeared to have been flung across the room, lying spine-up on the top of one of the surfaces.

As the woman lifted her head to make way for the emergency team, the sight was shocking, even to the paramedics. The face of the patient was blue and puffed, so discoloured that Ulysses Jones thought it was a black man lying there. His body was naked, except for a pair of gold pyjama trousers which had been yanked downwards during the attempts to revive him. The torso had bluish patches, not unnatural in a body where life had ebbed away perhaps three or four

14

hours before. He was a heavy man, with rolls of fat, and weighing perhaps 250 or 260 pounds. It surely wasn't Elvis Presley, was it? Jones puzzled to himself.

His face was set like a mask, his tongue was hanging from the side of the mouth, and he had bitten into it, as if rigor mortis was already setting in. There was a trickle of dry blood down the side of his face. The eyelids were open and could not be closed. The jaw was locked, and Jones and Crosby had difficulty prising open the mouth to insert the tubes of their breathing apparatus. They struggled for minutes in an attempt to revive some signs of life. There was no pulse, no breathing, no blood pressure. Nothing. The body was deathly cold. Crosby and Jones assessed later that he had been dead for some time, probably several hours.

There were about eight people in the room. Among them were Joe Esposito, foreman of Elvis's entourage, road manager and friend for seventeen years. Beside him was Sandy Miller, Vernon Presley's girlfriend and a trained nurse who, as well as attending the patient, was also calming Vernon himself, whom she feared might suffer another heart attack.

And there was Ginger Alden, ashen-faced and weeping. She was Elvis's current girlfriend who had woken at one-thirty p.m. that day, discovered that he was not where he should have been – in bed beside her – dressed herself, put on her make-up, and made two telephone calls before entering the bathroom at around two-ten to discover Elvis in a crumpled, foetal heap on the floor beside the black toilet pan, face down.

She would be questioned later about why it took so long to discover Elvis. How was it that he had lain unattended in the bathroom for perhaps three hours or more? Was it possible that someone had come into the room that morning, someone she did not recognise, perhaps? Vernon Presley asked her that very question. It was possible, she would say, because she was sleeping so soundly.

Crosby and Jones called for assistance to get the body on to a stretcher and to carry it downstairs to the ambulance. It took five men to move his hefty weight. As they bundled the lifeless form into the ambulance amid tearful wailing from the women, the men were silent but agitated. Dr George Nichopoulos skidded to a halt at the front door in his gold Mercedes, a present from his most famous patient. He clambered into the back of the ambulance as Crosby gunned the engine and began assisting Jones with the life-support mechanism inside the wagon. Pale and breathless, Dr Nick took up a quiet chant, 'Breathe, Presley, breathe.'

Presley did not breathe, nor would he ever again. Just over an hour later, his fans the world over were stunned by the announcement that Elvis Presley, the King of rock 'n' roll, was dead. Dr Jerry Francisco, the county medical examiner, joined a high-powered team of pathologists and medical specialists to begin an immediate autopsy. Later that night, he called a press conference to reveal the preliminary results of the autopsy on Elvis. Although certain tests were still to be carried out on body tissue, the doctor said he was confident in stating that Elvis Aaron Presley had died from natural causes – heart disease – unrelated to any external circumstances. It was, by any standards, a controversial verdict and one with which certain senior members of the medical team who examined the body strongly disagreed.

When it became known later that traces of a dozen or more identifiable prescription drugs were found in Elvis's body, there would be accusations of a cover-up, which Francisco loudly denied. But the findings could never be properly challenged because the autopsy report was never made public. It will not be available for public scrutiny until the year 2027.

No police investigation was ever initiated, in spite of the abundant local knowledge of Elvis's eccentricities and his long-standing abuse of prescription drugs which had caused to him to be hospitalised in Memphis for detoxification on at least five separate occasions. The police file was closed and what scant reports it contained were also kept locked away for years.

There would be no formal inquest or any other investigation into the actual circumstances of the death.

The lack of any real attempt to determine and authenticate a minute-by-minute account of events surrounding the death of Elvis merely led to a rash of conspiracy theories, mounted and speculated upon over the years, ranging from the serious efforts to show the cause of death, through to some preposterous suggestions, which have been treated with the derision they deserve.

Rumours abounded that there *were* documents proving that Elvis was in some way linked to a high-powered crime-busting operation, since criminology was his passion, and had not President Richard Nixon made him a 'special agent-at-large' for the federal drugs agency? That appointment was a bit of a joke, too, and the rumours were laughed off. No one paid much serious thought to the possibility that deep in the archives of local and national government offices, there were indeed documents which could reveal a possible reason for deception, or contain facts that were never made public when Elvis died. Had these facts been known, they would have caused the public clamouring necessary to instigate a thorough, forensic investigation into his death.

For when officialdom interferes, tries to manipulate and massage the facts, puts documents into secret files and will not let anyone look at them for up to half a century, it smacks of conspiracy. Events leading up to the demise of Marilyn Monroe, John F. Kennedy, Bobby Kennedy, Martin Luther King and others have provided unending, insoluble speculation for the conspiracy theorists.

The death of Elvis Presley never came readily to mind; though it should have. The circumstances of his death are surrounded by contradictions, and a very deliberate diversion of fact from the public arena.

After a visit to the FBI archives in 1991, I began my search, opening dusty old files, listening to tape-recordings with principal witnesses, made years ago, and re-interviewing some of those people today, including Dr Nichopoulos himself, FBI agents and members of the US attorney's office of the day, in an attempt to discover any hidden evidence that might throw credible new light on the Elvis saga.

I trawled through thousands of pages of official documents and reports made available to me by the FBI and other government archives in Washington. There were some intriguing inclusions.

The rumours were correct in alleging the existence of documents concerning Elvis, the Mafia and witness-protection programmes. The sequence of events, as it involved Elvis, is contained, with some still-secret exceptions and deletions, in a series of complex FBI reports.

It is a story packed with intrigue, avarice and criminal intent, of rumoured assassination attempts, of side issues and bad business deals, and of people always on the make, attempting to benefit from the moneymaking machine that was Elvis Presley. It is a poignant and often sad story of pressures bearing down on that immensely vulnerable person who was a victim of his own fame.

The original intent of this investigation was to re-examine the available material which dealt with a period immediately before and after his death, but the material I gathered from the FBI and elsewhere also provided such a revealing, though sombre, insight into Elvis's earlier life that I decided to begin at the beginning – among the earliest days of his career when, even then, he was unwittingly and unknowingly the subject of almost constant surveillance.

Authority was wary of him, and J. Edgar Hoover, director of the FBI, opened the book on what was to become an intensive watch on this new young star; here was the exuberance, the excitement and the anger of the early days, recorded in cold, formal jargon, as exploiters and leeches began to gather, not least in the area of officialdom and authority which spied upon him, even manipulated him, for their own ends.

So now let us go back in time, to April 1955, where the story begins . . .

1

Hoover's Hall of Fame

'Elvis Presley stepped on to the stage and immediately the soft-spoken kid with the nervous laugh disappeared and turned into a purple-coated musical demon who belted out songs as if his young life depended on it. The results were unbelievable. This kid, with jet-black hair, gleaming, darting eyes and dressed in New York clothes, stood for a moment and then let them have it. At the first tap of his leg the auditorium almost exploded. The listeners could not sit still. Every time he moved a muscle fifteen or twenty youngsters rushed forward and tried to break through the line of police to get to him. From then on, it was an even match to see who would entertain whom ... Elvis has somehow picked out a bit of teenage spirit and tucked it into his whanging geetar. You don't have to understand it. Just listen to it and the kids will tell you: This boy is crazy, man ... crazy ...'

La Crosse Register, 5 May 1956

I found the above news clipping relating to one of the early touring performances of a young Elvis Presley in the personal files of J. Edgar Hoover, self-appointed guardian of his nation's morals and director of the Federal Bureau of Investigation (FBI), the world's largest criminal intelligence organisation. True enough, such scenes that Elvis generated were pretty well unheard of in the mid–Fifties, but before we go on to discuss why Hoover should be remotely interested in a new young singer from Memphis, Tennessee, let us consider briefly the implications of the information contained in that news report. Those who were around at the time, part of that emerging generation of supposedly angry youth whose silver screen heroes were James Dean and Marlon Brando, can recall the moment when they first heard Elvis Presley.

19

Unless you happened to live in the southern states of America, where he was performing live, the only ear contact was by records, the jukebox at the local coffee bar or perhaps the briefest of clips on cinema newsreels. Those who were not even born, but who later became Elvis fans, could eventually peer back on those frivolous, exciting days, captured on the hundreds of hours of film and television footage devoted to one of the greatest – some say *the* greatest – icons of the music scene of this last half-century.

The sensation he was causing in the mid-Fifties sent shock waves across the country. His performances were branded as lewd and outrageous. Local politicians and religious leaders where he made his earliest appearances decided his stage act was so shocking, so lascivious, that it was sufficient to call in no lesser personage than Hoover to get this terrible young man stopped in his tracks.

The reasons were evident from the beginning of Elvis's FBI files, consisting of numerous contemporary newspaper reports, like the one above, sent to Hoover by disgusted members of local communities with suggestions that he should act immediately. It was the beginning of a new and frightening phenomenon that made the bobbysoxers who swooned over Frank Sinatra in his heyday look like a Sunday school outing.

The world was ill-prepared for Elvis Presley's swivelling pelvic region. Those in authority did not quite know what to do about it. He had become an instant icon of subversive rebellion, although that was a temporary assignment. In truth, he will hardly go down as one of the champions of American protest. As one who was in that scene as it happened – or, at least, observing it from the quieter climes of rural England – discovering these early accounts in the Hoover files had a special significance for me.

The first file was a fairly innocuous matter, containing letters of protest, newspaper cuttings pertaining to Elvis shows, threats from cranks who, even then, were going to kill him, and requests for advice from local law-enforcement agencies about how to deal with the new and unheard-of spectacle of thousands of kids screaming and swooning at Elvis concerts.

Reading those letters, meticulously noted and filed away in JEH's 'Private and Confidential' cabinets thirty-seven years on, I can liken the experience to recollections under hypnosis of times past, as stark facts which seemed incredulous and sensational at the time, are presented in a dour, almost Victorian manner. Discovering the contents of these old files, collected during the Hoover administration, was like raiding an old magpie's nest, filled to overflowing with an almighty collection of assorted gems in which the bird showed no discernment between the authentic and the phoney.

There are mind-boggling statistics about Hoover's FBI files, which talk in terms of enough sheets of paper to lay a bridge to the moon and back, and still have plenty left over to gift-wrap the White House and the British Houses of Parliament. Pick a name at random, any famous name, and there is probably a file buried away in the vast J. Edgar Hoover Building on Pennsylvania Avenue in Washington, or stored in some other archive close by.

The Freedom of Information (FOI) Act allows the media and the public access to literally millions of pages of documents which would, in many Western democracies, such as Great Britain, remain classified information until time blunted their impact and meaning. For comparison, files on the British Royal family can be locked away for 100 years or more without recourse to appeal, whereas in America FOI allows procedures to unlock the nation's secrets. Applications to view files of a particular person or organisation have to be made through the FOI office. There is already a huge library of pre-processed material which has been cleared. Applications to view known subject matter previously classified as confidential or secret may be made in writing, but even with this facility, many files and even parts of files remain classified and unobtainable under subsections of the act which protect national security and personal privacy.

There is an appeals system to which refusal of viewing rights may be referred, though the whole procedure can take three years or more with the current waiting list of applications.

The information I secured by persistent research and cross-referencing enabled me to piece together the FBI's early assessment of Elvis Presley. It emerged with remarkable clarity as I moved through the reams of documentation, prepared by agents of law enforcement, beginning with the discovery of the answer to Hoover's question: Who is this man? and on through the reports resulting from a watching brief they kept on his life without his knowledge. It progresses still further into the dark and secret areas of top-secret and dangerous FBI investigation in which Presley's name finally arises in the most unexpected and dramatic manner at the time of his death.

*   *   *   *   *

Before proceeding, it is necessary to describe the information-gathering techniques of Hoover personally, as opposed to the FBI as an institution, although at the peak of his power they were one and the same and only altered after his death. The brevity of this description does not do it justice and has been well-documented elsewhere, but I include it to provide a flavour of what needs to be borne in mind as we progress through the files up to the point when Hoover himself died in 1972. At that very time he was embroiled in deeply covert action against John Lennon, coincidentally inspired by Elvis Presley.

To Hoover, knowledge was power. He was not a large man in either thought or stature; he rose to fame fighting the mobs of the prohibition era and built the Federal Bureau of Investigation into what it eventually became, a domestic spying organisation to which – during his administration – fighting crime seemed to have become a mere subsidiary operation. I mention this now, because it becomes very relevant at a later point in our story about Elvis.

Hoover was in many ways a kind of model for George Orwell's Big Brother, watching and waiting, and compiling the files which he believed would, sometime, somewhere, be of use to him and the organisation. This power pervaded the FBI and scared the daylights out of successive presidents. Apart from the whole operational force of the bureau network itself, which he had at his complete disposal, he had official correspondents and unofficial spies in virtually every area of American life, who provided him which an incredible network of informants in his obsessional mission of digging the dirt in the cause of national security.

He was a chaser of criminals and communists, but he applied huge resources to the simple task of obtaining gossip from every available source. Friend or foe, it did not matter; whether the topic was a state secret or a matter of no apparent significance, details found their way into his private archive and he apparently derived great pleasure from letting his subjects know that he knew. Matters of least importance seemed to best illustrate the acquisitive facilities of the man. Examples abound. Lucille Ball and her husband Desi Arnaz were supposed to be his friends, yet he took enormous delight in informing Arnaz that his wife was pregnant before she had had a chance to tell him herself; the information came to him via a hospital where Lucille had undergone a pregnancy test.

He had discovered Rock Hudson's homosexuality long before the rumours started and, after a 'special report' on Hollywood vice compiled for Hoover by a team of agents, a film in which Hudson was to star as an FBI agent was suddenly cancelled. He let Errol Flynn know that *he* knew the star had escaped wartime service with the US army, by obtaining a phoney medical report classifying him as unfit – at a cost of five thousand dollars. He had files on Jayne Mansfield, Grace Kelly, Cary Grant, Spencer Tracy, Humphrey Bogart, John Wayne, Henry Fonda, Jane Fonda and, later, the rock 'n' rollers and musicians like Elvis, Jimi Hendrix and Janis Joplin – the list of stars who became the subject of Hoover's surveillance reads like a *Who's Who* of entertainment.

Never doubting that his personal files would remain secret for ever, he noted in the margin of a report on Jane Fonda, who was to appear in the film *Klute*, 'Certainly I don't want any reference to the FBI in any picture in which this tramp appears.'

People who thought they were his allies were not exempt from Hoover's attentions, especially in political circles. Joseph Kennedy was a special correspondent (informant) for the FBI, dating back to the days when he first began to mix with the Tsars of organised crime, when the Kennedys themselves became rich. Yet Hoover was watching the Kennedy clan, and tapping their telephones.

With this kind of information-gathering facility available, and when even the most powerful of politicians was no match for his electronic technology, what chance had the young and innocent rock 'n' rollers emerging on to the American music scene in the mid-Fifties and Sixties? Their lifestyles were abhorrent to him, and his mission to save the nation from their excesses became an obsessive vision.

★   ★   ★   ★   ★

Elvis Presley made his first appearance in Hoover's files in the late spring of 1956, when he was on his first tour of American towns and cities, causing great excitement among its youth and great anguish among their parents, as photographs and reports of outlandish stage appearances and outrageous teenage behaviour began to appear in the newspapers and on television.

Presley's emerging career is noted by a series of newspaper clippings and agents' reports, recording personal facts ... that he was born 8 January 1935 in Tupelo, Mississippi, into a family and neighbourhood which was just about the poorest place that white folks could live. His twin, Jesse, died at birth and he had an impoverished, uneventful childhood and adolescence.

The facts were stark and bland, almost clinical, and without the colour that was to be applied in later years as his story was told and retold in a million biographical articles and dozens of books. Looking back from the vantage point of three decades of great expansion in the boundaries of 'decency', and the developments in the music industry in general, it seems remarkable that an organisation like the FBI should concern itself in collating such a voluminous collection of data on a singer; but then Elvis was no mere singer.

There were traces of political undertones relating back to his early life in the cotton country of the old south, where a young black preacher named Martin Luther King – an upstart, in Hoover's view – was already making his mark by leading protests over segregation of schools and public transport and who, coincidentally, met his end not far from Elvis's home in Memphis.

When the nation's youngsters suddenly fell under the awesome spell of a southern white boy, who was a son of everything middle-class America despised in alleged 'white trash' and who was singing 'nigger' songs, Hoover accumulated a precis of the life of this young man.

Early childhood photographs clipped and included in the FBI files presented him as being almost waif-like. The story is undoubtedly familiar, but the key points of his early life are valid in any account. His parents were unimpressive and spent early life in the abject poverty that faced those on the wrong side of the economic divisions which lacerated the cotton-growing states in the Thirties.

Home was a two-room shack built next door to Elvis's grandfather's house, where they lived until his father Vernon, a lorry driver, was incarcerated for a three-year jail sentence at Parchman Prison Camp in the Mississippi Delta for forging a cheque, altering the sum from eighteen to twenty-eight dollars. Bringing up Elvis fell to his mother Gladys, the round homely woman of countless similar families, who was devoted to her son, and he to her, because he was the centre of her life, almost her only reason for living.

At the age of ten, Elvis Aaron won a school prize for singing at the county fair, crooning a country and western ballad called 'Old Shep', about a boy and his dog. In 1948, they moved a hundred miles north-west to Memphis, centre of the post-war boom which had attracted poor whites from all over the south, and the family lived in a one-room home in the poverty ghetto of the city centre, where whites and blacks waited vainly for their share of better times.

Segregation was still the rule. The poor whites had their hillbilly and country music; the blacks had their rhythm and blues. Elvis, who had lived his life tied to his mother's apron strings, mopped up the atmosphere, though never mixed with the rough crowds. He carried a guitar around in his early teens, mimicking the popular Grand Ole Oprey stars of the day, and Memphis was the magnet for and breeding ground of emerging musical giants.

He graduated from Humes High School in 1953, with no record of academic prowess; he followed his father into the employment wasteland of nothing in particular, at best driving trucks. When he had a dollar or two to spare, he wandered into the Sun label recording studio of Sam Phillips, who had a little sideline charging two dollars for anyone to come in and cut a disc. Presley made a few. Phillips, a local talent spotter, was unimpressed, until one day Presley and a couple of musicians that Phillips had brought in were playing some blues tunes; he started to sing 'That's All Right, Mama'. Later, Elvis could only equate it to the time when he was young, when they went as a family to the Pentecostal First Assembly of God, where the preachers used to get excited and jump around and up on the piano, belting out their message of salvation from sin.

Sam Phillips, according to legend, came rushing in while Presley was still singing and said, 'What the hell are you doing? Whatever it is hold it right there . . . don't lose it.' Popular music stopped dead in its tracks, and would never be quite the same again. Presley recorded ten songs, which to this day many believe were his best, and by the time the first record came out, he was already being discussed in the Memphis music scene as a wild kid.

The discovery of Elvis Presley in July 1954 coincided with Hoover's interest in other up-and-coming leaders of youth culture. Marlon Brando came out that year in *The Wild One*, leather-clad on a motorcycle, and determined to disrupt life in a quiet American town. And when he was asked, 'What are you rebelling against?' he growled back, 'Whadda ya got?' It was a catchphrase for a generation.

And James Dean was filming *East of Eden*, released in April 1955 as the green shoots of Presley's own career began to emerge. There was a correlation of the times between them all.

While Dean was the hero up there on the silver screen, with his mournful eyes moist from the effects of heavy dope-smoking, gazing down from a thousand movie-poster hoarding, Elvis was beginning his own movement. Elsewhere, there were louder noises coming from Chuck Berry, Little Richard, Bill Haley and, soon, that other Memphis genius, Jerry Lee Lewis. Elvis's first record for Sun, 'That's All Right, Mama', had reached number three in the Memphis country charts.

In May 1955, when he was on the road part-time, thousands crowded to see him at Jacksonville, Florida, and Elvis was mystified by his audience's reaction. 'Why are they screaming and shouting?' he asked repeatedly. It went on, and one of the best descriptions of that pre-fame era came from country singer Bob Luman, 'This cat came out in red pants and green coat and pink shirt and socks and stood behind a mike for five minutes with this sneer on his face before making a move . . . he hadn't done anything yet and these high school girls were screaming and fainting and running up to the stage. He made chills run up and down my back, man.'

One man who was to mould his life had a pretty good idea why Presley was attracting this kind of reaction. In the summer of 1955, the self-styled 'Colonel' Tom Parker, a cigar-chomping wheeler–dealer in a permanent trilby hat who ran circuses and carnival shows, stumbled by accident into becoming the manager of the world's hottest singing talent. He had recognised, just as all the angry parents and probably J. Edgar Hoover himself had, that the basic ingredient of Elvis's act was the old bump and grind of the vaudeville stripper. It was Gypsy Rose Lee, Johnny Ray and James Dean all rolled up into one overtly sexual package.

When interviewed in 1980 by Larry Hutchinson for the Memphis district attorney-general, Parker recalled the time he signed Elvis. 'Back in those days, I was booking shows and Elvis had a manager who came to see me, to see if I could use Elvis on some dates. He was pretty much on the Louisiana hayrides, being booked into small towns for 200 dollars a night. One night when he played Memphis, I went along to see him and met Elvis back stage. The next day, Elvis's father Vernon telephoned me and said they were looking for a new record contract and managerial arrangement, would I be interested?'

Parker was interested and he in turn persuaded RCA Records to take on Elvis. In November, they paid Sam Phillips 35,000 dollars – a small fortune then – to release Presley from his contract so that he could sign exclusively with RCA.

Parker said, 'I agreed a deal with Elvis and his father to become his manager and promoter, promising to handle his record contracts, tours, personal appearances and to try to get him into motion pictures. We had a contract for a while and then we went on a handshake. My percentages fluctuated. It started out as a flat twenty-five per cent of everything Elvis earned, but later as he became bigger, I took fifty per cent of some of the deals I arranged. We agreed a sort of partnership and my cut varied, depending on the deal; sometimes it was a quarter, sometimes it was half.'

Parker had struck gold, the richest seam in showbusiness history. On 10 January 1956, he took his boy into the RCA studios at Nashville and recorded his first international hit, 'Heartbreak Hotel'. It was as if the youth of the nation had been waiting for such an event: a white boy, exceedingly handsome, curiously homely and good ole boyish, but with the rebel greaser-look of Brando in *The Wild One*, singing songs which were a mixture of gospel and country with an undercurrent of negro fire. But for all the analysis of Presley's early music and the impact it made, he was more a creation of the times, unlike the styles of his contemporaries like Chuck Berry and Little Richard, who were the true creators of rock 'n' roll.

J. Edgar Hoover had one eye permanently cast in the direction of Hollywood and the entertainment industry, where he took great interest in the censorship of anti-society material. Hoover's files are punctuated by letters and petitions from a fair cross-section of society – from religious leaders and parents, through to right wing extremists – demanding combative action against rock musicians and films which portrayed youth and violence.

Why, for example, would the head of the FBI want to file away letters from youngsters published in local newspapers? There were several like the one from teenager Charlotte Jones, which prophetically read, 'Elvis is the King of popularity and we teens of America love him and we'll see he lives for ever. Not his body, perhaps, but his name . . .' The cutting was stamped and circulated among the higher echelons of the FBI administration, ticked as having been read – for whatever reason – by Clyde Tolson, Hoover's deputy.

Anything rebellious, subversive or pertaining to the national morals of society and the impressionable youth of the nation, was an area of special interest for Hoover and therefore his files reflect the shock of the nation when Presley exploded on to the scene early in 1956. Alarm bells began ringing all over the country as the new rock musician took to the road.

By then, James Dean was already dead, killed in his car on 30 September 1955, just as his second film *Rebel Without a Cause* was released across the world, with its message of crazy mixed-up kids, apparently crying out for parental love and crystallising the vague, ill-defined mood of youth. *Rebel Without a Cause* became a cult film; fans refused to believe Dean was dead and gathered outside Warner Brothers studios pleading for him to come out and show himself. Rumours abounded – the same kind that would be mirrored twenty-two years later when Presley himself died – that Dean was still alive and had faked his death so that he could retire peacefully from the pressures of life.

The film became a source of inspiration to Presley in that winter of 1955, leading up to his own emergence in the youth cult scene in January of the New Year. Nick Ray, who directed *Rebel Without a Cause*, related some years later in a Barcelona bar:

I met Elvis in Hollywood soon after he became famous; he came up to make some film tests in the spring of 1956. Jimmy had made a big impression on him. Elvis had seen *Rebel* forty-four times, bought a copy of the script and learned it off by heart. He could recite Jimmy's lines from memory and when he came back to do some filming later that year, he even began to date Natalie Wood, who was then around nineteen and had been Jimmy's girlfriend off-screen and on. Natalie told me that she could give him any cue-line from a certain scene and he would come straight back at her with the line spoken by Dean. She said it was uncanny. He deliberately sought out Dean's old haunts, and his old friends like Nick Adams. He had this big Harley Davidson and used to race up and down Sunset Boulevard with Natalie on the back. She told me she found him incredibly polite, not at all pushy.

By then, the dance halls of the nation, which had lain deserted in the fading era of big bands and crooning singers, were being warmed to new sounds and new small groups twanging guitars and bouncing around the stage. Soon they would be filled to capacity with gyrating performers and jiving fans. Reports of their activity and of Presley's in particular were soon dominating entertainment-news coverage.

Letters poured into local newspapers and eventually to the FBI. One correspondent wrote in April 1956 pleading with Hoover to do all in his power to strengthen laws of censorship: 'It is essential that some agency with sufficient influence do something to stop these people who will scarcely stop short of complete indecency ... and youth is not able to discriminate between right and wrong.'

An irate letter was the first notation of serious public outrage against Presley in the FBI files, dated 16 May 1956. Letter to The Director, FBI, from the publisher of the *La Crosse Register*, Wisconsin:

Elvis Presley played to two groups of teenagers numbering several thousand at the city auditorium here on 14 May. As a newspaper man, parent and former member of the army intelligence service, I feel an obligation to pass on to you my conviction that Presley is a definite danger to the security of the United States. All agree that it was the filthiest and most harmful production that ever came to La Crosse for exhibition to teenagers. The audience could not hear his singing for screaming ... his actions were such as to rouse the sexual passions of teenaged youth. One eye-witness described his actions as sexual self-gratification, another as striptease with clothes on ... gestures like those of masturbation or riding the microphone. After the show 1000 teenagers tried to gang into Presley's room at the auditorium; they were still milling around till five a.m. Indications of the harm Presley did just in La Crosse were the two high-school girls whose abdomen and thighs had Presley's personal autograph ... I would judge that he may possibly be a drug addict and a sexual pervert. There is also gossip that the Presley Fan Clubs degenerate into sex orgies. In any case, I am sure he bears a close watch ...

Hoover replied, thanking 'Disgusted of La Crosse' for his comments and the generous remarks he had postscripted about the FBI. Hoover added the letter to his file and it was soon to reflect the

29

way in which authority – local councillors, police and youth workers – were left open-mouthed by it all. They simply did not know how to handle the rising phenomenon. It was a kind of frenzy emerging from its roots in America and spreading worldwide.

Presley's success was rapidly repeated with a succession of number-one hit records. Between 1956 and 1958, when he went away for army service, he was top of the American popular record charts, fifty-five out of 104 weeks, and on the strength of his first, Hollywood beckoned. Hal Wallis, the famed producer of such classics as *Casablanca* and *Little Caesar*, screen-tested him for Paramount Pictures in March, put him under a personal contract and began making his first picture that summer. His first album raced up the charts; he was in demand for concerts all over the country, and on 11 July 1956, a coded message, no less, arrived at FBI headquarters for the attention of the director from his Louisville, Kentucky, field office:

Colonel Carl E. Heustis, chief of Police, Louisville, this day advises that Elvis Presley and Bill Haley and his Comets are simultaneously booked for appearances at Jefferson County Armoury and the Kentucky State Fairground Exposition Centre November 25, next. Colonel Heustis advises that he has received information that there have been riots at Jersey City, Santa Cruz, Santa Jose, Hartford and Jacksonville as a result of such simultaneous appearances. Riots reportedly resulted in many thousands of dollars property damaged. Colonel Heustis requests information appearing in [bureau] files to prevent such occurrences in Louisville.

Hoover suggested that Colonel Heustis should contact other police departments in towns where Presley had already appeared and try to formulate some kind of crowd control and property protection. By the time Presley was due to appear in Louisville, his first film, *Love Me Tender*, had been made and quickly released as the bandwagon rolled. On 14 November almost 2000 teenagers besieged the Paramount Theatre on Broadway, queuing behind the barricades manned by 300 policemen. The following day, Colonel Heustis called a press conference on the imminent arrival of Elvis Presley – noted in Hoover's files – and said that he would enforce a 'no-wiggle' ruling on the singer's performance, something akin to the stage censorship which strippers had faced in the past. He announced he would not permit any lewd, lascivious contortions that might excite the crowd.

To Hoover, Presley represented some unaccountable revolutionary force which even Elvis himself was apparently at a loss to explain. How was it that he'd suddenly found himself in the eye of a hurricane? Clipped in the files is an interview Elvis gave to C. Robert Jennings of the *Saturday Evening Post*, which discussed his effect on young audiences: 'I don't know what it is. I just fell into it. My daddy and I were laughing about it the other day. He looked at me and said, "What happened, El? The last thing I remember is I was working in a can factory and you were a truck driver." It just caught us up.'

American reaction on both sides of the divide reached something of a crescendo. Hoover took very seriously a threat which arrived through the mail to Elvis, postmarked Niagara Falls, which said simply, 'If you don't stop this we are going to kill you.' Investigations into the source of the note – the first of many similar threats on his life – produced no clues, and the police authorities found themselves in the ironic position of having to protect the young man they did not, according to Colonel Heustis, especially admire.

Though he had no powers to enforce censorship of anything, Hoover had a good deal of personal influence. With his armoury of secret files on major figures, he could move mountains in television and the big screen. He had 'friends' at all levels. The files reflect his continuing interest in calls for censorship of stage acts and films involving youth; he loved to receive the letters which began as this one: 'Dear Honourable Sir, Thank goodness you are still in Washington, serving us all as no-one else can ... Congratulations!' and he apparently showed special sympathy to a petition gathered by a group of housewives in Syracuse demanding that Elvis be barred from television shows. Elsewhere, other agents kept running reports on anything to do with Presley.

Hoover's man in Mexico, for example, filed a lengthy report on how the Communist Party there had started a campaign to stop Elvis Presley records being played on the radio, and that students from the city's university were planning an anti-Elvis celebration in which sheet music, records and magazines would be publicly burned; Presley had better not go to Mexico, the agent warned, otherwise there would be trouble and the US was in the middle of negotiating an air-flight deal which could be affected!

As Elvis reached superstar status, Hoover's good friend Ed Sullivan, whose variety show was the pinnacle of achievement for any entertainer, had earlier publicly announced that he would never have such acts on his show. But such was Presley's popularity that even Sullivan had to recant and booked him for three appearances at the then staggering fee of 50,000 dollars. But, for the first one, Sullivan stayed within the 'parameters of decency' recommended by Hoover by ensuring that the cameras only filmed the top half of Presley, thus denying the millions who tuned into that major coast–to–coast broadcast the opportunity of viewing the most controversial part of Presley's performance, his swivelling hips. The show received record viewing audiences, 82.6 per cent of American viewers, an estimated fifty-four million people.

Whereas Sullivan was quite open about his dislike, if not loathing, of all that Presley was doing and stood for, there was a definite pattern, which those of a suspicious nature might have identified as a concerted effort, in the media and on television, to cut the ground from under Elvis with the apparent hope and intent that he would collapse under the nation's derision and protest and never recover. Hoover must have approved wholeheartedly of this spontaneous reaction.

But that was the view of the establishment, the snobby reviewers, and was certainly not shared by most of the people he had come into contact with in Hollywood. Lizabeth Scott co–starred in his second film, another teenage exploitation flick entitled *Loving You*. In an interview taped by Professor Ronald Davis for the DeGolyer Institute of American Studies, she waxed lyrically:

I just thought Elvis was the most remarkable young man I had ever, ever encountered. He was very young and very adolescent but he had the most mature eyes. I shall never forget his eyes, so beautiful and exquisite. And so talented. Elvis had an entourage of young men around him and he was untouchable. He was also one of the most polite young men I have ever met in my life: 'Ma'am this and Ma'am that'; 'Yes sir and no sir!' As an actor, he was excellent for what he was doing. He came in prepared and had a photographic memory. He was a gentleman to the very core of him. He was also a simple man, a simple little boy. But I feel that he could have been so much more than he was, because he had the potential.

By November 1957, he had sold twenty-eight million copies of his singles, not counting the albums which also ran into millions. MGM paid him 250,000 dollars, plus fifty per cent of the profits for his third film, *Jailhouse Rock*, plus all the marketing of sheet music and records, to Elvis Presley Music Inc. It had not escaped J. Edgar Hoover's attention that Elvis Presley had just achieved the record of the most money earned by a star on a single film.

That he was a money machine was carefully reflected in his acquisitions. He bought Graceland, a plantation-style home which the previous owner had named after his wife, for 100,000 dollars in the summer of 1957. He had a fleet of cars, the familiar Cadillacs, Lincolns, a Rolls Royce and other expensive toys. His topsy-turvey world in which night became day had already begun. He was by then unable to enjoy the delights of normal life, like bowling or going to the movies. He could not move without a massive crowd gathering and the fleets of Cadillacs with their shaded windows carrying him around had become commonplace.

So Elvis and his entourage began a pattern that was to remain for the rest of his life; when he wasn't working, they would stay up all night and sleep during the day. He would rent a bowling alley, or an entire cinema. Or they'd go to Whitehaven High School football ground and play under the arc lights. Kids near the school slept with one eye on the window and when the lights went up, they would sneak out and watch him and his friends play.

The girls were innumerable, but the shy, polite boy who Natalie Wood and Lizabeth Scott discovered was nervous about kissing, took some time to lose his inhibitions. Natalie Wood recalled that on their first date, he merely kissed her on the cheek and said, 'Goodnight, Ma'am.' The child star who had grown up in Hollywood, and had played around James Dean and Nick Adams, with whom she used to smoke a joint and bathe naked in champagne, was jolted by his behaviour. She found Elvis a novelty at first, but when he took her home to Graceland one weekend to meet his mom, she telephoned her own mother and pleaded, 'For chrissakes, get me out of here. These people are nuts!'

The FBI kept track of everything, even the girls. Reports in December 1957, for example, noted the presence of two houseguests at Graceland. Photographs of the girls, a dancer named Kathy Gabriel who was that year's Miss Ohio, and Hannah Melcher, who was the current Miss Austria, appear in the Presley file. In reports flagged 'secret', their movements were tracked from Las Vegas, where Presley met them at the Tropicana, on through Salt Lake City and finally to Memphis, where they stayed at Graceland for two days before moving to New York, where it was established they were going to audition as dancers at a nightclub.

Why the FBI should take such an interest in the movements of two beauty queens during this brief association with Presley was never made clear in the files. A possible explanation was that Miss Austria was working in the country without suitable papers. Whatever the reason, they were just two more names who flickered in and out of Elvis's life, and in and out of FBI surveillance, undoubtedly apparently unaware that they had been watched.

But that was only the start of it all . . .

2

The Blackmailer

'When the time came for drafting, Elvis had it in his mind that he was going to go into the special services, so that he could continue his career. I sat down with him, and said, "Elvis, a lot of these guys who opt for the special services find that their career is shot when they come out because they're ducking the job." He eventually agreed with me that he should go off and volunteer for the army, do his service as a soldier with no performing of any kind for the duration, absolutely none at all – not even for the army. So off he went and I barely saw him for the next two years. There was very little contact, especially after he left for Germany. He called three or four times. I never got any letters. Elvis was not in the habit of writing letters. I got one thank-you note one time, but that was all he ever wrote. So he did his duty . . . and it helped him tremendously when he came out.'

Colonel Tom Parker, 1980

Tom Parker, a bluff, confident, ebullient man, made one of the most curious decisions of contemporary showbusiness when he took his star, then at the zenith of his career, suddenly and abruptly out of the public eye and banished him to military service for two years. It was all the more curious in that he need not have done it. Even before he reached the point of call-up, there were notes of top-brass discussions about the singer appearing in the service records of the forthcoming draftee, *Presley, Elvis A*. It was a recorded fact that, like the subject himself, the military did not actually expect Elvis to undertake the two-year term faced by other young American boys, for whom the draft became a reality. There were two choices facing teenagers and young men of the day. They could volunteer as soon as they came of age and show what true red-blooded young Americans they really were, or alternatively they could await the arrival of the buff coloured envelope informing the recipient that he had been randomly drafted for military service.

There were no wars, no emergencies and it was surely true that the army could manage without the dubious soldiering abilities of one hip-swinging singer. They could make better use of his talents during his two-year term. He could best serve his country in some other way than kicking his heels on some far-off military base. He was, after all, the most successful entertainer of modern times. He had made seventeen straight million-selling singles, his records had sold over forty million copies worldwide, and his first three films had all been massive box-office hits. Nothing less was expected of the fourth, on which he was currently working.

The military was ready to do a deal and allow him to fulfil his commitment in the special services, where he could have continued his career, cutting records in his off-duty time and remaining in touch with his fans. It was a route to military service taken by a number of stars and the one preferred by Elvis himself.

There had long been speculation that he would not be required, and *Billboard* magazine published an authoritative article a year before he was called up, giving what appeared to be a well-sourced account of the arrangements that the army were planning for their most famous new recruit. Elvis, according to *Billboard*, would be drafted in December 1957. He would be expected to complete six weeks basic training and would then be released into special services, from where he could continue his career with minimum intervention to complete his army commitment.

Colonel Parker and executives at his record company, RCA, decided otherwise. Parker insisted that, in the long term, Presley's career would benefit from public acclaim and respect if he volunteered to do his duty and serve his country as a buck private. It was certainly true that when the *Billboard* article received wider publicity, there was a strong upsurge of protest from service veterans about Elvis ducking his duty to the country. Privately, Elvis was worried that in two years, his fans would have forgotten him. Parker virtually instructed him to go, and on 24 March 1958, Elvis Presley, amid great media hype, reported for duty at the Memphis draft board, having secured a sixty-day postponement of his call-up to allow him to finish making his fourth picture, *King Creole*. His co-star, Carolyn Jones, almost accidentally sabotaged the great rush to complete the film by coming down with flu. To the DeGolyer Institute of American Studies, she said in recollection:

Oooh, that was an experience. We had been down on location in New Orleans and they were going to grab him off the set to take him into the army. I caught a bug and had a temperature and a heavy fever. So I was doing love scenes with him, with a hundred and four, and whispering in his ear, 'I hope you've had a shot of penicillin.' He was very nice, very kind, and like the biggest thing going. And he was very much the amateur. He played it. He came to me before we were starting the shoot and said, very shy – shit-kickingly shy – 'Listen . . . you're such a marvellous actress. I know I've got so much to learn. If there's anything you can do to help me I would sure appreciate it.' And I thought, 'Oooh boy, are you full of shit?'

His managers had already set up heavy promotional activity, having Elvis drive up to the draft board in an open-topped Cadillac, with two attractive young women at his side. Parker had made certain that there would be a substantial press presence, and he had arranged for some strategically placed promotional material, blaring the message SEE ELVIS IN *KING CREOLE*, which could be picked up by the newsreel cameras.

Parker kept making the point to all present that his boy had volunteered, rather than wait for the formal drafting papers to arrive. The military joined the exploitation exercise, having the world's hottest male entertainer in their ranks, and co-operated fully with the publicity opportunity, as crowds of photographers and television cameramen were on hand to record his surrender to army service – accompanied by his mother, father, manager and record people. The shaving-off of his sideburns and long hair, swept back into the customary duck's arse, into the GI short-crop style was featured on every front page the next day.

A crucial point of Parker's promotional activity arrived when Elvis stood in front of the cameras to read some congratulatory messages which applauded his all-American image. They included one telegram from the state governor which read: 'You have shown that you are an American citizen first, a Tennessee volunteer and a young man willing to serve his country when called upon to do so . . .' Elvis was supposed to read it out to the waiting world on the other side of the camera lenses. But he could not bring himself to do it and stuffed it into his pocket.

The files reflect another curious aspect of Elvis's sojourn in the army, which only Parker could explain, but never has. He and the army itself began to be inundated with internal requests for appearances by Elvis at services-related functions and to entertain US troops posted in far off places. There was also a facility available to take time off to cut new records. There was no reason on earth why he should not have issued new discs whenever he wanted, just as he did when he went into Nashville for a recording session during a five-day furlough after completing his basic training.

All these possibilities were rejected. This session was to be the last for the whole of Presley's time in the army. As far as Parker was concerned, Elvis's career was in limbo. The army had to turn down all requests. Elvis was shipped to Fort Hood, Texas, the pre-arranged point closest to Memphis, along with twenty or so other rookies aboard a Greyhound bus. There, the army co-operated with another two days of promotional activity, showing just about every possible aspect of Elvis in the army. Elvis put on a brave smile, but as soon as the cameras were off, he was gloomy and sullen. Apart from the millions of fans who wept over his departure, his mother Gladys was beside herself. It was the first time she had been parted from her son for more than a few days since he was born. Even during the heady days of the past two years, she had always been close at hand and had daily contact with him, waiting up until he called.

It was a closeness that came from his early life, when his father was often away earning a living. And, for much of his impoverished formative years, and even into adolescence, he had shared her bed. The prospect of Elvis going away for two years hit her badly. She suffered severe depression to the extent that when Elvis moved to Fort Hood, the family followed. Vernon and Gladys rented a mobile home near the base and later Elvis rented a large house for 1400 dollars a month, into which he moved his parents and grandmother; he promised to move them again for his overseas posting. Gladys, however, was already ill.

In trying to come to terms with the life into which the family had been thrust by her son's stardom, she had taken to heavy bouts of drinking, aggravated by overdoses of appetite-depressant pills, which she consumed in an attempt to get her weight down and make herself more presentable. Within a few weeks of moving to Fort Hood, Vernon had to take her back to Graceland for constant medical care.

Her health deteriorated and she died on 14 August 1958, from heart and liver failure, to which the drink and pills had contributed. Presley's anguished grief over his mother's death led to the almost embarrassing scene at the cemetery. He fell weeping upon her coffin during the graveside service and had to be literally pulled clear for the burial to proceed. It was this emotional trauma of losing the only important woman in his life that was to be identified as the starting point of some of his own problems.

The compassionate leave ended and he returned to the military base, red-eyed and grief-stricken, to prepare for the overseas posting that was already in the offing – to Germany. When it finally came at the end of September 1958, Colonel Parker was on hand to make sure that the event was given suitable hype. Amid the scenes of farewell, as hundreds of relatives of Elvis's fellow soldiers being sent to Germany crowded the army Marine Terminal in Brooklyn, an army band played some of his hits as the young soldiers trooped up the gangplank of *SS General Randall*, in full dress uniform. Elvis was smiling, but truly nervous and unhappy. He hated the prospect of Germany. The cameras were running, the flashguns popped and hundreds of fans wept.

★   ★   ★   ★   ★

In spite of all the line fed to the media that Elvis would be just another soldier, it was never like that. Charlie Hodge, a singer and guitarist who, in 1980, was another subject for questioning by the Memphis attorney-general's investigator, Larry Hutchinson, spoke these reminiscences into the tape-recorder:

I first met Elvis when I was with a country quartet. We used to appear on a show on the ABC network, calling ourselves the Foggy River Boys. In 1957, when we were playing in Memphis, Elvis came backstage and we were all introduced to him. We were all around the same age, in our early twenties. Next time I saw him was when we were both in the army. We were in Fort Worth, Texas, in different outfits which were both posted to Germany. As we were being shipped out, I discovered he was on the train and I went along to his compartment to say hello. When we boarded the ship for the passage across the Atlantic, Elvis asked if I would move in with him for company. They'd put him in the sergeant's quarters to keep him away from the troops and he had no friends. So they moved me in with him and we became real good friends. And that's the way it stayed. I was one of the last people to see him alive. We weren't stationed together in Germany, we were in different posts but I met him almost every weekend.

His military service contained no real thrills, once the novelty of thrashing around the countryside in Jeeps and tanks had worn off. There were a few exciting manoeuvres and excursions into Germany's heartland but, by and large, the routine of army duty soon became exactly that – a daily drudge which required his attention from early morning to evening.

Elvis looked to his social life for compensation, and being who he was, the army allowed him a certain leeway in his private time. Initially, he took rooms at local hotels for himself and his cronies to stay at weekends. But very soon he acquired his own personal residence off-base. He rented a pretty, three-storey house in the small, cobbled-street town, Bad Neuheim, and there began to gather a coterie of aides who encouraged his rich-kid life that barely bore comparison to that of the average American GI. He bought himself a BMW sportscar for the duration, which the local newspapers nicknamed *Der Elviswagen*.

Once his address became common knowledge, girls flocked to the house surrounded by its white picket fence at Goethestrasse 14. Fans starved of Elvis records and films began travelling from all over Europe to try to catch a glimpse of him. Eventually, a notice was pinned to the front gate with a message in German spelling out the request: 'Autographs between seven and eight p.m. only'. The press and locals would turn up to witness this nightly spectacle.

The notice had a double-edged effect. Early in the evening, a large crowd of fans, mostly young girls, began to gather; often, one or two of the lucky ones were invited in to meet Elvis and his friends, who had turned the house into an off-base centre for their parties. Elvis was no different to a thousand other rookies posted abroad for the first time and sought the pleasures on offer from local life. The military,

The Blackmailer

throughout this period, kept their own observations on their star, largely as a protection measure for fear of any untoward event while he was in their care.

They had already been alerted to this possibility by the FBI. The threats and warnings of assassination attempts had to be investigated, even if they were thought to come from cranks. One such investigation listed in the FBI files and passed on to the military investigations unit in Germany alleged that a Red Army soldier serving in East Germany had been trained and briefed for a special mission – to go into Bad Neuheim and kill Elvis – to cause friction between West Germany and the United States. Later, the surveillance was to take on a more salacious tone.

The arrival of Vernon and Elvis's grandmother, Minnie Mae Presley, along with other aides imported from Memphis, did little to quell his mission to compensate for the boredom of army life, and search for companionship. Albert Goldman, Presley's controversial biographer who raked heavily through the less appealing aspects of his subject's life, caused something of a furore with his claims about Presley's predilection for the white panties of teenage girls. This allegation stemmed originally from his time in Germany, where young girls were ever-present.

In spite of the crowd which gathered at his front door, Presley did send out scouts to bring English-speaking female company, an aspect of his life in Germany which eventually resulted in blackmail, a case fully documented, though kept secret at the time, in army intelligence and FBI files.

The newspapers had already been alerted to his quest for young companions. He was photographed dating a sixteen-year-old German girl, Margrit Buergin, who had approached him one day while he was walking in a local park. Later, at a cinema, he met Elisabeth Stefanliak, aged eighteen, whose parents were German. Her mother had recently divorced her father and married a US army sergeant, and they had lived in America for a number of years before returning to Germany for a posting. Elvis, who was looking for a secretary to help with the sackloads of fan mail arriving daily at the house, appointed Elisabeth to the job, promised her a salary of thirty-five dollars a week, and moved her into the house to join the family and the rest of the mini-entourage.

There, Elisabeth joined the routine of life with Elvis that his aides

41

knew well – a routine in which he was served and waited upon, from the moment he woke to the moment he finally went to sleep, surrounded by his relatives and servants who saw to his every whim. The daily programme barely changed. He was up at dawn to report to the base, and returned when his duties ended. Life was punctuated by mealtimes, which were always an event. On weekday evenings, he would often go to the cinema; he rarely mixed in army company. At weekends, selected cronies would come to the house.

★   ★   ★   ★   ★

It was there in Germany that Elvis began to assemble the entourage who would remain his closest companions for pretty well the rest of his life. Three of his aides from Memphis, cousins Red and Sonny West, and Lamar Fike, had travelled to Germany to give Elvis the off-base protection he required while outside army jurisdiction. Others who now joined the 'boys' included Joe Esposito, a thick-set and darkly handsome young soldier of Italian extract from Chicago.

Charlie Hodge was Elvis's closest companion. He was a smaller version of Elvis, standing only five feet, three inches, and he hailed from Decatur, Alabama. He too loved gospel music, which he sang beautifully, and played guitar. So, the gang was all here – and the fun started.

The last of the new arrivals into the Elvis companionship club that was to last for years to come was Priscilla Ann Beaulieu, the fourteen-year-old stepdaughter of an air force officer who, unknown even to her, would soon figure in reports filed by both the FBI and military intelligence. She met him through an introduction to the singer which was an extraordinary event in itself. Her family had arrived in Germany a few months earlier when her stepfather, Captain Joseph Paul Beaulieu, had been posted from Bergstrom air force base, Texas, to Wiesbaden, where she attended the local school for the children of US personnel in Germany. At the time, Priscilla was still in the ninth grade. One afternoon, she was sitting in the garden of her home with her brother Don when she noticed a young man in his mid-twenties observing them.

After a while, he walked over and introduced himself as Currie Grant, an American who, like her father, was serving in the air force. After some small talk about Germany, he asked her if she liked Elvis

Presley. She jokingly half-swooned and then he said he was a good friend of Elvis and how would she like to meet him? He and his wife would be chaperones and he would arrange for her to visit him at his house in Bad Neuheim. Barely believing what she was hearing, Priscilla reported this conversation to her mother and stepfather, who eventually agreed to let her go.

She arrived at Goethestrasse for the evening, and in a room crowded with others, including Vernon and Minnie Mae, Elvis proceeded to serenade her at the piano. Afterwards, he took her into the kitchen where Grandma Minnie was cooking bacon, which Elvis devoured at great speed in five huge sandwiches. They talked about the current pop charts, and Elvis, she reported back to her parents later, was a 'perfect gentleman' throughout.

A few days later, she received a telephone call inviting her back. This was a set procedure – first the 'vetting' stage and then the dating. Every girl who went with Elvis for longer than a one-night stand would go through it. This time he said he wanted to be alone with her and took her up to his own room, where they sat talking. Eventually they began petting, though Priscilla, in her own description of this and the many other meetings that followed, insisted that there was no sex.

Later she took Presley and his father home to meet her parents and, for the next few months, she spent a great deal of time in his company, invariably at his house, which had become something of a retreat when he was not on duty. One of his entourage would call and collect her, sometimes it was Vernon himself, to bring her to Goethestrasse.

Eventually, Priscilla's stepfather requested that Presley report to their home, where he asked him exactly what his intentions were, pointing out that Elvis was the world's most eligible bachelor, with women throwing themselves at his feet wherever he went. Why did he prefer the company of an impressionable schoolgirl? 'Don't worry Captain, sir,' Elvis replied. 'I just happen to be very fond of her and I enjoy her company. It hasn't been easy for me being away from home an' all. I just need someone to talk to, and I'll take good care of her.' Thereafter, Priscilla continued to see Elvis as often as he was able, and her visits often kept her out until the early hours.

Late nights began to affect her ability to stay awake at school and Priscilla admitted that after she told him that she was only getting four or five hours of sleep on the nights she came around to his house, Elvis offered her pills which he said would give her extra energy. He gave her a phial of dexedrine, which he obtained through an army contact. Presley told her that before he was drafted, he had been taking sleeping pills for his insomnia brought on by his unusual working hours and dexedrine had helped to get him going again. In Germany, he told her an army sergeant used to dish out dexedrine to help his soldiers stay awake on guard duty.

In spite of her apparent naïvety over his drug use, in which she did not indulge, Priscilla provided a rather homely account of life at Goethestrasse 14, and the only deviance from her descriptions of a loving, caring relationship with Elvis was the night when one of his aides tried to rape her while driving her home. The man was sacked and the whole affair covered up so as not to attract either bad publicity or the wrath of her stepfather, who would undoubtedly have banned her from seeing Elvis again. Yet, ultimately, rather more lurid descriptions of Elvis's stay in Germany, when Priscilla was not present, became the topic of military intelligence reports.

According to one informant, Elvis's house was constantly the scene of rampant sexual adventures for himself and his friends, who surrounded themselves with girls. They got all the amphetamines they required from an army pharmacist, to whom Presley paid 100 dollars a week.

Some curious hangers-on were present, not least was the latest arrival, a man from South Africa who claimed to be a skin-care specialist and masseur, who we shall call Lawrence. He wrote to Elvis in the summer of 1959, offering his services. The letters, later handed to military intelligence by Elvis's father and now in the FBI files, were in untidy handwriting. He attached numerous references which he claimed were from satisfied customers, including many from the world of showbusiness. In a letter to Elvis in August of that year, he wrote, '... I will be of great service to you ... enclosed please find recent references from two more satisfied ladies ... I have given up my business and cancelled many new bookings in order to attend you.'

This was apparently sufficient for Elvis to accept the man's claims. Elvis dictated to Elisabeth a reply to Lawrence expressing his interest in his treatment. Elvis was concerned about acne pockmarks on his skin and the first signs of crows' feet around his eyes. Lawrence replied by airmail, 'I feel honoured and very privileged in having been chosen for this important task. In fact, I am greatly enthused by my mission and assure you that I am going to work wonders on your skin . . . it is certainly my cherished ambition to give you a complete new skin, and I swear to achieve it within the quickest possible time . . .' A third letter reported that he had obtained a passport and was awaiting Elvis's instructions.

From the batch of letters I read, it would not require an expert eye to discern that he was hardly a man of either professional or worldly substance and, yet, when he eventually turned up on Presley's doorstep, Elvis invited him in to sample his treatment. It was another example of his gullible and trusting nature, enhanced by his narcissism, that he was taken in by the South African's claim of being able to rejuvenate Elvis's face with his secret treatment.

Priscilla described Lawrence as a 'half-mad quack', who was suddenly spending hours on end with Elvis. Elvis himself insisted that he was doing good by treating large pores, the legacy of adolescent acne. Vernon, who was signing the cheques, complained that the fees he was charging were exorbitant and they would be bankrupt if it went on. Elvis waved aside the objections of his aides and every evening for six weeks, Lawrence treated Elvis's face and gave him a body massage.

Then, on Christmas Eve 1959, there was a huge shouting match coming from Elvis's room during a session with Lawrence. The masseur had apparently made homosexual advances towards Elvis. He came crashing down the stairs, with Presley screaming, 'Get this queer out of here.'

Soon afterwards, Elvis received letters from Lawrence, who had taken up residence at the Hotel Rex in Bad Neuheim, stating that he had been advised by lawyers to take him to court for breach of contract. He added, 'I have been very much hurt because things did not work out the way I expected . . . that I have given up my business to attend to you . . .' It was made clear that certain allegations would become public; he claimed to possess tapes and photographs, and if the story ever leaked to the newspapers, Presley's career would be over.

According to FBI reports, Lawrence threatened to implicate Presley's American girlfriend, a reference to Priscilla. The letters continued until 28 December. By then, Presley had paid over 15,000 dollars in 'compensation' to Lawrence. Vernon, worried that his son would continue to be fleeced, called in the US army police. On 3 February 1960, Major Warren E. Metzner, chief of the army's investigation branch, filed the following report, marked 'secret, for official use only':

Elvis Presley was interviewed on 28 December 1959 concerning a complaint that he was the victim of blackmail. Presley indicates that [Lawrence] had made homosexual advances to several of his enlisted friends and admitted that he was bisexual ... On 24 December, Presley decided to discontinue the treatment. At the same time he told [Lawrence] of his decision, he censured him for embarrassing his friends ... [Lawrence], in a rage, threatened to expose Presley by publishing photographs and tape-recordings which were alleged to present Presley in compromising situations, which he denies. He threatened to involve the fourteen-year-old daughter [Priscilla] of an American air force captain ...

   The day following the interview Lawrence was visited by two US officers at the Hotel Rex and was quietly escorted out of Germany. Before he left, he posted Presley a last letter, 'I have decided since this morning to take no action against you. I am deeply sorry for you and I know that you miss something big in your life ...' The letters were filed away with the rest of the evidence in a folder marked secret and the whole affair swept under the carpet to avoid a damaging court case.

*   *   *   *   *

By then Elvis was totally bored with army life. Early in 1960 there were big headlines about him being rushed to hospital during manoeuvres in the freezing German countryside. It was a fake illness, designed to release him from the drudgery of playing soldiers and into a warm hospital bed, where he remained for a week. He told Priscilla there was nothing wrong with him and that he had simply had enough. They were now together as often as possible, in spite of the possibility that publicity about their relationship could blow up into a major scandal. His friend Jerry Lee Lewis had virtually wrecked his career recently by announcing his marriage to the thirteen-year-old daughter of his best friend. He was virtually drummed out of

Britain, where he faced a hostile press and a police investigation.

Elvis was not far from a similar plight. Priscilla, still only fifteen, had been spotted with him on numerous occasions and with the military now keeping close observation of both, there was gossip that leaked back to the media.

There was also an aura of potential scandal surrounding Vernon, whose own romantic inclinations had not passed unnoticed by the military. Routine observations of Elvis for security reasons had noted the arrival in the household of Dee Stanley, the young and very attractive wife of army master sergeant Bill Stanley and the mother of three young sons. The Stanley family was well known to military top brass. Sergeant Stanley, a career soldier whose well-decorated past included service as a bodyguard to General Patton during the invasion of Europe, was also a heavy drinker. He lived with his family at Wiesbaden, though his marriage was heading for the rocks.

Dee, bored with the life of an army wife, sought excitement outside and one day decided she wanted to meet Elvis Presley. She wrote to him, telling him she too came from Tennessee. Elvis invited her for supper, but in the end he did not go. He sent Vernon instead. She was past thirty and hardly within the age group that Elvis preferred. A friendship developed. Vernon even met Bill Stanley, who later tried to enlist his help to try to save his marriage. Instead, the relationship between Dee and Vernon strengthened and they decided they wished to marry. Dee parted from her husband and sent her three sons – David, five, Ricky, six, and Billy, seven – into a temporary home back in America, the Breezy Point Farm for young boys at Newport News, Virginia.

She had soon become Vernon's constant companion but, according to Priscilla, the relationship and the thought that Gladys was being replaced so soon after her death had 'upset Elvis terribly'. They turned up at the Frankfurt Military Hospital, where Elvis was supposedly being treated for tonsillitis, and asked his permission to marry. He told Dee that anything that made his daddy happy would make him happy too, but privately he was set against it. He questioned whether Dee's motives were, as he put it, 'honourable', since she was twenty years Vernon's junior. But Vernon was lovesick.

He wrote Dee long love letters, and before they all left Germany in March 1960, there was no question that she would become his second wife, just as soon as her divorce came through. The marriage, in July

1960, which Elvis pointedly did not attend, provided him with three stepbrothers, two of whom were eventually to become star witnesses of events on the day of his death seventeen years later.

When Elvis returned to America before his discharge from the army in March, Priscilla was very much in evidence at the airport and was seen being escorted in tears from the tarmac by a military policeman. In this way, she suddenly became the focus of press attention.

Colonel Tom Parker who had remained in America throughout Elvis's term in Germany and had never once made an attempt to visit him – for reasons which would only become apparent later – was furious with the publicity and the scandalous potential of the love-lives of both Elvis and Vernon. Parker had been setting up all kinds of new deals and contracts in readiness for his boy's return to civilisation and the money-making. He was, not unnaturally, concerned about this friendship.

When he learned of Priscilla's importance to Elvis, he raged angrily at Elvis, and at Vernon for allowing it. 'Look at what happened to Jerry Lee,' he fumed. 'The pair of you are either stupid or mad – or both.' Elvis warned him to stay out of his private life and to concern himself only with his business affairs.

Parker retaliated that if he carried on like that, there would be no business affairs to manage. If it was discovered that Elvis had brought the girl into his household while she was under the recognised age of consent, he could kiss goodbye to a promising future. The music business might stand the kind of media attention he could expect, but in Hollywood, at the start of the Sixties, phoney morality and one-foot-on-the-floor bedroom scenes were still the order.

J. Edgar Hoover's beady eye remained cast in their direction, as did the ever alert religious communities of the bible belt. On-screen sex and violence was already a subject of mass discussion on both sides of the Atlantic and the boundaries were being extended by the new wave of young writers and directors. That was the movies. The studios still worried about their stars' morals. Universal went to great length to cover up any suggestion that Rock Hudson was gay, and hadn't Joan Collins just secretly terminated a pregnancy by Warren Beatty, for fear of scandal that could have ended their careers? It was that bad. And Elvis bringing home a high school girl would not have endeared him to the money men who, as the colonel kept insisting, they needed to keep sweet. Whatever his feelings were for Priscilla at the time and regardless of the motives for his friendship with her, Presley did as the colonel commanded, and did not see Priscilla again for two years until, as he stipulated, she had reached a respectable age.

Parker temporarily resolved the publicity situation by feeding a fictitious leak to the newspapers that Elvis was being welcomed home by Nancy Sinatra and romance was in the air. It wasn't, although the rumours were fired again by a television special, entitled 'Frank Sinatra's Welcome Home Party for Elvis Presley', which was a schmaltzy vehicle aimed at edging him back into public life, and in which he appeared nervous and uncomfortable.

Priscilla had no doubt about the causes for their separation. Parker had ranted so loud that Elvis was still worried that the blackmail story might break in scandalous form. He was apprehensive about how he would be received by his fans and whether he could resume his career with the same status that he had left it, and he was anguishing over his father's decision to remarry.

3

Hollywood Capers

'When we were discharged from the army, I went down to Nashville to help Elvis work on the first album. I also went to Florida with him for the Frank Sinatra show, and then he was going out to Hollywood to make his new picture, GI Blues. *The day he was leaving, I was at the Memphis train station to see him off with his father. I was just standing there waving goodbye when he looked down at me and said, "Do you want to go with me?" I didn't have any clothes with me or anything, but I said I sure as hell would, and he said, "Well, get on the goddamn train ..." That was it. He put me on the permanent payroll, I moved into his house and I stayed for seventeen years ...'*

Charlie Hodge, 1980

Charlie Hodge was Elvis in miniature. He was a fine singer of gospel songs and played a good guitar. And he was around for the beginning of a new era for Elvis Presley, a life so different from two years of heel-kicking in the forces, and different again from the mad, mad whirl of his early career. Another of his ex-army buddies, Joe Esposito, had also joined Elvis's private staff and would remain as the senior and most influential member of the entourage for the rest of Elvis's life. While Charlie became a companion and one who could rehearse Elvis's new songs with him in private, Joe's role was altogether more responsible.

In his taped statement, Esposito said:

I suppose you could say that I became his foreman. The job he gave me when we came out of the services was generally overseeing this operation. I would take care of all Elvis's personal business, looking after his personal money, paying the bills, fixing up transport, running the house he had rented in Los Angeles, making sure everything ran smoothly. I was next in line to Vernon on the personal side and had contact with Tom Parker on the business side. When I first started, there were really only four of us in the post-army entourage; myself, Charlie Hodge, Sonny West, his bodyguard, and his cousin Jean Smith, who helped with business matters. Vernon had complete control over the money, and he wrote all the cheques.

The phrase 'TCB' – Taking Care of Business – became the adopted motto of his private entourage, and Elvis had solid gold bars with those words engraved upon them, presenting one to anyone who eventually passed into service as one of his personal aides.

And so, here we begin another portrait of Elvis, switching from the stark and cryptic notes of the FBI and military files, to the colourful archives of movieland and some early recollections of those closest to him. I found some excellent, previously unpublished accounts in the DeGolyer Institute of American Studies, and in the superb collections of the Doheny Facility at the University of Southern California, which throw a revealing spotlight on the way Elvis's new career was planned.

From the time he came out of the army until he made his 'comeback' in 1969, Elvis appeared before a live audience only twice – for benefit concerts. It was a carefully controlled period of his life which became known as 'the Hollywood years', and during that time, everything he did was geared to generating income from his films. His personal ambitions were totally subjugate to the direction of others and it marked the beginning of many problems of a psychological nature that he tried to block out with chemical aides. This sojourn in tinsel town was, in the end, to leave Elvis angry and disillusioned, or, as Albert Goldman put it in his assessment of Elvis's films, 'the laughing stock of the entertainment industry'.

While he had hopes of becoming a 'serious' actor, like his pre-army idol, James Dean, his management team had decided to make him a Hollywood product, aimed solely at generating the largest amount of revenue, from box-office takings, film-linked albums and merchandising, for the least possible outlay. There was no secret in that; it was obvious to all who followed Elvis's films and have seen them on television over the years. What is pertinent now in terms of the scope of this work is the way the whole thing was set up – where the interests of Elvis were actually a very minor consideration.

The money was a crucial factor to his managers, but not so much to Elvis himself. All he ever wanted was a bank balance that allowed him the freedom to do what he wanted. He would willingly have sacrificed the fees he drew during the Hollywood years for greater personal satisfaction and achievement, that provided him with help and tuition as an actor instead of the lightweight material he became saddled with and which he admitted was within the capabilities of a performing monkey.

The course of his life had already been set by the time he left the army by the joint aspirations of three men who had shaped his career over long discussions in smoke-filled offices in Beverly Hills – Parker, producer Hal Wallis, and Abe Lastfogel, president of the William Morris Agency, then one of the most powerful organisations in Hollywood. Elvis's future was mapped out to the finest detail – they could have been marketing a box of soap powder. What they knew, and what Elvis had long ago feared might happen, was that he had returned to a vastly altered pop music scene, one which was already discarding the raw rock 'n' roll that brought him to fame.

New sounds, new stars and a new thing called soul were rising and the old barons of Tin Pan Alley had been sent scuttling for cover, rocked by the exposes of corruption and manipulation in the music business. Even as the King stepped back from exile to the mass greetings of his people at Memphis, payola and DJ bribery was being investigated on a vast scale, and Memphis itself was among the key centres of trouble.

Purist Elvis fans would have preferred him to have been relaunched as a rock singer, updated and refreshed and ready to do battle with the Beatles and the rest. In fact, the man who had inspired many of the guitar-twanging groups of the Sixties offered virtually no opposition. Parker had already held up his hands – on Elvis's behalf – in surrender. It was pretty clear to all concerned that Elvis could not return as the hip-swirling rock 'n' roller, which had formed the basis of his stage act when he'd left. In fact, his managers did not even want him to go on stage. They all agreed that his appeal should be broadened, modelled on Frank Sinatra, who had been the idol of the bobbysoxers and who, in the Fifties, had moved into films. He'd had the added good fortune to be involved in some classics, such as *From Here to Eternity*. That was the example they held up to Elvis on his triumphant return to Memphis in March 1960. The results were obvious: here was Sinatra paying Elvis 25,000 dollars for a one-slot appearance on his television show. They sold him the tale of silver-screen greatness and Elvis naturally believed them.

He was excited at the prospect. Joe Esposito said he was totally taken by the thought of becoming a great actor, a big movie star, and the re-direction of his musical appeal became evident in the first two singles released after his return, 'It's Now or Never' and 'Are You Lonesome Tonight?'. It moved him out of the bawdiness of bumping and grinding into the centre ground of pop, largely populated by the ageing crooners of the day like Bing Crosby, Perry Como and Tony Bennett, and more youthful singers like Pat Boone.

There were actually a number of film critics around who agreed that Elvis had great acting potential. He could, perhaps, have become a decent actor with the same sort of schooling and lessons that were drummed into some of the major stars of Hollywood in the golden days of the studio system, when the likes of Rock Hudson had to attend daily coaching in speech, diction, movement, dancing, and even ballet. But the studio system had already collapsed when Elvis returned from the non-war, and anyway there was never any intention on the part of his management team to turn him into a serious actor. In fact, there was never the slightest thought of it, in spite of his personal aspirations when he set out on that Sixties route to a new kind of stardom. He was to become the victim, and there is no other word, of commercialism and exploitation.

Parker and his partners talked money the size of telephone numbers and mapped out a system which was based upon a pyramid, with each aspect of financial income linked to and boosted by the next – so that he made films in which he played lightweight parts and sang at least twelve songs. He had to sing twelve songs because that was the minimum requirement for the next stage of the marketing operation, the album – the great Sixties boom industry – and from each album there would be a hit single. The films and the records provided the basis for the third stage of the marketing, the merchandising, with every film carefully analysed and ticked out to inspire the manufacture of dozens of Elvis lines, from *Blue Hawaii* T-Shirts to *Viva Las Vegas* playing cards.

Elvis was the key to unlocking this dormant hoard of wealth, and three of the greatest deal-makers in Hollywood at the time were taking care to ensure that the direction, the films, the marketing was right in every respect – not necessarily for the advancement of Elvis, but for the product he was to become.

Hal Wallis, in later years, confessed that he would have preferred doing a deal with the devil than Tom Parker. But they were all pretty much of the same fabric. Parker negotiated hard because he was on a large slice of Elvis's income. This became even more important when the films took off and he formed a merchandising company in 1963. Parker signed a new contract with Elvis which provided him with a broad-based fifty per cent cut of everything Elvis earned, from films to merchandise. Elvis and Vernon had for some reason best known to themselves agreed that Elvis and the colonel were a partnership. At least, that was how the colonel himself explained their relationship, when he had to account for these rather large commissions years later, when a probate court was examining Elvis's financial affairs. Parker said they went fifty-fifty on everything because, eventually, the management of Elvis's career occupied his entire working life. That is what Parker claimed.

And so, he had the incentive of negotiating as much for himself as for Elvis when he said he wanted a million dollars a picture for Elvis at a time when even Elizabeth Taylor wasn't getting that money – she first achieved that magical sum for *Cleopatra* – and actors like Sean Connery, who had just become an overnight star as 007, had accepted six thousand pounds (about ten thousand dollars) for his first Bond film. Warren Beatty, another up-and-coming star, had just completed his first major picture with the girl Elvis wished he could have married, Natalie Wood, and was making a mere 200,000 dollars a picture. In fact, Elvis's money went higher. When he signed with MGM, he was put on a massive salary of 75,000 dollars a week, and got a fifty per cent share of the profits of each picture. He was provided with a house, limousines, everything he wanted. He was, without doubt, the highest-paid movie star in Hollywood by the end of 1963.

Abe Lastfogel, of the William Morris Agency, was the man charged with transferring this demand into actuality; he was the one who went to the film studios and put forward the package for which he collected a ten per cent fee of the gross. Lastfogel was especially important to the development of Elvis's film career. He was at the absolute peak of his substantial power and influence in Sixties

Hollywood and, more importantly for the colonel, had the reputation of absolute honesty. Hal Wallis, who had discovered such stars as Burt Lancaster and Charlton Heston, was, of course, the first movie producer to spot Elvis's potential when he signed him back in 1956. His task was to bring Elvis alive as an actor, find the right material, get the scripts written and bring the whole package to the screen. There was a great deal of speculation and publicity at the time about the prospects for Elvis in Hollywood, that he had very real potential to become a good actor. In truth, the possibility was dead in the water almost from the word go. He would not be provided with the opportunity. Neither did he possess the toughness of a Hollywood upbringing to kick against what his managers were bestowing upon him. Basically, he did just as he was told.

He accepted Parker's view as sacrosanct, never argued with Wallis and turned up at the studios on his best behaviour, extraordinarily polite and desperately eager to please. He was never concerned about the money; he just wanted to be the new James Dean.

The true intentions were revealed by Hal Wallis in two tape-recorded interviews he made for inclusion in university facilities for study and research, which have never been published. The way in which Elvis's career was planned in advance emerges from these tapes, both recorded in 1982. Wallis, who died in 1986, was remarkably frank about their intentions and how Elvis became one of the most manipulated stars in Hollywood history.

First, he admitted his close friendship with Tom Parker. He said:

He's what you would expect of a carnival showman. It was as if he had stepped right off the midway. A big rough kind of guy, but big-hearted. We are very good friends to this day. I see him frequently. We would make a deal on a handshake and the papers would come through four or five months later. We would be making pictures under a handshake deal. And he always kept his word. He made sure Elvis was always there ... never had a problem, considering that every picture we made with him was a success.

Wallis provided a far greater insight into the intentions of the two men, that existed right from the outset of Elvis's film career. He noted:

55

Elvis was a great personality who had undoubtedly revolutionised the music business in 1956, and that is what I knew when I bought him for the movies. Everyone remembers those scenes of fan worship and the public adulation. Well, I envisaged that kind of reaction being transferred to the movies, and the movie theatres. I remembered way back when we first tested him that there was a kind of magic, an excitement which was similar to when I first tested Errol Flynn in the Thirties. I remember very well the similarities. It came through in a different way; but very powerful. It was the look of him, the eyes – with flickers of Rudolph Valentino – the way he moved, there was just excitement about him. We never had a problem with Elvis. He was easy to work with, he was always there on time; he had learned his lines and was exceedingly polite to everyone, and especially his co-star.

When a woman came into the room, he would stand up and address her as he would have done his schoolteacher. He called the men 'sir' and the women 'ma'am'. He was anxious to succeed as a motion-picture star; very co-operative. He loved acting and there were people who were saying that he was in the exact mould of Marlon Brando and James Dean. Well, perhaps he could have been with different material. But I never felt that he was that good an actor; in fact, I would go so far as to say that he wasn't an actor in the real sense. We just about pushed him to his true limits. We first cast him in toughish, angry sorts of roles, which he performed naturally. He had a range, sure, but the fact is that we did not hire him as a potential actor. When we bought him, it was not in our mind to use him as you would a conventional actor. It was the personality and his ability as a singer and a performer. We looked specifically for material in which he could sing his songs, have a romance with a girl and live happily ever after, so that his fans would leave the theatre with a warm glow, wanting more, and dash out and buy the soundtrack.

Wallis agreed that the films written for Elvis were all largely variations on a theme, built around the songs. And the films were used as a vehicle to revamp Elvis's total image as he arrived back home. There was a marked difference in the films he made before going into the army and those when he came out. In the early films, he was cast as the snarling, angry young man which was the theme of young people's movies then.

The post-army films were deliberately designed to be much lighter, so as not to force either his acting or his character. He played himself, as a singing personality, cast in undemanding scripts, usually set in exotic, escapist locations and surrounded by girls. His first film was already lined up for production when he arrived home from the army; it was *GI Blues*, unashamedly geared to cash in on the all-American boy who had just completed his service to president and country. If his fans from the early rock 'n' roll era were expecting the same hip-swirling, lip-curling Elvis, then they were to be sorely disappointed.

It was a loose story of a singing soldier, which even Elvis did not like. But, of course, it was commercially successful and like many of his films has remained constantly among the re-runs on television.

Elvis dearly wanted stronger roles and his next, *Flaming Star*, in which he appeared as a half-breed Indian, gave him that opportunity. The script did not match his hopes and it did not fare as well as the last; his managers felt it was a mistake to change the formula. Another so-called serious film, *Wild in the Country* – his third after the army – about a rebellious hillbilly boy, was also a box-office failure and even *Monthly Film Bulletin* was moved to retort, 'One can't help feeling he was better off prior to his misguided bid for class.'

This, of course, gave his managers the ammunition they needed to prevent any further deviation from the formula pictures. So they went back to the froth, and Elvis was destined to churn out production-line movies, one every four months, that did nothing for his burning ambitions, but made all concerned a great deal of money.

*   *   *   *   *

With the Hollywood situation pretty well established, Elvis paid some attention to his domestic arrangements. His girls were legendary. They arrived in abundance for his private parties and he could have had his pick of any one of a dozen top female stars of the day. And yet, his thoughts roamed back to Germany where he had left his school-age girlfriend waiting for his call. She had to wait almost two years, until she turned sixteen. Priscilla Presley's own account of life behind those walls is *Elvis and Me*, one of the most reliable and honest of all the many books written by his former associates. Her awe-struck descriptions of her arrival to spend the summer holidays of

1962 with him at Graceland conjure up visions of a Dickensian story of a child being sent to spend time with a distant relative. The house was full of Elvis's entourage. Vernon had married Dee Stanley by then and her three sons had moved into the house that Elvis had bought for them not far away.

Her father had needed some convincing that he should allow his teenage daughter to travel from their home in Germany, where he was still serving, to join a star whose name and photograph was seldom out of the gossip columns. After a thrilling and successful holiday with Elvis at Graceland that summer, Priscilla was desperate to return for the Christmas holidays – and for good! With Elvis's assurances that she would be well cared for, and her own pressure and desire to go, along with increasing hostility towards her German surroundings, her mother and stepfather eventually gave in and allowed her to move to Memphis. She arrived early in the New Year, 1963, after her stepfather had received Elvis's faithful promise that he would make all the arrangements for her to complete her schooling. It was, to be sure, one of the strangest romances in the annals of modern showbusiness history.

Priscilla was kept virtually hidden away. When visitors came to Graceland, she would move out and stay with Vernon and Dee, or with one of his friends. In Memphis, where everyone knew he had a teenage 'protégée' who he was putting through high school, the gossip was kept low profile, as was everything in Elvis's life in that city. For years, the local newspapers and reporters assigned to the Elvis Watch, kept a discreet silence about the things that they knew would damage him if they ever got out.

Priscilla's presence remained an unpublicised item. The cover story was Elvis's romance with Ann-Margret, which also served the purpose of warding off the discovery of the dark-haired little schoolgirl who he had enrolled at a Catholic school for girls. Parker was, of course, steaming through fear of scandal.

Jerry Lee Lewis's episode with the child bride had not been forgotten and he was still suffering the effects. He was ostracised from the higher strata of showbusiness for almost a decade and his problems only increased as the humiliation of these pressures drove him ever more firmly into the grip of drugs. It was still a touchy subject, and it arose again in 1961. Chuck Berry was similarly struck by self-inflicted catastrophe at the height of his career when he was given a three-year jail sentence and fined 5000 dollars for transporting a fourteen-year-old across the state line.

And so, Elvis's own little flower of youth, the child who was delivered to her classroom every morning in Elvis's big blue Cadillac to the great envy of her schoolfriends, was nurtured and cultivated in readiness for the great day, when she was old enough to become his bride without causing a sensational scandal that would wreck his Hollywood career.

In the meantime, she adjusted to the routine of schooldays interspersed with the strange life of the man who lived at night. When he wasn't working in Hollywood, he would sleep by day and then hire a cinema or an amusement park by night, and take the entourage along. Priscilla used to go to school, sometimes still half-asleep from being awake all night, attend class and then go back to Graceland and slip back into bed with Elvis to be at his side when he awoke from his pill-induced slumbers, usually around four p.m. It affected her schooling and her looks. Once, when her parents came for a holiday, her stepfather took one look at her and declared that her heavily made-up eyes looked like pissholes in the snow. If her stepfather had known the truth, he would have ordered her home.

★ ★ ★ ★ ★

The quality of Elvis's films remained one of his most continual causes of anguish. *Blue Hawaii*, another GI picture, telling the tale of a lonesome soldier returning home, was based on a flimsy plot, carefully punctuated to accommodate songs which could be made into a soundtrack album, from which a couple could be selected for a single. The 'Girls, Girls, Girls', scantily clad, and being whisked around the countryside in a variety of flash automobiles and motorcycles, were the young and beautiful of the day, like Ann-Margret, the former Miss America, who co-starred in *Viva Las Vegas*, and Tuesday Weld. Hal Wallis made no bones about their aim:

We set what was considered a reasonably good budget to make his pictures and tailored them for colourful backgrounds; we made them on various locations. We did three in Hawaii, we did one in New Orleans, we did one in Germany, and all of those were, I believe, first-class pictures which fared very well commercially. The films were all relatively expensive to make. We did not reduce the cost or make cheap pictures just to hype the profit. We did try to make decent pictures and I think, by and large, we succeeded. I have no apologies to make for them at all. If I had to do it all over again, I would make the same kind of pictures with Elvis. I reckon we correctly assessed his ability and stretched him as far as we could. We weren't hiring an outstanding new actor. We knew that. Some of his more ardent admirers have said that he could have dealt with that kind of material, stronger scripts which were less reliant on the Elvis entertainment value.

Frankly, I doubt he could have gone much further. He tried hard, but I would say that I found him somewhat embarrassing to watch in some of his love scenes, the nice-guy scenes. The fact was, you could not compare him to any real actor; he was never going to be a Richard Burton or a Peter O'Toole, not even a Danny Kaye, because they were actors and great in the things that they did. They were very selective in material, too. Elvis never stood up against anything we did. He never directly asked me to put him into a different kind of picture or into dramatic parts. That was whipped up by critics or columnists; it never happened with me.

Now, later in his career, when some of his pictures did not hit the mark and his popularity as a movie star tailed off, it may be that he was tiring of them. After the nine I did with him, he made other pictures which were not made to that formula, and were made on a lesser scale, smaller budgets which seemed commercially aimed at squeezing the most revenue out of Presley for the least possible input of capital. I had nothing to do those. I can only be responsible for the ones I did. I repeat, he never complained while he was working with me. He never kicked. By and large, he just did as Colonel Parker wished, and, of course, Parker was ever anxious to please the Hollywood moguls.

It always amuses me the way the Monday-morning quarterbacks go on about things they cannot alter. I would like to have seen any one of them create something out of Elvis, some dramatic presence, instead of letting him be natural, which is what he was. There was absolutely no point pushing him. We knew what we were doing; hell I'd been around there long enough.

I know what it takes to be a star of any magnitude, one who can take on the kind of picture Dean and Brando were doing when they started out. Or the likes of Charlton Heston, who I signed when he first came to Hollywood in 1950; he was an actor. Presley was not. We did not sign him as a second Dean or second Brando. We signed him as the number one Elvis Presley. Full stop. I think possibly the best film was *King Creole* and the most successful one was undoubtedly *Blue Hawaii*, which some of the carping critics found fault with. But it grossed over thirty million dollars, and the response from the fans was probably the best of all Elvis's pictures.

Alan Weiss, who wrote five of Elvis's pictures, agreed with Wallis. He said it wasn't just the sexual attraction that made Elvis so appealing to his fans. It was transcended by an indefinable energy. The question was, would it show on film? Weiss concluded that it would and believed the transformation to be quite incredible. They knew that they were in the presence of a phenomenon; electricity bounced off the walls of the sound stage:

One felt it as an awesome thing – like an earthquake in progress, only without the implicit threat. Watching this insecure country boy, who apologised when he asked for a rehearsal, as though he had done something wrong, turn into absolute dynamite when he stepped into the bright lights and started lip-synching the words of his familiar hit. He believed in it, and he made you believe it, no matter how sophisticated your musical tastes were. To deny his talent would have been foolish, like sticking your finger into a live socket and denying the presence of electricity.

As the writer of some of his best films – including *Blue Hawaii* – Weiss was more conscious than most of the need to tailor the part to fit Elvis's ability. While he was more than competent in his early dramatic pictures, such as *Love Me Tender* (1956) and *King Creole* (1958), he was much more comfortable and successful in lighter pictures. Some Elvis liked, some he did not, but Weiss said he was 'far too polite or fearful of offending to object'.

*   *   *   *   *

The Hollywood years were also the fun years, well-documented by Elvis chroniclers. They were years of a thousand girls, of one true romance, with Ann-Margret, which she refuses to this day to discuss after he broke it off. There were other names mentioned, like his early encounter with Natalie Wood, which was brief, and a publicity affair with Tuesday Weld. But the latter, like most of his gossip-column encounters, was generally the figment of a publicity man's imagination. In reality, Elvis usually steered clear of the actresses. There were some wild parties, but they were only ever Elvis's parties. He refused to associate with the glitterati, as one of his publicists discovered when he was provided with the daunting task of getting Elvis to join the standard Hollywood social scene. This was as much due to Colonel Parker as it was to Elvis. Parker's attitude was, 'If you want to see Elvis, buy a ticket.' And this also suited the star. He just did not want to go anywhere outside of his group.

To prove a point, there came a time when the Hollywood mogul Spyros Skouras, head of Twentieth Century-Fox, tried to get Elvis to make a personal appearance to promote his movie. The colonel refused to allow it, and Skouras said he would appeal directly to the star. 'If you can get Elvis to do it,' said the colonel, 'you can have him.' Elvis stayed home.

He brought his own party to Hollywood, the entourage of relatives and friends which he had gathered in the intervening years, and which had grown around him like a tribe. He had houses in Bel Air and Palm Springs. So the parties were always his own, with the Memphis Mafia — so-called because they were a collection of young men who always accompanied him everywhere he went, wearing dark suits and black sunglasses, like secret servicemen protecting the president of the United States. They were his companions, his servants, his fetchers and carriers, his procurers of a plentiful supply of female company. They attended his every need, his every whim. They slept when he slept. They wrestled and played games.

When they weren't in Las Vegas or Hollywood, they were back at Graceland where mobile homes sprouted in the grounds to accommodate the ever-growing numbers. Graceland, designed like an old plantation house, had become exactly that, with his staff and aides at close call. This was his castle where he escaped from the world and the fans and the pressures. Life was insular, protected. Outside the two huge gates there were the gate persons, the sightseers who gathered day and night to catch a glimpse of Elvis. Some were in virtual residence on the street outside, and Elvis would often stop and talk, or sign autographs as he arrived home.

Throughout these years, Priscilla remained in the shadowy corners of his life, within Graceland or on the ranch he had bought nine miles outside of town, where they would go riding together. She seldom joined him in California and only occasionally went to Palm Springs. That was his other life, the one from which she was largely excluded.

He had also established a routine of medication which matched his lifestyle and his feelings. Riddled with insecurities and disappointments over his films, and trapped by the desires of his nightlife, he had to take several strong pills to sleep and then a handful of 'dexies' to get moving when he woke up. His experimentation with pills and prescription drugs had begun in Hollywood, partly out of boredom, partly in pursuit of social pleasures, and occasionally to help him meet the needs of his masters. He had always suffered from insomnia and in recent years it had merely been exacerbated by his intake of dexedrine; one was needed to counteract the other and vice versa. The pattern became all too predictable.

Joe Esposito said he did not consider drugs to be a problem then; Elvis was no worse than many others in that showbusiness world of pressures and crazy hours, and his intake was certainly controllable. He said he had seen Elvis go thirty days without taking a pill, and it had never affected his work. When interviewed by Larry Hutchinson, members of his entourage recalled few problems with drugs during these years. They were there in his life for whatever reasons were applicable at the time. No one, not his father, Tom Parker, nor Joe Esposito seemed to think it was a problem that Elvis could not handle.

The habit became a worrying factor for Priscilla, however, as early as 1966. She saw it close at hand, in the bedroom where the medication was consumed out of sight of everyone else. When she spoke of her concern, he would pull out a thick medical book, the *PDR – Physicians' Desk Reference* – from which he could quote the ingredients and effects of every conceivable pill. Priscilla was 'impressed' by this knowledge and soon she, like many others in the entourage trying to keep up with his lifestyle, found it necessary to take the pills, too. 'Two placidyls for him, one for me. A dexedrine for him, one for me. It soon became as normal as watching him eat a pound of bacon with his Spanish omelette,' she later wrote.

So commonplace had this extraordinary life become, that she took a dexedrine to get her through the examinations before school graduation. She passed, and on the day she graduated Elvis bought her first car, a red Corvair. Later, he bought a Mustang for her brother. Even with Priscilla out of school, they could not marry for many more months.

Publicly, Elvis's affairs when he was in Hollywood were still high profile; it was all part of the Hollywood story for public consumption and promotional publicity. It wasn't until Christmas 1966 that he and Priscilla became engaged – four years after she had first moved into the house as a sixteen-year-old. Colonel Parker gave his nod of approval to the wedding the following spring and they were married in Las Vegas on 1 May, in a hotel suite before a select group of guests, at a ceremony conducted by an old friend of the colonel's, a Jewish judge.

By then, Elvis's film career was already showing the first signs of decline. Hal Wallis and Weiss parted company with Elvis and left him to the devices of others. The movies became weaker, the reasons for doing them became overtly commercial, and he was pumping out three films a year. With new producer Sam Katzman, well known for his low-budget, quick-fire movies, the production time for an Elvis picture was cut to less then a month so that expenses were minimised.

Elvis made thirty-one films before they finally ran out of steam and the fans began staying away in droves. By the end of 1968, he was sick and tired of the self-styled crap. Also, Parker could find no new producers willing to take up a new Elvis contract at the price he was asking.

During their time, the money which the films generated was enormous, estimated at over four hundred million box-office dollars alone, a figure which in today's terms could well compare with a modern blockbuster series. To this was the added bonus of the record and merchandising spin-offs. But the chicken that was laying all these golden eggs had himself been diverted off course to such a degree that once Hollywood had sucked him in and spat him out when his usefulness had been drained, his career was balanced on a knife-edge.

Each film became less successful than the last, and album sales declined against the Sixties' competition of the groups: the Beatles, the Rolling Stones, the Beach Boys. Alongside them, Elvis, the original rock 'n' roller, looked wan and old-fashioned. He became bitter and cynical. His whole attitude had changed in these past few disappointing, treadmill years as he watched the new wave and listened to the wall of sound. He was the face at the window, like a child looking through a window at a party to which he had not been invited.

The incredible, underlying loyalty of his own fans had been sorely tested. Those around him also felt the pain in a way they had never experienced before. He had changed. He had always been arrogant, autocratic, and demanding of all those around him, sometimes even physically cruel. When he went too far, he would try to make amends with his gifts and tearful apologies. The bitterness was an added trait, and it made life difficult for those in the company who, it must be added, had lived well during Elvis's fun years.

Several left, marriages broke up and the whole Elvis organisation had edged closer to breaking point. Not least among the causes of his anger was the continued success of the new groups. Though he professed to love the Beatles for their music, he despised them for knocking the King off his throne, and the day would come – as we shall later observe – when he would attempt revenge. More importantly, he had to consider whether he too should return to basics, and join the crowd.

4

Death Threats in Vegas

'I first met Elvis in 1969 when I conducted a lie detector test on him to investigate allegations made regarding a paternity suit. We ran a polygraph which was a controlled reconstruction on the night in question when the lady claimed she had sex. Results of that test exonerated Elvis Presley. Not guilty. However, we did think at the time that he was probably on barbiturates. His cardio pressure was completely subdued and shortly before the test he did something that I would not normally allow. He went into the bathroom and came out after about five minutes, relaxed . . .'
John O'Grady, former Los Angeles drugs cop, 1980

It was the moment that John O'Grady, renowned drugs buster of the Los Angeles police force, formed a unique friendship with Elvis. It was also a friendship that would challenge O'Grady's principles, on the question of his professional ethics: How should he handle the knowledge that Elvis Presley, superstar, was a heavy user of prescription narcotics?

O'Grady was a retired police sergeant with the Los Angeles police, and in the last ten years of service, he had specialised in drugs. He led a narcotics detail and was the veteran of hundreds of drugs busts in the LAPD area. He had studied narcotics extensively, and was the first certified narcotics instructor in the United States; he lectured at the police academy for five years, was a member and officer of the International Narcotics Enforcement Officers Association of America, and, when he retired, set up in business as a private investigator and polygraph consultant, used extensively by defence lawyers.

His meeting with Elvis in that all-important year of 1969, when the star was on the brink of relaunching his career, aroused his suspicions but nothing more. He was a private investigator in Los Angeles by then and had been asked by Elvis's lawyers to conduct the lie detector test to prove that he was not the father of a certain child, as claimed by a woman who had filed a paternity suit against him. The incident was one of many such claims. This one was unsuccessful, although, as we will see, it was to have a deeper significance a year later. O'Grady said that during the test there was nothing in Elvis's general demeanour to suggest he was a severe user, other than the low blood pressure. So, he let it go.

Elvis kept in touch, however, because for one thing he was a police groupie, and loved stories of drugs busts and other experiences that O'Grady was able to relate in their long conversations. Elvis told him he was an honorary police officer in several states, and had a very large collection of police badges. For the time being, O'Grady continued his association on the basis of becoming a friend, as indeed he was, but he could not have imagined then how deeply he would become involved in the final saga of Elvis's life, which was then at the very beginning of a slow and desperate drama.

As the income from the movies stopped virtually overnight, he needed a new source of funds. True enough, he also needed a new direction and a new challenge. He had realised long ago that the appalling movie plots no longer had any kind of relevance to young people, or to the age in which they lived. The movies were old hat, washed up. Elvis knew it better than anyone and it angered him that he should have remained in them for so long. He was in limbo, hoisted between generations.

The flower children, Timothy Leary's tune-in, turn-on and drop-out brigade, had no time for Elvis or his kind of music, and as the decade neared its end, Jack Nicholson, Peter Fonda and Dennis Hopper caught the mood emphatically with *Easy Rider*, the marijuana-drenched road movie that almost melted the celluloid and made Elvis's efforts look like a bible class.

Priscilla recalled that he would return home from filming filled with disillusionment and anger. He would call the guys together and tell them to get the bikes out. There were now eleven of them in the entourage, and he had bought them all motorbikes – Triumphs and Harley Davidsons – along with all the leathers. And they would get dressed up and go roaring off around the Hollywood hills, Presley's own 'Hell's Angel' gang.

He couldn't escape the notices, which were getting worse. *Charro!*, which he made in a quick shoot in 1968, was massacred by the critics: 'a dismal western with a singing star playing straight. A bad experience.' His final film, aptly entitled *Change of Habit*, with a star-studded supporting cast including Mary Tyler Moore and Ed Asner, was a one-last-try, in which Elvis made a valiant but vain effort to rescue his movie career. The *Monthly Film Bulletin* said the movie sounded the death knell for Elvis's career. And they spoke generally. Outside, it was being said that Elvis was as good as washed up, with nowhere to go. His lucrative contract with MGM was at an end, and all the studio-supplied trappings that went with Hollywood stardom disappeared.

He returned to Memphis to consider his position, and with all the millions he had made out of the movies, those eight hectic years, it ought to have been possible for him to have done whatever he pleased – take a break, sail around the world with his wife and new daughter Lisa Marie, lounge around, relaxing in some Caribbean hideaway. He could do none of those things.

The fabulous money, the tens of millions he had personally earned from the films alone, not counting the record royalties from dozens of singles and albums with multi-million sales, had been unwisely and rashly discarded in his orgies of generosity and extravagance. It seemed a barely credible fact, but absolutely true, that he did not have a great deal of spare cash.

When, a couple of years earlier, he insisted upon buying a ranch nine miles from Memphis, where he and Priscilla could go and relax, Vernon had to go, cap in hand, to his local bank to borrow 500,000 dollars – set against Graceland, as collateral – to complete the deal.

While the world talked about how wealthy Elvis must be, he was already talking with Colonel Parker about what they could do next. Basically, it came down to his never-ending spending spree, the generosity motivated by a mix of kindness and showing off that led him to give cars to people he had never met. William Morris, at one time sheriff of Shelby County, Elvis's local district, has a favourite story. They were in a car showroom one Christmas where Elvis was placing a order for several sedans to give away as presents when he saw a black woman ogling a car.

'Do you like that vehicle, ma'am?' asked Elvis.

'Why I sure do,' said the woman.

'Would you like to drive away in that vehicle, ma'am?' asked Elvis.

'I sure would,' said the woman, 'but there ain't no way . . .'

'Well, I'll tell you what, ma'am,' said Elvis, 'you just get into the driving seat o' that vehicle and drive away, 'cos I just bought it for you . . .'

It was a typical story, and one which was repeated over and over again. Elvis just liked spending. He also had a very large family to support, his father and Dee and her three sons, a couple of uncles and aunts, a grandmother, several cousins, plus the increasingly expensive entourage, and a full complement of servants at Graceland. As we have already noted, he also gave half of most of his income to Colonel Parker, and up to forty per cent of his share went in taxes. Elvis's share of the proceeds was coming in the front door, and going straight out of the back. But there were other reasons why his seemingly bottomless pit of wealth diminished at such a fast rate, and this would only become apparent after his death. We will visit the documents relating to his finances in a later chapter.

$$\star \quad \star \quad \star \quad \star \quad \star$$

He had to do something to earn a living, and much as he initially disliked the thought of it, he finally had to go along with his manager's only solution to their woes – that Elvis should stage a comeback to live entertainment, which he had walked away from in the spring of 1961 and had never returned to.

He made a television special at the end of 1968, his first for eight years, and it was a great success. Then he decided, at last, that he was going to 'kick some ass', jettison the kind of songs he had been turning out for the movies, and get back to his roots. He had long ago struck up a friendship with Tom Jones, who was one of the few singers whom he would fly specially into Las Vegas to see.

Tom had been inspired originally by Elvis, and now it was the pupil teaching the master. Jones had introduced spectacular raunchiness into his act that brought a flurry of women's knickers fluttering on to the stage. While Elvis did not want to go quite that far, he drew some pointers from Tom Jones as he prepared to carve out the third stage of his career – going back on the road.

Charlie Hodge said that after watching Tom Jones in Vegas, Elvis was quite sure of his direction. He was to put together a classy stage act, with a big, loud sound, backing singers, glitzy costumes and powerful numbers. This was going to be a new Elvis, said Hodge, and they all disappeared into the studio and devoted several weeks to recording new material. For the first time in years, Elvis was motivated by the music and there was another distinctive turning point – instead of going into the RCA studios, he decided to record at the American Sound Studios, in Memphis. This was a black company where many major artists of the day, including Aretha Franklin, had recorded their most recent hits.

For Elvis, it was a journey back in time. The musicians were mostly youngsters – like the ones who had accompanied him on his earlier and most acclaimed work. He built up a strong rapport and was soon turning out some fine songs. He had discovered a new level of performance, mature yet appealing, with a flavour of the Elvis of old, but staying in a range that was a cut above Tom Jones and Engelbert Humperdinck. He and Charlie would stay at the studio for hours. They seldom came home until the middle of the night, and would go back the following evening, every day, for weeks.

His voice seemed to be improving as each day went by. Elvis was infectiously happy and full of fun. Sometimes, even the musicians applauded and Elvis would get so excited by an especially good track, he would play it over and over again.

At the end of six weeks, Elvis had recorded so many good songs that it provided RCA with enough material for the next year and a half, and was sufficient to account for a third of the company's income for the following year. The songs included massive hits like, 'In the Ghetto', 'Suspicious Minds' and 'Kentucky Rain'. He zoomed back into the charts again. Success bred success.

After his television special and the inspiration gained from his new songs, he was ready and anxious to return to the throbbing, pulsating excitement of a live audience, which he had not experienced since 1961. He wanted to show everyone, and particularly some of the newer stars like the Beatles – and to a degree even Tom Jones – that he had not lost it.

So Tom Parker flew to Las Vegas to negotiate a season's engagement for Elvis, and came back with a signature on a contract from the International Hotel for him to appear twice nightly for a month, for half a million dollars.

It was exactly the kind of challenge Elvis needed to get him out into the public arena again, and to show that he could still capture the attention of a live audience. It scared him and excited him at the same time, and ultimately led him down a road that would destroy him. But that was way off in the future; for the time being all that mattered was Vegas and getting his voice up to strength. He had made no demands on his vocal cords for years and to undertake a straight run for so long and under such intense pressure might cause problems with his voice. That wasn't all that worried him. The big stars who were booked into Las Vegas – Sinatra, Dean Martin, Tony Bennett – were there because of their ability to pull in sell-out audiences at fifteen dollars a head, who would also drink and gamble. Elvis wondered if his pulling power remained. It had been so long since he'd been tested in a live situation that he feared the crowds might just walk by. Even if he got them inside the hotel theatre, would he be able to sustain their interest for two whole hours?

These fears and insecurities mounted as the first night approached. Elvis rehearsed at RCA Sound Studios for ten days, took a break and then spent another week polishing his performance. Everyone agreed he looked terrific – and sounded great. It was billed as the event of the summer in Las Vegas. Colonel Parker stoked up the publicity to fever pitch and Elvis's face peered down from hoardings all over the city.

The only shock was the way the interest was building. Some of the trade pundits had unwisely suggested that Elvis had kept his fans waiting so long for a public appearance that they might stay away in protest. It was also quite possible that he might discover he was about to become the forgotten man of pop. No such eventuality seemed likely, as early bookings at the International were surveyed. It was being said that no other entertainer had ever created such excitement.

Meanwhile, Colonel Parker was doing a roaring trade on the merchandising front, and the hotel lobby was festooned with Elvis pictures, posters, T-shirts, balloons, records and souvenirs.

A huge opening-night celebration had been planned from Graceland, and every single member of the entourage had to be there. The audience cheered wildly from the moment he stepped on to the stage and for two hours Elvis had them spellbound with a mixture of his original hits and new songs. He astounded everyone with his performance and, as he came off, Colonel Parker stood in the wings crying as the two men embraced. Later that night, Joe Esposito bought morning papers, unanimously awarding him rave reviews. John O'Grady, who watched Elvis at Las Vegas, said, 'His condition in 1969 was the most fantastic I have ever seen him. The guy was thirty-five and looked twenty-two. He was a new man; I should have known then that it might not last . . .'

Anyway, Elvis was back.

On the strength of the first night, the International produced a five-year contract for Elvis – he would play two seasons each year, in January and August, with sixty shows, twice nightly for thirty days, at the then top-of-the-house fee of a million dollars. Spurred by his success in Las Vegas, the colonel had already begun arranging tours, putting Elvis back into the countryside, back among the people of America and, initially, he loved the thought of it.

He was a changed man; the bitterness and cynical arrogance that had developed in his personality during the last few years in Hollywood began to subside. He said he felt humbled by the way the crowd had reacted to him. For weeks at each new performance, genuine tears rolled down his cheeks until the novelty of the public acclaim wore off. The old confidence about himself as a performer began to return.

It gave him a new feeling of self-respect; he was feeding off the crowd and off the quite astounding reaction he drew from his fans as the tours around America began. He seemed bent on staying healthy. He had cut back, though by no means eliminated, his intake of chemicals. In fact, the very thought of the new life gave him some sleepless nights, which could only be overcome by the use of barbiturates. However, he began trying to compensate by working out with members of the entourage every day. He started to watch his weight and took a new interest in karate, which he developed as part of his act.

He was healthy and happy, and occasionally actually ventured into the world outside, which he had seldom done in the past few years, choosing instead to remain reclusive, in the sheltered protection of the entourage.

The tours were something else, bigger and better than anything he had ever tackled in the Fifties. Joe Esposito recalled, 'After Las Vegas we went straight out on the road. He made me his road manager, responsible for his personal welfare on the tours. They were invariably one-nighters, and we got into the routine of playing 100 towns a year. We would do them in sequences of twenty or so successive days, playing a different town each night. It was a huge challenge to Elvis's stamina.'

Joe explained that the roadshow routine was always the same. They would work out a route that allowed no more than 200 or 300 miles between stops. They would arrive at the first town, do the show, get what sleep they could and then travel on to the next town the following morning. There were up to 100 people in the tour group. The road crew, who travelled in three trucks with the stage and sound equipment, went on ahead with Colonel Parker. The security men were also in the advance party, to check out the hotel and make sure the whole floor blocked off to Elvis was clear. Next came the musicians and the singers who would follow on behind, to be there in time to set up in the afternoon. Then came Elvis and his entourage, usually arriving late afternoon, with just enough time for Elvis to get a sleep before showtime.

Unless he had called a special rehearsal for new songs, it was likely that when he went to the show venue and out on to the stage, it would be his first glimpse of the arena and he would have to stand for a second or two to get his bearings. Elvis preferred to travel by road. He had a specially converted bus that they had used to travel between Memphis and Hollywood during the movie years. It was a long drive. On the tours, it became impractical and eventually they had to use aircraft, as the distances grew longer.

In the first year after his arrival in Las Vegas, they completed more than 120 show nights, thirty of them with two shows a night. The ticket sales and merchandising quickly ran into millions; the records were given a new boost and Elvis was back on top. 'The pressures were enormous,' said Joe. 'The hours were crazy, the travelling was endless and no one could come through it without feeling the effects. It was during this time, towards the end of that first year, that Elvis's health began to deteriorate, but I did not think much about it at the time.'

There was another problem. The renewed fame brought fresh dangers to Elvis, which ultimately meant additional worries and pressures. There had been a couple of security scares, logged in by the FBI in the first part of the Seventies, when threats were made against Elvis's life. His personal security was doubled. Red and Sonny West were the prime guards, two big and tough men who were constantly at his side. Red and Sonny had become – initially by necessity and then by impatience – increasingly offhand and belligerent about keeping unauthorised people away from the boss. Their concern for Elvis's safety was heightened on his next visit to Las Vegas in 1970 – when a double threat of kidnap and assassination emerged. The FBI was alerted by Las Vegas police and agents moved into the Presley entourage for additional protection. The FBI files show that both threats were treated with utmost seriousness. J. Edgar Hoover requested a full appraisal of the situation, and asked to be kept informed of all developments.

The first alert developed on 26 August, when a security officer at the International Hotel received a telephone call in which an anonymous male alleged that associates of his were planning to kidnap Elvis and hold him to ransom. The caller said he had originally been approached to take part in the operation, but wanted nothing to do with it. The threat was repeated with some urgency by a second call the following day by a male with a southern accent who telephoned Colonel Parker's office.

And while this scare was in progress, another threat arrived. This caller warned of a forthcoming attempt to shoot Elvis. The would-be assassin was apparently a woman who had previously accused him of fathering her child, a claim which he had rejected. The FBI report states: 'Call was received at twelve noon, stating that this individual who is going to kill Presley . . . had already departed from Los Angeles airport and has apparently made a reservation for the Saturday evening performance of Presley. The potential killer, a woman, is carrying a pistol fitted with silencer.'

FBI agents were sent to the International. John O'Grady, Elvis's detective friend, was flown in from Los Angeles to complement his personal bodyguard, and the hotel threw a cordon of specially hired security men around Elvis and Priscilla, who were warned to stay in their hotel room except during showtime. The FBI men pointed out that he was a walking target, especially during his stage performance. Elvis, when told of these developments, insisted on continuing his act, and for several days, the additional security protection and FBI coverage was kept in force.

He was told to stay alert while performing his act and he and his bodyguard went through a pre-arranged plan, in the event that there was an attempt. Sonny West and Jerry Schilling, another member of the entourage, were stationed in such a position that they would jump in front of Elvis at the slightest sign of untoward movement in the audience. Elvis said the last thing he wanted was some crazy person to become famous for shooting him. Red West, meanwhile, was posted along with the FBI agents, at strategic positions in various parts of the auditorium. Priscilla sat in the front, at her usual table with other wives, while Vernon Presley stood backstage.

The massive security ring that had been thrown around Elvis surely put paid to any attempts at either plot, and from that time on Vernon insisted that Elvis would need extra protection. The fear of assassination was such that they worked out a routine to keep Elvis's contact with the public down to an absolute minimum. Where there was open space between the limousine and the show venue entrance, for example, the entourage would crowd around him.

In hotels, security guards were posted at the lift entrances and along the corridors leading to his suite of rooms. No one without an identity tag was allowed near. They introduced a grading system for security purposes, whereby people with red tags were allowed backstage, people with blue ones were allowed only around the stage area, and those with none were not permitted within the immediate area that Elvis might walk. Every member of the show group eventually had to carry a photographic identity card and without it they could not get into the theatre. The entrances and exits to any venue where Elvis was performing were all carefully checked. Where possible, entrances to backstage areas were made through kitchens and side doors. The tension was such that Elvis's closest guards, Red and Sonny West, became almost 'frenzied' – according to Priscilla – about their duties, diving upon any suspicious people in the crowds that gathered wherever Elvis went. All of Elvis's personal guards were provided with shoulder holsters and pistols and Elvis himself invariably carried a gun, sometimes two or three. The mounting fear, almost self-feeding from within the group through hot-tempered actions of Red and Sonny West, merely added to the pressures of those long tours and nightly performances.

What had begun, a year ago, as an exciting new adventure – often shared by Priscilla, the other wives and their children, who would all fly out in family groups to join their husbands – had turned into an absolute nightmare.

It caught up with them all very quickly, and conflict developed in that tight-knit group surrounding the King. They battled to stay loyal to him, and yet were torn between staying with him at all times and retaining some sort of a home life. The two weeks of inactivity between tours became a sort of no-man's land for the married members of the entourage. Elvis needed them around him even during the off-duty period. The hyperactivity of the tours left him suspended with inactivity during the resting periods, a condition merely aroused by the increasingly large doses of chemicals which he used to control his routine. Everyone in the group found the pressure increasingly unbearable, especially those who were married. The warning signs of trouble ahead were already very evident.

5

The Nixon Papers

'*The concern about Elvis's health emanated largely through his stage appearances. I suppose at the root was the medication which he believed was helping him cope. Elvis was extremist in all that he did. He was either going flat out twenty-four hours a day, or he was a recluse. It all started to catch up with him. He took amphetamines to get him up for a show and then to counteract the amphetamines he would take barbiturates. And when he was on these tour situations where he was working night after night, he would build up immunities to them and require more and more, and then stronger medication. He would look them up in the* Physicians' Desk Reference *and try to discover what he should take. But in no way did he consider himself an addict. He would ball anyone out if they were discovered taking any kind of street drugs on the tour. He was absolutely against hard drugs . . .*'

Jerry Schilling, Elvis's friend and aide, 1980

There was simply no way Elvis could have accepted any suggestion that he was addicted to 'drugs', or anything else for that matter. His pills and potions, his feelgood injections and his amphetamines were 'medication', and he would become furious if anyone had even mentioned the possibility that he might have a 'drugs' problem. He hated the word. To him it meant mainlining and fixes; dirty pushers and kids out on the street stealing to feed a habit. Elvis a drug addict? No way.

Jerry Schilling, one of Elvis's long-time aides, trusted by the whole family, is quietly spoken, and gives restrained answers, often erring on the side of understatement. He made the very pertinent point that Elvis operated a blatant double standard, but that he personally was simply unable to see it. Before his deterioration began to run out of control, he considered street drugs to be one of the greatest threats to youth, and in part he blamed the Beatles. He made the point repeatedly. He had done some public work around Memphis calling attention to the dangers of drug taking and actually did, from time to time, make public warnings from the stage.

All of this may have seemed pathetically idiotic, coming from a man whose orgiastic parties during the movie years had been boosted with an abundance of pills of every description and occasionally some of the best-quality Mexican grass.

But, in 1970, Elvis was consumed by some sort of need to go out into the world and do some good, and Schilling, who had known Elvis from high school and had worked for him through the Hollywood years as a general aide and stand-in, figured in one of the most remarkable episodes of Elvis's life. It began a few days before Christmas, in 1970. The family and friends were gathering for the festivities at Graceland. There were, apparently, several rows and indeed Jerry Schilling himself had temporarily left Elvis's employ. Vernon Presley, struggling with the household accounts, was complaining about the bills he was receiving for Christmas gifts, charged by Elvis on another of his impulsive spending sprees. There were ludicrously expensive presents for everyone, including himself, and not least among the bills Vernon was wrestling with was a 19,792-dollar account for the purchase of thirty-two handguns and assorted other weapons from a gun store in Los Angeles, which Elvis had added to his collection of armoury. There was a bill for 85,000 dollars due to a local car dealer for the purchase of ten Mercedes cars, which he had given away to friends and associates.

Then, there was a row with his manager, Colonel Tom Parker, over the incessant sameness of his routine, the tours, the one-night stands, the repetitive nature of his act. They were beginning to build up. Parker said there was nothing that could be done. That's the way it would always be. Elvis's reaction was incredible. He stormed upstairs and reappeared in a dark blue suit and cape, and set off with a huge gold belt which had been presented to him by the International Hotel, Las Vegas, for breaking attendance records. Priscilla recalled that he just 'stomped out of the front door, never returning that night or the next. We were mystified.' No one knew where he was going, or what he planned to do.

They discovered later that under his arm he carried a Colt .45 pistol in a shoulder holster, and another gun, a Second World War Colt .45 in a presentation case. He wore the darkest of sunglasses and carried a silver-topped cane. He jumped into one of the cars parked outside and raced off down the drive of Graceland to Memphis airport, where he dumped the car and went to the American Airlines desk. He purchased a first-class ticket to Washington on his American Express gold card, and went into the VIP lounge to await his departure.

Elvis had decided he would go to Washington, where he intended to change his life, and was consumed with one ambition – to become a federal agent and to carry the badge and the credentials to prove it. It had been a recurring theme of his conversations in the past few weeks, since the occasion in Los Angeles when he was dining in a restaurant with Priscilla, a couple of his bodyguards, and his friend, the former drugs detective, John O'Grady. O'Grady had told him how the federal drug enforcement administration had undercover men all through the drugs supply network on the street.

That night, O'Grady introduced Elvis to Paul Frees, an actor and singer better known for his voice-overs in television commercials and Walt Disney cartoons. Frees was also a police buff, like himself, and had followed the activities of the drugs squad for years. As the conversation developed, Frees took from his pocket a leather wallet which carried documents identifying him as an official 'agent at large' of the Bureau of Narcotics and Dangerous Drugs, signed by the bureau's director, John Ingersoll. Beyond his role in the entertainment industry, Frees operated as an undercover federal 'narc'.

Elvis was fascinated by this and decided immediately that he must be one, too. He wanted to become a federal agent, and he needed the papers to prove it.

So here he was in Washington, just before Christmas 1970. He landed that afternoon and took an ordinary cab to the Washington Hotel, where he checked in as Colonel John Burrows, one of his favourite aliases when travelling. So far, he had enjoyed his journey, free of the minders and all the ballyhoo. But here he was alone in a Washington hotel room, with no one but himself.

Elvis became nervous; panicking, he decided he needed some company. He checked out of the hotel and went back to the airport, catching a plane to Los Angeles to make contact with Jerry Schilling, who was now working in Hollywood. Schilling got his call in the middle of the night, and Elvis insisted that he should tell no one. In particular, he should not tell the family at Graceland. This was a secret mission. He talked with Schilling about his ambitions and asked if he would travel with him back to Washington. Schilling said it would be difficult because he was working on a film, but eventually he agreed, and they caught the overnight flight back to Washington. They flew American Airlines from Los Angeles. Elvis was completely enveloped by the desire to pursue the fantasy that had gripped his imagination. It was total irony and a perfect example of the double standards by which he ruled his own life and those around him, in almost dictatorial fashion.

Elvis, the policeman.

It was laughable, but he treated it earnestly, and now he was determined to achieve official recognition for what he described as his 'drugs work'. It must be said that those around him knew that his ambitions were not entirely honourable. There was revenge, too, in his plans to become an undercover agent. He talked about wanting to nail John Lennon and the Beatles, whom he blamed specifically for knocking him off the top of the charts in the mid-Sixties and he had harboured a grudge against them ever since. Lately, John and Yoko Ono had been getting a lot of publicity for their 'Love Not War' message. Lennon had become the hero of the American subculture and the left-wing groups sprouting throughout the country.

Elvis Presley was going to tell the President of the United States that he believed the songs of Lennon and the Beatles promoted drug use and communism and were the real force behind the growing anti-American spirit, fostering subversiveness and supporting the communists and peace movements. Elvis wanted it stopped. His plan crystallised with conversations he had with two fellow passengers on his journeys between Los Angeles and Washington. The first was with a young soldier just back from Vietnam, who poured out his heart about the services. At the end of the conversation, Elvis told Jerry Schilling to give him all the money they had between them. It amounted to 500 dollars, and he handed it straight to the soldier and wished him good luck.

The second passenger he enjoined in conversation was George Murphy, the Republican senator for the state of California, who was returning to Washington on the red-eye after duties in his home state. Presley spoke of his concern for the youth of America, and told Murphy how he intended to offer his services as a federal agent.

Could Murphy help?

Certainly. He suggested Presley write a letter to the president and take it personally to the White House. He, Murphy, would then telephone J. Edgar Hoover, director of the FBI, and John Ingersoll, director of the Bureau of Narcotics and Dangerous Drugs, and suggest that they both enlisted his assistance and consider appointing him a special agent. Elvis explained that he was in the perfect position to be an undercover man, in the midst of the highest-profile members of the entertainment industry. He could spot users and pushers alike, and make reports to the federal authorities; he could also use his stage appearances to spread the anti-drugs message. It all sounded too good to be true.

Murphy nodded enthusiastically, and added some of his own ideas; by not being a member of the establishment, and accepted by young people the world over, Elvis was perfectly placed to assist. The use of drugs had become an epidemic.

They talked about the problems. Marijuana and LSD were commonplace on the university campuses and on every street corner. And just as Presley himself had been the cause of great consternation among parents and authoritarians when the rock 'n' roll era arrived, fifteen years earlier, hippies, peace campaigners, civil rights demonstrators, black militants and left-wingers were all being parcelled up in America as a common force against the Nixon administration and America itself.

In another era, Elvis Presley's ambitions might have been treated as something of a joke, laughed out of town, especially since confidential FBI files – it can now be seen – already reflected much coverage over his own drug use and even more about his 'debauchery' involving young women.

They were not. After his conversation with Murphy, Elvis called a stewardess and asked for some notepaper. She said that the only paper they had carried the American Airlines logo. Would that do?

'That'll be fine,' said Elvis, and grinned. 'It'll give you a good plug. I'm writing a letter to the president.' She gave him a pen and with George Murphy's assistance, he began to write his letter, which is now lodged in a small collection of documents relating to Presley in the US National Archives in Washington, where more than fifty million pages from the Nixon administration are stored.

A mere dozen pages records one of the most remarkable exchanges imaginable between a president and a pop star. It provides an intriguing insight to both Presley's own mental state at the time, and to Nixon and his aides, who were quick to spot the public-relations opportunity ahead of the 1972 American presidential election. The letter ran to five pages, and his handwriting was untidy and childlike; Elvis wrote:

Dear Mr President:

First I would like to introduce myself. I am Elvis Presley and admire you and Have Great Respect for your office. I talked to Vice President Agnew in Palm Springs 3 weeks ago and expressed my concern for our country. The Drug Culture, the Hippie Elements, the SDS, Black Panthers, etc, do not consider me as their enemy or as they call it the Establishment. I call it America and I Love it. Sir I can and will be of any Service that I can to help the country out. I have no concern or motives other than helping the country out. So I wish not to be given a title or an appointed position. I can and will do more good if I were made a Federal Agent at Large, and I will help best by doing it my way through my communications with people of all ages.

First and Foremost I am an entertainer but all I need is the Federal Credentials. I am on the Plane with Sen. George Murphy and we have been discussing the problems that our Country is faced with. So I am staying at the Washington Hotel Room 505-506-507. I have 2 men who work with me by the name of Jerry Schilling and Sonny West. I am registered under the name of John Burrows. I will be here for as long as it takes to get the credentials of a Federal Agent. I have done an in depth study of Drug Abuse and Communist Brainwashing Techniques and I am right in the middle of the whole thing, where I can and will do the most good. I am Glad to help just so long as it is kept very Private. You can have your staff or whomever call me anytime today tonight or tomorrow. I was nominated this coming year one of America's Most Outstanding young men. That will be in January 18 in My Home Town of Memphis. I am sending you the short autobiography about myself so you can better understand this approach. I would Love to meet you just to say hello if you're not too busy.
Respectfully
Elvis Presley

PS I believe that you Sir, were one of the Top Ten Outstanding Men of America also. I have a personal gift for you also which I would like to present to you and you can accept it or I will keep it for you.

Elvis read and re-read his letter, made corrections and then folded the five sheets neatly and placed them in an American Airlines envelope. When the plane landed in Washington, he shook hands with George Murphy and thanked him for his help. Murphy promised he would recommend Elvis to the appropriate agencies and suggested that he should go personally to the gates of the White House and hand in his letter.

Disembarking from the plane in Washington airport for the second time in two days, he was ushered across the airport terminal through the VIP exit, where a chauffeur was waiting with a limousine which Schilling had ordered in advance. Elvis hollered, 'Take us to the White House.'

The chauffeur blinked, but said nothing. This was Elvis Presley and no one argued with Elvis. So he said, 'Yessir', gunned the engine, and slid off gathering speed towards his destination on the traffic-free roads. It was a dark, chilly December morning four days before Christmas. Elvis was in jocular mood. 'I'm gonna get to see the president,' Presley boasted all the way there. 'I'm gonna get into that Oval Office, this li'l ole boy from Memphis, and I'm gonna volunteer for the feds. Elvis Presley, special agent.'

But the stupidity of the whole situation was compounded by the fact that Elvis was sitting there, high as a kite, on speed. His eyes were glazed, partly from the mirth and the giggling, but more from the roll-on effects of the uppers and downers that were the inherent part of his world, of living by night and sleeping by day.

The extent of his programme of 'medication' – or, more accurately, the drugs upon which he relied to maintain the routine that demanded so much from the star – was then known only to the doctors who serviced him with his pills, and the closest members of his circle of family, friends and bodyguards. It had been going on for so long that it was part of 'life with Elvis', and a necessary facility for those in his entourage. His closest companions had to take them, just to keep up with them.

But, in his mind, they were not drugs.

It was acceptable medication, and as Jerry Schilling testified in his statement to the district attorney's investigator, he considered himself to be an expert on the pills and chemicals upon which he relied to sustain the life. Yet he was curiously unable to understand that the cause of his problems was the effect the chemicals had upon him. Heavy doses of sleeping pills and narcotic medicines to knock him out were followed by the dexedrine, amphetamines and the most potent forms of the drug known on the streets as 'speed' to wake him up. They were being taken, as the world would discover soon enough, in increasing quantities; it had become the norm, and on those days when he was up and around during the hours of daylight, the uppers were consumed like jelly beans. There was nothing unusual about it. It happened most days and such a day was 21 December.

They had landed at six a.m., and Elvis had had no sleep for almost two days. But it didn't matter. He was going to see the president and the car sped along to the White House, arriving at its north-western gate at around six-thirty a.m. that same morning. He got out of the limousine. The guard on the gate looked in amazement as this familiar figure, wearing sunglasses at that hour, and still dressed in the dark blue suit, gold International belt and carrying the silver-topped cane, stepped out and approached him.

'Good morning, sir,' said Elvis, smiling and saluting the young officer. 'Cold around here today. I want you to make sure this letter is delivered to the president's office just as soon as possible.'

The guard said he would make sure that it was, and Elvis retreated into his car and sped off to check in at the Washington Hotel to wait for the president's call. He was also to meet up with his bodyguard, Sonny West. Schilling had persuaded Elvis to allow him to call Graceland the night before, and West was dispatched immediately to Washington. Elvis, by now, was anxious and impatient. He paced around and finally told Jerry Schilling to telephone the Bureau of Narcotics and Dangerous Drugs and tell them that Senator Murphy had recommended him, and to fix him an appointment to see the director, John Ingersoll, on a matter of great importance. The word came back that Ingersoll could not see him, but his deputy, John Finlater, could spare time for a brief discussion.

Elvis went alone to the agency building, saw Finlater, described his mission and how important it was that he should be appointed a special agent. Finlater replied that while he appreciated Mr Presley's concern for the youth of the country, he could not agree to his request.

They shook hands and Elvis, angry and depressed, telephoned Schilling at the hotel. He was near to tears when he said, 'He won't let me have a badge.' But Elvis was immediately cheered by the news that President Nixon had agreed to see him. He was to report to the White House soon after noon.

The events of that morning at the White House, following the delivery of Elvis's letter to the president and the subsequent invitation for him to call, are meticulously described in a series of memos now filed under PRESLEY, in archives of the Nixon administration. The first was:

December 21, 1970
Memo for: Mr H.R.Haldeman (President Nixon's chief of staff)
From: Dwight L. Chapin
Subject: Elvis Presley

Attached you will find a letter to the President from Elvis Presley. As you are aware, Presley showed up here this morning and has requested an appointment with the President. He states that he knows the President is very busy, but he would just like to say hello and present the President with a gift. As you are well aware, Presley was voted one of the ten outstanding young men for next year and this was based upon his work in the field of drugs. The thrust of Presley's letter is that he wants to become a 'Federal agent at large' to work against the drug problem by communicating with people of all ages. He says that he is not a member of the establishment and that drug culture types, the hippie elements, the SDS, and the Black Panthers are people with whom he can communicate since he is not part of the establishment. I suggest that we do the following:

This morning Bud Krogh [a Nixon aide] will have Mr Presley in and talk to him about drugs and about what Presley can do. Bud will also check to see if there is some kind of an agent at large or credential of some sort that we can provide for Presley.

After Bud has met with Presley, it is recommended that we have Bud bring Presley in during Open Hour with the President to meet briefly with the President. You know that several people have mentioned over the last few months that Presley is very pro the

President. He wants to keep everything private and I think we should honour his request.

I have talked to Bud Krogh about this whole matter, and we both think that it would be wrong to push Presley off on the Vice President since it will take very little of the President's time and it can be extremely beneficial for the President to build some rapport with Presley. In addition, if the President wants to meet with some bright young people outside of the Government, Presley might be a perfect one to start with.

The memo passed rapidly to Haldeman, who clearly held some scepticism for the whole idea, having written in the margin next to Chapin's suggestion that Presley was the perfect one for rapport: 'You must be kidding'. However, he also quickly approved the recommendations in their entirety, clearing the way for Presley to meet the president at twelve-thirty p.m. that day.

Another memorandum was prepared for Nixon, to get him ready for his meeting, with some ideas of topics and suggestions for what Nixon might say to Presley.

Memorandum for: The President
Subject: Meeting with Elvis Presley
December 21, 1970, 12:30 p.m.
1) Purpose
To thank Elvis Presley for his offer to help in trying to stop the drug epidemic in the country, and to ask him to work with us in bringing a more positive attitude to young people throughout the country.

In his letter to you, Elvis Presley offered to help as much as possible with the growing drug problem. He requested the meeting this morning when he presented himself to the guard at the North-west Gate bearing a letter.
2) Participants
Elvis Presley; Bud Krogh [staff]
3) Talking points
A. We have asked the entertainment industry – both television and radio – to assist us in our drug fight.
B. You are aware that the average American family has 4 radio sets; 98 per cent of the young people between 12 and 17 listen to radio. Between the time a child is born and he leaves high school, it is

estimated he watches between 15,000 and 20,000 hours of television. That is more time than he spends in the classroom.

C. The problem is critical: As of December 4, 1970, 1022 people died this year in New York alone from just narcotic related deaths. 208 of these were teenagers.

D. Two of youth's folk heroes, Jimi Hendrix and Janis Joplin, recently died within a period of two weeks reportedly from drug-related causes. Their deaths are a sharp reminder of how the rock music culture has been linked to the drug subculture. If your youth are going to emulate the rock music stars, from now on let those stars affirm their conviction that true and lasting talent is the result of self-motivation and discipline and not artificial chemical euphoria.

E. Suggestions for Presley activities:

1) Work with White House Staff.

2) Co-operate with and encourage the creation of an hour Television Special in which Presley narrates as stars such as himself sing popular songs and interpret them for parents in order to show drug and other anti-establishment themes in rock music.

3) Encourage fellow artists to develop a new rock musical theme, 'Get High on Life'.

4) Record an album with the theme 'Get High on Life' at the federal narcotic rehabilitation and research facility at Lexington, Kentucky.

5) Be a consultant to the Advertising Council on how to communicate anti-drug messages to youth.

The memo was typed with urgency and delivered to the president's desk shortly before the meeting with Presley was scheduled to begin. Nixon's aide, Bud Krogh, was present in the Oval Office and took notes of the conversation, which he later transcribed into memo form and placed in Nixon's files. It read as follows:

Memorandum for: The President's file
Subject: Meeting with Elvis Presley
Monday December 21, 1970, 12:30 p.m.
The meeting opened with pictures taken of the President and Elvis Presley. [A White House photographer was summoned and he took twenty-eight pictures of President Nixon and Presley together, some of which were later released to the press for maximum publicity value, though the true reason for the meeting was kept secret.]

Presley immediately began showing the President his law enforcement paraphernalia including badges from police departments in California, Colorado, and Tennessee. Presley indicated that he had been playing Las Vegas and the President indicated that he was aware of how difficult it is to perform in Las Vegas.

The President mentioned that he thought Presley could reach young people, and that it was important for Presley to retain his credibility. Presley responded that he did this thing by 'just singing.' He said that he could not get to the kids if he made a speech on the stage, that he had to reach them in his own way. The President nodded in agreement.

Presley indicated that he thought the Beatles had been a real force for anti-American spirit. The President nodded in agreement and expressed some surprise. The President then indicated that those who use drugs are also those in the vanguard of anti-American protest. Violence, drug usage, dissent, protest all seem to merge in generally the same group of young people.

Presley indicated to the President in a very emotional manner that he was 'on your side'. Presley kept repeating that he wanted to be helpful, that he wanted to restore some respect for the flag which was being lost. He mentioned that he was just a poor boy from Tennessee who had gotten a lot from his country, which in some way he wanted to repay. He also mentioned that he is studying Communist brainwashing and the drug culture for over ten years. He mentioned that he knew a lot about this and was accepted by the hippies. He said he could go right into a group of young people or hippies and be accepted which he felt could be helpful to him in his drug drive. The President indicated again his concern that Presley retain his credibility.

[Not recorded in the memo was the fact that at this point in the conversation, Nixon spoke into his intercom and ordered that a badge of the BNDD (Bureau of Narcotics and Dangerous Drugs) and a set of credentials be prepared for Mr Presley and delivered to his office.]

At the conclusion of the meeting, Presley again told the President how much he supported him, and then, in a surprising, spontaneous gesture, put his left arm around the President and hugged him. [Presley broke into tears at this point.]

In going out, Presley asked the President if he would see his two associates (Jerry Schilling and Sonny West). The President agreed and they came over and shook hands with the President briefly. At this meeting, the President thanked them for their efforts and again mentioned his concern for Presley's credibility.

In this manner was recorded the remarkable meeting between Elvis and the president of the United States, from which Nixon and his aides managed to extract the maximum publicity value. There was an amusing note in the White House files. An employee in the Nixon office had written a note to another secretary:

Lucy:
Elvis Presley (believe it not) was granted an appointment with the President on Monday Dec 21. He left these autographed photos with the President. I don't think any acknowledgement would be necessary. For good disposition. Bev.

And, finally, on his return to work after Christmas, Nixon dictated the following letter to Presley:

December 31, 1970,
Dear Mr Presley,
It was a pleasure to meet with you in my office recently and I want you to know again how much I appreciate your thoughts in giving me a commemorative World War II Colt .45 encased in the handsome wooden chest. You were particularly kind to remember me with this impressive gift as well as your family photographs and I am delighted to have them for my collection of special mementos.
With best wishes to you, Mrs Presley and to your daughter Lisa for a happy and peaceful 1971.
Sincerely,
Richard Nixon

Elvis was elated. The president had over-ruled John Finlater's decision not to give him a federal narcotics badge and had ordered one to be sent over to the White House. He presented it to Elvis before he left. Meanwhile, Senator George Murphy was as good as his word and telephoned the office of the director of the FBI and the director of the Bureau of Narcotics and Dangerous Drugs later that day to suggest that both would like to meet with Elvis. It became curiouser and curiouser . . .

6

Mr Hoover Regrets

'Presley's sincerity and good intentions notwithstanding he is certainly not the type of individual The Director would wish to meet. It is noted at the present time that he is wearing his hair down to his shoulders and indulges in the wearing of all sorts of exotic dress. A photograph clipped from today's Washington Post *is attached and indicates Presley's personal appearance and manner of dress . . . [however] Presley noted that in his opinion no one has ever done as much for his country as The Director and that he, Presley, considers The Director to be the greatest living American . . .'*
Memo to J. Edgar Hoover from an aide, December 1970

The FBI and J. Edgar Hoover treated the whole idea of Elvis Presley becoming a special agent – or even the possibility of a meeting with Hoover – with derision. But Elvis's comments about the Beatles had struck a nerve with President Nixon, and would have far greater implications than Elvis could have imagined, especially for John Lennon. Now, by marrying the memos from Hoover's personal files with those from the president's office, it is possible to track Elvis's final elevation to being appointed an official agent which, though treated in a satirical vein when it eventually became known, was at the time a serious and potentially dangerous undertaking.

The FBI records of the event begin with the following inter-office memo from Hoover's administration assistant, M.A. Jones.

Date: 22–12–70
Subject: Elvis Presley
Senator George Murphy (R–Calif) telephoned your office late yesterday to advise that captioned individual [Elvis Presley] who is, of

course, the prominent entertainer and motion picture personality, had accompanied him to Washington on a flight to Los Angeles and expressed an interest in meeting the Director during his stay in Washington. According to Sen. Murphy, Presley, whom he describes as being a very sincere young man, is deeply concerned over the narcotics problem and is interested in becoming active in the drive against the use of narcotics.

Senator Murphy was advised that the Director [Hoover] was out of the city until January 1st and Senator Murphy suggested that someone from the Bureau get in touch with Presley and express the Director's regrets. This was done ... Presley expressed appreciation for the call ... he suggested that should the Bureau ever have need of his services, they should contact him through the pseudonym of Colonel John Burrows, 3764 Highway 51 South, Memphis, Tennessee [private telephone number inserted].

Bufiles [bureau files] reflect that Presley has been the victim of a number of extortion attempts which have been referred to this bureau. Our files also reflect that he is currently involved in a paternity suit pending in Los Angeles California and that during the height of his popularity in the later part of the 1950s and 1960s his gyrations while performing were the subject of considerable criticism by the public and comment in the press. The files of our Identification Division fail to reflect any arrest record for Presley.

Elvis had more luck with the narcotics bureau. Its director, John Ingersoll, now granted him a tour of the building, along with a description of the bureau's work, and though he was given an official badge denoting his appointment as an agent of the drugs agency by the president, Elvis still hoped to receive official recognition as an agent for the FBI. He retired from Washington and went back to Memphis for a family Christmas, but he could not let it rest. He talked constantly about becoming a federal agent and he returned to Washington immediately after the holiday with influential reinforcements to try once again to fix an appointment with J. Edgar Hoover.

On 30 December 1970, the FBI's M.A. Jones filed the following memo to Hoover's office:

Mr William N. Morris, former Sheriff, Shelby County, Memphis, Tennessee, telephoned Assistant Director Casper from the Washington Hotel today and advised that he was in town with Elvis Presley and six others and inquired concerning the possibility of a tour of our facilities and the opportunity to meet and shake hands with the Director.

There was a summary of the previous recent contact with Presley, and Jones added the following observations at the end of the memo: 'Recommendation: That the Director permit someone to advise [Sheriff Morris] ... that we will be pleased to afford Presley and his party a special tour tomorrow (December 31, 1970), and that it will NOT be possible for the Director to see them.'

When Hoover eventually read the memo, he scrawled at the bottom, 'I concur. H.' He was then kept fully informed of the exchanges and personally approved the tour programme. He kept well out of the way when Elvis and his party duly arrived at the FBI. The grand tour was not commonplace, and Elvis was reminded that it was an honour, not to be taken lightly.

It is also worth noting that Hoover was an absolute disciplinarian, especially on the morals and appearance of his agents. Shabby agents might be sent home, suspended or even fired if they were repeatedly unkempt, and therefore the matter of Presley's personal appearance came through in the memo reporting to the director on the visit of Elvis and his entourage:

January 4, 1971
From: M.A. Jones
Subject: Elvis Presley; Bureau tour 31-12-71
Presley and Morris and six individuals who provide security for Presley visited the FBI headquarters and were afforded a very special tour of facilities in accordance with plans approved by the Director. Presley indicated that he has long been an admirer of Mr Hoover and has read material prepared by the Director including *Masters of Deceit, A Study of Communism* and *J. Edgar Hoover on Communism*. Presley noted that in his opinion no one has ever done as much for his country as Mr Hoover and that he, Presley, considers the Director the greatest living American. He also spoke most favourably of the bureau ...

The memo goes on to describe Elvis's comments during the tour, throughout which M.A. Jones had clearly taken copious notes to be reported back in full to his boss. These reflected much of what Presley had told President Nixon in his meeting at the White House, with added grandiose comments, stating that he, Elvis Presley, was living proof that America was the land of opportunity and that he had risen from truck driver to prominent entertainer almost overnight. From that position he was able to influence young people. Jones's memo then reports on a private conversation held between Presley and other FBI officials at the conclusion of the tour, in which once again he drew attention to the Beatles and directed J. Edgar Hoover's attention to John Lennon.

Elvis saw the opportunity of inflicting revenge for being toppled by the Beatles in the mid-Sixties, and virtually spelled it out as the conversation veered towards the most devastating part of Presley's ambitions – his vow to inform the FBI of the activities of others in the entertainment industry, and his pledge of commitment to J. Edgar Hoover personally. The memo concluded:

Presley privately advised that he has volunteered his services to the President in connection with the narcotics problem and that Mr Nixon responded by furnishing him with an Agents Badge of the Bureau of Narcotics and Dangerous Drugs. Presley was carrying the badge in his pocket and displayed it. Presley advised that he wished the Director [Hoover] to be aware that he, from time to time, is approached by individuals and groups in and outside of the entertainment business whose motives and goals he is convinced are not in the best interests of this country . . . In this regard, he volunteered to make such information available to the bureau on a confidential basis whenever it came to his attention. He further indicated that he wanted the Director to know that should the bureau ever have need of his services in any way that he would be delighted to be of assistance. Presley further indicated that he is of the opinion that the Beatles laid the groundwork for many of the problems we are having with young people by their filthy unkempt appearances and suggestive music while entertaining in this country during the early to middle sixties. He advised that the Smothers Brothers, Jane Fonda and other persons in the entertainment industry of their ilk have a lot to answer in the hereafter for the way they have poisoned young minds by disparaging the United States in their public statements and unsavoury activities . . . Presley advised that he was in a unique position. He spends a substantial portion of his time in the Beverly Hills, California and Las Vegas, Nevada.

Elvis again reiterated his willingness to help, and gave M.A. Jones a piece of paper for the files with his 'codename' Colonel John Burrows, and contact addresses and telephone numbers printed upon it. That day, 4 January 1970, J. Edgar Hoover read the memo from Jones and took notice. He dictated the following letter to Elvis, warmed perhaps by the singer's observation that he believed Hoover to be the greatest living American:

Dear Mr Presley,
I regret that it was not possible for me to see you and your party during your visit to FBI Headquarters; however, I hope you enjoyed your tour of our facilities.
Your generous comments concerning this bureau and me are appreciated and you may be sure we will keep in mind your offer to be of assistance.

On the same day, Hoover sent out a memo to all special agents in charge of FBI field offices, alerting them to Presley's offer of assistance, and passing on details of his codename and telephone numbers.

Presley now believed, and boasted as much, that he was a fully fledged federal agent, authorised to make drug busts by the Narcotics Bureau, when in reality it was nothing of the kind. Though Nixon's staff may have considered the badge an honorary presentation, no one had actually said as much to Presley himself. He had been fêted by three of the most powerful offices in the land and as far as he was concerned, it was an official appointment. He was President Nixon's personal drugs spy; he was an informer and drugs cop for the Narcotics Bureau, and Special Agent Colonel John Burrows of the FBI.

It was total fantasy, of course, but Elvis began to act it out.

Very soon, his bodyguards discovered that they were being instructed to bring out the car late at night, or in the early hours of the morning – when Elvis was often high on chemicals himself – and they would tour the streets of whichever town they were in – Memphis, Las Vegas, Los Angeles – looking for drug dealers. If they saw any,

Elvis might fire potshots out of the window to scare them off. If he saw kids looking for a connection, he'd jump out of the car and give them a lecture, get back in and take another dose of dexedrine to keep him awake.

It was later rumoured that famous personalities in the film business and the pop world suddenly discovered that the police were becoming increasingly active and seemed to be obtaining information on their drug habits. Covert and well-to-do suppliers to the movie industry of topline cocaine and heroin were being picked off one after another in the period after Elvis volunteered his assistance. It is impossible to know if Elvis supplied such information. Details of his activities have never been made public, nor will they be, on this side of the next century.

Many pages of FBI documents in the Elvis files for this period remain classified. If he had turned informer, utilising his knowledge of Hollywood and Las Vegas, heartlands of the west coast Mafia, he was sailing perilously close to danger; perhaps he knew it. The FBI certainly would have known.

There was another immediate reaction to Presley's conversations with Nixon, the Narcotics Bureau and the FBI, to whom he had expressed his disgust at how he believed the Beatles had corrupted the youth of the nation, and his feeling that John Lennon should not be allowed in the country. Reading those documents now, it is evident that Elvis may have inspired some thoughts in this respect among the FBI hierarchy and the president himself. It may well have been considered by some of Nixon's aides that Elvis's own behaviour was odd, even fanatical. But he was a national monument with a massive following among the country's under-forty age group, who Nixon himself was targeting for the forthcoming election. Though his motives may have been dubious, Elvis's intervention at this point was obviously seen as a heaven-sent opportunity.

Hoover and Nixon discussed Lennon and the Beatles in the early part of 1971, when Nixon himself had his eye on re-election. Hoover was already keeping watch on the Beatles. He had long ago concluded that they were undesirables. America had enough subversives among its own pop culture without importing others from England, and he had no qualms at all about saying that they should make every effort to keep Lennon out of the country. Only the previous year, Hoover had tried, and failed, to initiate prosecution against John and

Yoko. Under interstate laws, he'd tried to have them arrested for the transportation of obscene material – the cover of their album *Two Virgins*, which showed them both naked. He was advised by his legal office that a prosecution would not stand up in court.

In the wake of Presley's visit, Hoover ordered an immediate review of all the FBI files on John Lennon, and grasped at the one serious, though flimsy, piece of information they had on him – that Lennon had been granted a visa to enter the United States with the Beatles after being granted a discretional waiver against a drugs conviction for possessing marijuana in Britain.

There was virtually nothing else to go on; nothing at all. In spite of all the intense activity that followed, the US authorities never produced a scrap of evidence to prove the Beatles were involved with drugs. Up to the end of 1970, the FBI files on Lennon and the Beatles amounted to a mere handful of pages. It seems, therefore, hardly a coincidence that after Elvis's visit to Nixon and the FBI, from the early part of 1971 onwards, the Lennon file suddenly began to explode with activity, with page after page containing memos and instructions from Hoover to his agents, descriptions of Lennon's movements and contacts, reports of his associations and affiliations, especially with prominent peace campaigners.

In the space of the following eighteen months, the FBI file on Lennon expanded to over 500 pages of reports, of which, in 1992, only 196 pages were released to me under the Freedom of Information Act. The remainder are still classified, including the whole contents of one file running to 207 pages, which has been retained at FBI headquarters. A further 1800 pages specifically relating to John Lennon are contained in the archives of the Immigration and Naturalisation Service and are not available for public inspection.

Those who provided information concerning Lennon, and it is reasonable to suggest that one of the informants was Elvis himself, were to have their identities protected by an instruction from Hoover that information received was to be classified as 'confidential to protect sources ... of continuing value whose disclosure would be prejudicial to the security of the United States.'

The visit by Elvis was also followed by Lennon's own attempts to secure a longer stay in the United States. And while it would be wrong to blame Elvis for all that followed, his spirited allegations certainly helped Hoover to focus his mind. A close reading of this

Above left: The two-room shack where Elvis was born. Today fans queue round the block to get a glimpse (*Elvis Presley Fan Club*). *Above right*: Elvis as a youth; who could ever guess what he'd become (*Elvisly Yours*). *Left*: Elvis aged three; his twin brother Jesse died at birth and he would speculate upon the loss often in his lifetime (*Camera Press*).

A young Elvis Presley – before the hips started swinging and the bucks poured in (*Camera Press*).

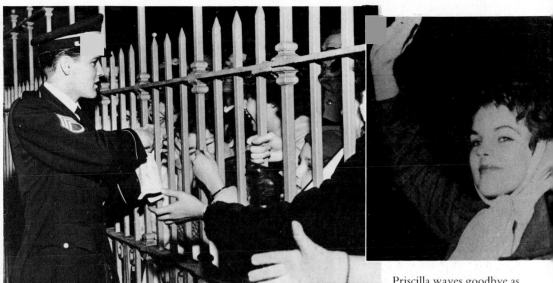

Above: GI Elvis greets adoring fans (*Camera Press*).

Priscilla waves goodbye as Elvis leaves Germany, never guessing she'd one day be his wife (*Elvisly Yours*).

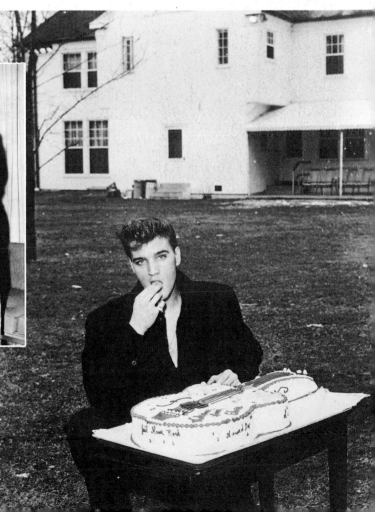

Above: In his family home, Elvis comforts his mother the night before he leaves for the army. Vernon Presley looks on (*Elvis Presley Fan Club*).
Right: Elvis is welcomed back from the army with a spectacular cake (*Elvisly Yours*).

Centre: Elvis signs with RCA as Vernon (left) and an adviser look on (*Elvis Presley Fan Club*). *Left*: Frank Sinatra welcomes Elvis home to America in an extravagant TV special (*Elvis Presley Fan Club*). *Right*: Elvis at the Beverley Wiltshire Hotel in California, 1960. Already he is surrounded by an entourage, most of whom would remain with him for the rest of his life (*Elvis Presley Fan Club*).

Top: Elvis playfully cocks a gun at Colonel Parker on the set of *Follow that Dream* (*Elvis Presley Fan Club*). *Bottom*: Vernon with Dee and David Stanley; a ready-made family for only-child Elvis (*Elvisly Yours*).

Clockwise from the Top: Elvis Presley with co-star and real-life girlfriend Tuesday Weld, in *Wild in the Country* (*Elvis Presley Fan Club*). Elvis examines his motorcycle for a studio shot – he later bought a cycle for each of his substantial entourage (*Elvis Presley Fan Club*). Guitar was his mainstay, but Elvis could turn a hand to anything, including keyboards (*Camera Press*).

Top: Elvis and Priscilla Presley. Some of
their attendants include Joe Esposito (far
left), Marty Lacker (left), George Klein
(right) and Billy Smith (centre right)
(*Elvisly Yours*). *Above*: Elvis and Priscilla
pose for another shot, at their wedding
breakfast, 1967 (*Elvis Presley Fan Club*).
Right: An informal snapshot taken at the
wedding (*Elvis Presley Fan Club*).

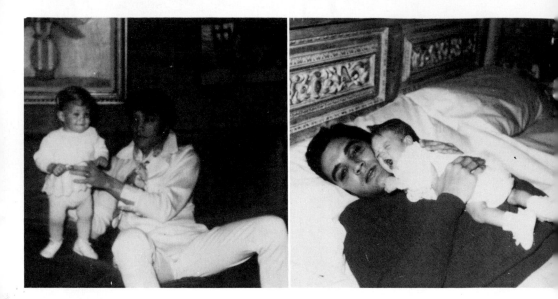

Elvis poses with his daughter Lisa Marie at Graceland. Always a doting father, Elvis was troubled when his tours took him away from home for long periods of time. *Below right*: Vernon Presley eyes his grand-daughter with affection. Both he and Elvis were shattered when Priscilla left with Lisa Marie in 1972 (*All pictures Elvisly Yours*).

material demonstrates without question that Hoover decided that drug use was the key to keeping Lennon out of the country and ensuring that he was never allowed to return for more than a fleeting visit. And there began a most remarkable surveillance operation against John and Yoko, which Hoover pursued with a vigour that verged on vendetta until his own death in May 1972. Lennon was spied upon, his phone was tapped, and he was followed, at the peak of the operation, twenty-four hours a day, as this memo from Hoover to every single field office in the FBI network illustrates:

Date: May 13, 1971
Subject: John Lennon
[Every agent] should remain alert for any activity on his part of a potentially illegal nature . . .

This was a follow-up to an earlier memo sent personally by Hoover to special agents in charge of his New York and Los Angeles field offices at a time when Lennon and George Harrison were planning a trip to the United States. The detail of the following memo reflects the closeness of the observation maintained by the FBI:

Date: April 23, 1970
Subject: John Lennon, George Harrison, Patricia Harrison
These individuals are affiliated with the Beatles musical group and Lennon will be travelling under the name of Chambers and the Harrisons are using the name Masters. [They] will remain in Los Angeles for business discussion with Capitol Records and other enterprises . . . they will travel to New York for further discussion . . . waivers were granted by the Immigration and Naturalisation Service . . . in view of the ineligibility of these three individuals to enter the US due to their reputations in England as narcotics users. While Lennon and the Harrisons have shown no propensity to become involved in violent anti-war demonstration, each recipient [of this memo] should remain alert for any information of such activity on their part or for information indicating they are using narcotics. Submit any pertinent information obtained for immediate dissemination.

In the event, Lennon left America and returned to England with the Harrisons. In July, he made application to return to New York for a specified period of six weeks, giving as his reasons that he wanted to edit a film, conduct business negotiations with his record company and attend a custody hearing over Yoko's child by her former marriage. He was admitted as a temporary visitor until 24 September, but thereafter applied to have his visa extended until February. This was granted by US Immigration, much to the chagrin of J. Edgar Hoover.

He contacted the immigration department, angrily criticising them for allowing 'this individual' the facility of getting back into the country. He said he was firmly of the view that Lennon was a continuous narcotics user and, further, that the question of a custody hearing over Yoko's child was just a front to allow them to stay, and eventually settle, in America. He suggested that every effort should be made to ensure that prosecution could be undertaken for the breach of local or federal laws, and that agents and other crime agencies should pay particular attention to Lennon's narcotics use and to the possibility of a charge being brought for perjury over the child custody case.

From the moment of Lennon's entry into the United States, his movements were tracked, his television appearances monitored, his songs noted, and his comments taped and recorded for the FBI files. Towards the end of the year, Lennon was witnessed as 'associating with' leading figures in the New Left, a group called the Allamuchy Tribe, which had just renamed itself Election Year Strategy Information Centre (EYSIC), and other student groups and peace protesters, whose organisation and support was growing.

In December, Lennon's presence at a freedom rally at the University of Michigan was noted; he was also said to have been 'associating' with members of a group known as the White Panther Party, all reported in earnest tone and virtually detailed down to the colour of his underpants, as if the FBI agents were dealing with a major Russian spy.

A new and separate Lennon file was opened under the heading: 'John Winston Lennon, Revolutionary Activity' and thus, with Hoover ranting about the continued presence of Lennon in the country, a deportation order was finally served upon him and Yoko in January 1972. Hoover continued the onslaught.

When that date for expulsion came and passed, Lennon was still in the country, and Yoko was still firmly embroiled in her custody case, the child having been abducted by his father. Hoover was furious; he accused them of delaying tactics and fired off another memo to all senior agents:

Date: 16-3-72
Subject: John Winston Lennon
It appears that subject and wife may be preparing for lengthy delaying tactics to avert their deportation. In the interim a very real possibility exists that subject . . . might engage in activities in the US leading to the disruption of the Republic National Convention . . . for this reason . . . locate subject and remain aware of his activities and movements. Careful attention should be given to reports that the subject is a heavy narcotics user . . . Afford this matter close supervision and keep Bureau fully advised by most expeditious means warranted.

Hoover persisted with his surveillance of Lennon until the day he died, collapsing from a heart attack on the night of 12 May 1972. For the time being, his deputy Clyde Tolson and the new administration continued to prosecute their cause with the same vigour, as demonstrated in a memo to the acting director from the special agent in charge at the New York field office of the FBI. It pertained to the reports that Lennon was to appear at a rock concert outside the Republican party convention to re-elect President Nixon, in Miami:

Date: May 25, 1972
Subject: John Winston Lennon
Miami should note that Lennon is a heavy user of narcotics . . . this information should be emphasised to local law enforcement agencies . . . with regards to subject being arrested if at all possible on possession of narcotics charge. The local INS [Immigration and Naturalisation Service] has a very loose case in NY for deportation of subject . . . INS stressed to Bureau that if Lennon were to be arrested in possession of narcotics, he would become more likely to be immediately deportable . . .

In the event, Lennon did not go to Miami. He was never arrested for the possession of drugs, and he and Yoko hired a team of lawyers who sought to show the full extent of the unwarranted surveillance which they had suspected since the beginning of 1971. Lennon's lawyer even attempted to prove that the FBI had been illegally tapping Lennon's telephone. The FBI denied the claim.

The FBI backed off, noting by internal memo that it might prove to be a considerable embarrassment if any FBI agent was called before a court hearing. Nixon was re-elected by a landslide.

Elvis Presley, meantime, continued to embroil himself in the fantasy that he had created around the federal badge presented to him by Nixon.

$$\star \quad \star \quad \star \quad \star \quad \star$$

Early in 1973, the entourage was in Las Vegas when two of Elvis's rings went missing. He suspected one of his aides, James Caughley, of theft after a 19,000-dollar thirty-carat sapphire ring was found in his briefcase. Caughley said he had found it lying around and had put it in the case for safekeeping. Another ring was also missing. By then, Caughley had just left the Las Vegas hotel to return to Memphis. Elvis decided he was going to arrest him.

He left his hotel with Red West and a hotel security guard, and drove at high speed to Las Vegas airport. The flight the aide was supposed to be on was just preparing for take-off. Elvis flashed his badge and ran through the airport control out on to the tarmac. Elvis waved his arms and held up his badge again, eventually being allowed on to the plane, only to discover the suspect was not on board.

It was the wrong plane.

The suspect was still in the airport lounge. He was taken outside to the car, where Elvis flashed his badge once more and started to go through the arrest procedure: 'You have the right to remain silent . . .' and then he couldn't remember the words and broke into giggles.

Caughley was taken back to the hotel for interrogation, with Elvis conducting the questions, while one of his aides had the man covered with a .357 Magnum revolver. Eventually, his temper subsided. Caughley stuck to his story and refused to confess to theft. He was put on a plane back to Memphis with the instruction that he should keep his mouth shut or face the consequences.

When Elvis returned to Memphis, he showed his federal narc badge to the local police force, with whom he had a very good relationship. Occasionally, they allowed him to accompany them on a drugs bust, on the condition that he disguise himself so he could not be recognised. The first time he went out with them, he turned up wearing a dark blue jumpsuit and a ski-mask, through which only his eyes and mouth were visible.

'Gee, man, I'm a G-man,' he kept giggling.

7

Into Decline

'*Elvis had become a part-time husband. From adolescence, he fashioned me into the instrument of his will. I lovingly yielded to his influence ... accustomed to living in dark rooms, hardly seeing the sun, depending on chemical aids for sleep and wakefulness, surrounded by bodyguards who distanced us from reality, I yearned for more ordinary pleasures ...*'

Priscilla Presley, in *Elvis and Me*

Elvis was becoming impossible and the previous nine months had been torment. The tours were becoming more demanding and Elvis's own attitude had worsened as each month passed, to the point where he demanded a kind of relief from the boredom that Priscilla could not provide. He was looking for excitement, like in the old days of Hollywood, and he chose to revisit some of those experiences by resorting to the weekend orgies laid on at his house in Palm Springs. When he began to say that he was going away for the weekend to rest, Priscilla knew what was happening. In the spring of 1972, she finally called a halt to the marriage, just ten years after she first moved into Graceland as a teenager.

She, in turn, had found a new focus for her affections, a karate champion named Mike Stone, whom she had met during Elvis's last concert at Vegas. Ironically, Elvis himself had suggested she should go to see him for lessons. To most in the entourage the moment of her departure was identified as the turning point, the moment at which Elvis lost control. For months afterwards he was raging about Priscilla's treachery, running off, as he put it, with a pauper. He was impervious to counter-suggestions that his own selfishness had been a cause of the marital breakdown, with his refusal to live his life any other way than in the pursuit of his own pleasures – derived from his chemical support system and his voracious, though declining, appetite for young women.

In the weeks and months following the separation, Priscilla was bombarded with telephone calls from Elvis, threatening all kinds of retribution. Most vocal were his intentions towards Mike Stone, who he said would not live to see the year out. One particularly bad night, he telephoned Priscilla and told her that he and the guys were coming hunting; he would be carrying his M-16 automatic rifle and they were going to put Mike Stone up against a wall and execute him. The threats went on and on. There were some bad times for the entourage, attempting to control Elvis. The night he called Priscilla warning her that they were coming to get Mike Stone, the scene in the penthouse of the International Hotel, Las Vegas, was one of bedlam. Elvis was rampaging about with the rifle, and shouting that Stone had to die. Linda Thompson, his new girlfriend, was so scared that she pleaded with Red West to do something.

They called the local doctor, Elias Ghanem, who often treated Elvis. He arrived within minutes, since he was also the house doctor for the hotel, and gave Elvis an injection of a powerful sedative. The night was calmed, and eventually the battle moved to an arena controlled by lawyers.

The sadness for Priscilla was that in her innocence and guilt that she had had an affair, she told Elvis she would not want a large settlement, just sufficient to live on and to buy a house in Los Angeles – plus an allowance for Lisa Marie. When tempers cooled, there were meetings with Elvis's Los Angeles lawyers and she agreed to a 'property division' settlement providing her with 100,000 dollars in cash and a combined alimony and child support payment of 1500 dollars a month. Priscilla had no experience of money. In the past, she had just signed for whatever she wanted. Vernon was always hovering in the background to control the purse strings. Very soon, she discovered that the settlement was nowhere near sufficient for her needs. She hired her own lawyer in Los Angeles to seek an increase to these payments. When he saw the documents which she had signed, he was literally amazed at the figures. The fifty-fifty split when couples parted had existed in California for years. There was no such law in Tennessee, where the wife could expect only what her husband chose to pass on. In May 1973, Priscilla's lawyers filed a suit in the superior court for the state of California, claimed intrinsic fraud, and Priscilla had to go on to public record for the first time with a statement in which she said:

Since I was sixteen years old I have been living with my husband's family and during that time I have developed a trust and confidence in my husband, his father and other persons associated with them. During our marriage, I was never involved in my husband's business and financial affairs. I was never informed of my husband's income nor the nature and amount of property which he had accumulated. My expenses were paid through unlimited chequing accounts upon which I wrote cheques . . .

The statement went on to claim that Priscilla had been wrongly advised to sign the property division settlement, and she now sought a fairer division of her husband's assets. The case had the makings of a lengthy struggle, with arguments raging about whose law governed the situation – California's or Tennessee's. In the end, there could be no dispute that Priscilla had accepted a ridiculously low sum and eventually she was awarded a 1.5–million-dollar settlement, with half of that sum paid immediately and the remainder in monthly instalments. She was also to receive a very substantial increase in her alimony and child-support payments, and was awarded a five per cent stock holding in two of Elvis's music companies, which received royalties from his records.

During these months, Elvis had become enraged and almost uncontrollable. His quest for medication and his violent changes of mood and temperament were a worry to all around him. His music was becoming sterile, with only occasional flashes of the old brilliance. The stories emanating from this period of his life, retold after his death, were of a sensational and lurid nature; the calmer recollections of four people closest to him during the months surrounding his divorce, recounted for Larry Hutchinson during his investigations for the district attorney, provide a more objective view. For this reason, I will devote the rest of this chapter to their own words, transcribed as I listened to the hours of taped conversations now lying in the archives of the Memphis district attorney-general's office.

I will begin with James Caughley, otherwise known as

'Hamburger James', because he used to bring Elvis his favourite snack, or 'Fetchum Bill', because he was the one called upon so often to run errands. He was also the aide Elvis accused of attempting to steal one of his rings – which Caughley strongly denies – and who had a pistol held at his head and was told he would be shot unless he 'confessed'. His testimony provided a graphic, if sometimes unpleasant, insight into life with Elvis.

Caughley first went to Graceland and became head valet and dresser in 1970, remaining until he was fired in 1973. These are his words:

I suppose you could say I was head valet, personal aide, wardrobe organiser, errand boy and general factotum, and during the period from 1970 to September 1973, there was probably not more than twenty days in the whole time that I wasn't with Elvis. The outfit ran like the military. Joe Esposito was the number-one man; he knew everything that was going on, I mean everything. So did Charlie Hodge, who was Elvis's shadow. But anything Vernon Presley said superseded their orders. I started off as an aide, just running errands and looking after Elvis's personal stuff. Then, later on, as we lost employees, I was put in charge of the wardrobe, keeping care of jewellery and all personal items when we were travelling. When we weren't working, I went back to being a personal valet, making sure he was fed, running errands – that was basically my job. It was constant daily contact, twenty-four hours a day, sometimes. I was involved in the dressing of him, sometimes physically. I also had to clear up the mess behind him, which was at times rather embarrassing and distasteful.

Caughley was referring to a period when Elvis was suffering from colon problems, and the treatment he received affected the control of his body functions. It was a matter of fact, Caughley told Hutchinson, that it was necessary to change bedclothes and mattresses quite regularly. He said he had been told about Elvis's eccentricities even before he went to work for him. He had heard he was getting difficult to work for, because of his temperament and to a lesser degree because of the entourage who were with him. At first, said Caughley, it wasn't too bad, but any observer of the man's habits and tempers had to be around him twenty-four hours a day to appreciate what was going on. 'Then you'd see the problem mounting slowly, and the problem was drugs, sure,' he said. 'Nineteen seventy-one wasn't too bad; 1972, the year Priscilla left, it started to get worse and the last nine months I had with Elvis, it was unbelievable. It was like a graph – there would be highs and lows. Sometimes, when we were back in Memphis, he would stay upstairs for twelve days at a time and never come down.'

In those periods, Caughley classed himself as an errand boy. It often fell to him to get the prescriptions filled. During the time he was with Elvis, he estimated that he had brought back hundreds of pills to Graceland. There were Percodan tablets, codeine, Demerol in pills and liquid, some amphetamines, occasionally Seconal, Valium, and there were a lot of throwaway syringes. Elvis would get a great deal of prescription medicine from outside of Memphis. It would arrive in packages from Las Vegas, Los Angeles and other cities. Caughley notes:

I used to see his personal physician Dr George Nichopoulos – we called him Needle Nick – on most days. When we were at home, he would arrive to visit Elvis early evening. He also travelled on the eight different tours I went on. He seldom came to Vegas. It was too long a time for him to be away from his practice in Memphis. We'd be there thirty days at a stretch, whereas we'd only be on the road about fifteen days at the most. I never saw Dr Nick administer anything to Elvis, never once. But they used to disappear into Elvis's private room and you'd be able to notice the change in attitude.

Once on tour, Elvis collapsed and Caughley believed it was through an overdose. He had to send for Dr Nick, who was travelling with them. Dr Nick was certain that Elvis had obtained some pills from another doctor and taken them in addition to those prescribed by Nick. He barely had a pulse. Caughley had seen him 'far out' before, but never this bad. Sometimes, he was so far gone that he would have to sit him up in bed, and run a vibrator over his back to wake him. This time, he could not rouse him. Some of the guys got him into a chair while Caughley called the doctor. Joe Esposito sent him outside and closed the door. Dr Nick, he said, did seem to care about Elvis, and what happened to him. He was angered by the fact that Elvis was getting stuff from other doctors.

Caughley also became angry. When he was cleaning up the pill bottles and syringes, he would discover bottles with his own name on them. Elvis used other people's names to get drugs when they were out on tour – to protect the name of Elvis Presley, so that no one knew it was really him getting them. Back in Memphis it didn't matter so much, because it was a regular thing for the pharmacies there to provide pills for Elvis – hundreds of them. No one seemed to care. Caughley went on:

In the summer of 1973, we were preparing for his thirty-day engagement at the Hilton International in Vegas. You know, it was pretty hard work, getting all the clothes and costumes and souvenirs ready for so many concerts, twice nightly. That's a lot of concerts by any standard. When we got there he called local doctors, who would be placed on alert to visit Elvis daily. One or other of them would come in and give him what they said was a B12 vitamin shot and, doing two shows a days, his ass was like a pin cushion. In addition, I might be sent to get prescriptions from Dr Max Shapiro, a dentist who lived in Palm Springs. He used to come and visit Elvis, too. I filled all the prescriptions at the Landmark Pharmacy right across the street from the hotel. We had a charge account there.

A lot of times, the pharmacy would simply send over a package which would be addressed to Joe Esposito. Mostly it would be class-two drugs, narcotics. They would be in everybody's name but Elvis's, although his name was on the charge. Regardless whose name they were in, the drugs were all destined for Elvis. Sometimes, he would get anxious, during the bad periods, waiting for stuff to arrive. But I'll say this, for all the time I was with Elvis, all the drugs that I ever saw coming in, apart from a little grass, were all prescription drugs, provided by registered doctors.

Caughley said he knew that Vernon Presley was worried. The colonel knew what was going on, too, because he was kept informed by some of the guys. On bad days, Elvis would be a like a zombie, just sitting in front of the television, doing nothing, going nowhere. He was in a sort of twilight stage, brought on by taking controlled substances. During these periods Dr Nick would drop by and give him something to bring him out of it. But the twilight times grew longer, and closer together.

At Christmas, in 1971, Jo Smith, the wife of Elvis's cousin Billy, bought Caughley an address book and diary. He began to keep a diary of the tours, until Joe Esposito saw him writing in the book and told him not to put anything in it about Elvis. Joe was ever vigilant about preventing any leaks about Elvis's erratic behaviour getting out – as they eventually did – and the stories describing him shooting out the televisions when he didn't like what was on, were just the tip of the iceberg. Caughley explains:

I have sat there and watched him shoot out the lights at the Hilton. [The International Hotel in Vegas became a Hilton hotel in 1972]; sitting at the breakfast table in his suite with a 22,000-dollar gold engraved pistol in his hand, shooting at the chandelier. We were all in the penthouse. Now the management didn't normally complain, but they made him stop that because it was causing a leak. Once, he got up mad one morning. He and Linda Thompson, his girlfriend, had been rowing and he started firing the pistol in the bedroom of the Hilton suite while he was eating breakfast, firing at an ornament, a pot owl.

Linda was in the bathroom and I was cleaning up the room, getting her dirty clothes together for the laundry and so on, when that goddamn gun went off. Linda screamed and I called out to her. Her bathroom backed up to the television area where the owl was positioned, and one of the bullets missed the owl and went straight through the cheap wall, through the door to Linda's bathroom, and just missed her. Elvis did crazy things, but you can't blame it all on the drugs. He had a very emotional temper, and could be riled sick. Nobody would stand up and tell him, 'no'; and he was like a little kid sometimes.

*   *   *   *   *

Joe Esposito's recollections of his years with Elvis were kinder, and provided Larry Hutchinson with a rose-tinted view of life with Elvis. But it was an interesting conversation, pinpointing the moment in Esposito's mind when he believed Elvis's problems began to get serious. 'To me, everything started, the erratic behaviour, after his divorce,' he said, in his statement for the district attorney, and by implication dismissed what had gone on in the past as not especially worrying. It was dangerous at times, perhaps, but controllable. Priscilla's departure was followed by his health problems, with a twisted colon in the early Seventies, and he was admitted to hospital in Memphis. He also had a blood pressure problem.

But Elvis could never sit still; he would be up and flying around different parts of the country at a moment's notice.

Dr Nick first arrived on the scene when they started touring. He and Elvis got along pretty well, and about a year later, he became Elvis's personal physician. Joe said that Nick started to go along on the tours, and looked after Elvis's health from then on. Elvis firmly believed that he needed a doctor around for himself, and for the entourage and the show people. It wasn't just Elvis he cared for, and there were three or four other doctors on the west coast, some of them Elvis first met while making pictures.

Elvis needed these doctors for his Vitamin B12 shots, Joe told Hutchinson. He also required medication for his throat, and pain-killers for aches and sprains caused by the vigorous nature of his act, when he used karate movements. He also needed sleep medication when they were on the road. Hutchinson pressed this most important member of the group about the extent of Elvis's reliance on drugs, but got nowhere. 'I would not say Elvis was hooked on narcotics, never ever,' said Esposito:

He took a lot of pills. We all did because of the crazy hours. Otherwise we'd never have got any sleep. There was erratic behaviour on his part, but it was due to the life we were leading. He had a lot of emotional problems. He'd get angry like anyone else. If he got mad, he might walk off the stage. Sure, he did that. But that was down to the work, the emotional stress. It became a problem sometimes to get him to sleep and we would have to give him the medication. Sure, I'd seen the doctors give him medication to knock him out. Afterwards, he might have a problem getting up. Before he went on stage, he'd have shots. I was always told that the injections were B12, but no, I can't say definitely what they contained. When he came off the doctor would give him a tranquilliser to bring him down, because Elvis used to get really hyped up on stage. I have never seen him overdose, never in my life. I don't know where that story came from.

The times we went to hospital, it was for real medical problems like exhaustion, not overdosing on drugs, definitely not. Some members of the entourage had spoken to me about it as his intake increased and I frankly I had to tell them there was nothing I could do about it. I tried to help him out, we all did. I talked many times to Dr Nick about it. He said it was a problem, because he was getting drugs from other people, outside of Memphis. He said he was trying to control it by giving him placebos and sugar pills. Dr Nick asked us to keep watch and try and keep track of what he was taking. I know Dr Nick called Dr Ghanem and other doctors to see what they were giving him. We even went to see his father about it. But Elvis was a very strong guy, you know. When I spoke to him about it, he'd say he wasn't doing anything wrong. In the end, he'd just tell me if I didn't like it to get the hell out. I left a couple of times over personal rows, but came back . . .

*   *   *   *   *

Linda Thompson was twenty-three years old when she met Elvis Presley. She was a local girl who had, naturally, followed his career, but was not a fan. Elvis was a bit out of her age range. She worked in a nearby business until she met Elvis at the Memphian Theatre in July 1972, six months after Priscilla had taken Lisa Marie and moved to Los Angeles. George Klein, a local disc jockey, had for years arranged introductions to young female companions for Elvis. When he saw an attractive girl he thought Elvis would like to meet, he would go over and talk to her. The pattern was always the same; she would be brought to Graceland where there would be introductions in a crowded room. Elvis would signal his approval or otherwise, and if he liked the girl, she could expect a telephone call soon afterwards, with an invitation to visit him. Linda Thompson had just become Miss Tennessee of 1972, and Klein who met her through this connection, asked if she would like to meet Elvis Presley.

Klein intimated that he was doing her a great honour and favour, selecting her for such an audience, but actually Linda would have been just as happy not to go; in a word, she was unimpressed. Anyway, that night, she accepted his invitation to go to the Memphian Theatre, which Elvis had rented, as usual, for an all-night screening which had been his practice for years. Again, there was always a pattern for this event. The film would be booked for a certain time, guests would be invited, the lights would go down and Elvis would arrive with his entourage and sit in the row of seats reserved halfway down the auditorium.

On this occasion, Linda was introduced and she left soon

afterwards. Just as she arrived home, the telephone rang – it was Elvis. He was desperate to see her again and could she come around the next night? She did, and their relationship took off from there. According to most in the Elvis entourage, Linda was the best thing that could have happened to him, and they all believed that he saw in her a trust and reliance that had been missing from his life since his mother died.

At the time, in 1972, Elvis was still struggling with the loss of Priscilla and he also had weight problems, fluctuating between 210 and 230 pounds, which was the heaviest he had ever been, though he would get heavier. In part, the amphetamines were supposed to be part of the combative action to suppress his enormous and continual appetite for junk food – the hamburgers, ordered up at any time of the day or night and the huge piles of burned bacon and eggs he had for breakfast.

Linda gave this recollection of events:

A couple of days after that first meeting, I started seeing him, going to Graceland for chats and watching films and so on. After about three weeks I faced a choice. He had to go to Las Vegas for the summer show. I agreed to go, and from then on, I was with him constantly, and so it remained for the next four and a half years. It came as a total surprise to myself and my family. I was never a particular fan. But from thereon in, I was with him all the time. I travelled with him on most of the tours, all the time. I wasn't aware he was taking all those pills when I first met him. In fact, that first night when I'd met him he called me at home and he sounded very groggy. I had no idea then what it was and I asked him if he had been drinking.

The first I realised what it was was when I went to Las Vegas with him. He was very groggy and not really together. I had absolutely no experience of being around people who drank or took drugs. I asked him what was wrong, and then I saw the pills. It was totally foreign to me. I asked him why he had to take medication like that, why he had to take it every night. It was clearly excessive.

As time went on, I would see him take as many as twenty or thirty pills during the course of an evening. I started to do my own investigations to find out exactly what he was taking. It was primarily sleeping medication and painkillers. He was getting the pills from all his doctors, in Memphis, Las Vegas and Los Angeles.

There was always a supplier of medication on hand. He

periodically used injections, some were vitamins, B12, but I think a lot of them were amphetamines, the Dr feelgood mixture. Any of the doctors might inject him. His behaviour was constantly erratic. His temperament was volatile and variable, but I must say a lot of the time quite lovable. He had a bad temper, and sometimes it would be the interaction of the drugs. It was basically the Marilyn Monroe/Judy Garland syndrome, you know. He would take sleeping pills to knock himself out and then wake up groggy and take dexedrine. The erratic behaviour involving the bad temper, the shooting-out of television sets, that kind of thing, resulted.

When he woke up after a long sleep, he would generally take something to rouse him and maybe during the day, maybe once or twice, he would take pain medication and then at night he would take sleeping medication. That was the general routine of an average day. On show days, it was different again, more excessive . . .

Linda said that eventually the problem was not one of merely trying to control the medication, but also making sure that he did not choke on his food. On several occasions, he would fall asleep while they were eating and she would have to take the food out of his mouth to stop him choking. Sometimes, she had to call the doctor. Even so, there were innumerable times when Elvis choked, so many times she could not recall how often she'd had to put her fingers into his throat. One time, she woke up and he wasn't breathing properly. She called the nurse, who called Dr Nick, and he had him removed to the hospital.

On another occasion, in Las Vegas, he had choked and 'was completely out of it'. Linda called the Las Vegas doctor and he came to the hotel penthouse and gave him some injections to help. He was out for hours. On a different date, when they were flying back from Vegas to Memphis, Elvis was taken ill on the plane. He could not breathe properly and was admitted to hospital as soon as they landed. The story they put out was that there was a problem with the air-conditioning on the aircraft. Sometimes he was admitted to hospitals in other people's names, so that no one would learn that he had gone in. Linda expands on this:

When we were on tour or in Las Vegas, there was always a doctor present before the show. The routine was that he would see the doctor and they would go into a private room. I never actually saw Elvis injected by doctors, but the general assumption was that he was receiving medication. Elvis was very sensitive about his medication. We talked about it from time to time. He said he had suffered with insomnia since he was a child. Then, when he became a star, there was so much going on, so much pressure that he had taken medication to help him keep going, or to sleep. I know other members of the tour had to take medication to keep up with him.

When we were on tour, Elvis always carried a little black bag that contained his medication. He never went anywhere without it. There were a couple of times when he asked me if I wanted to take a sleeping pill or something because we would be out on the road and the routine was so erratic; I never did, though.

There were times when he was ready to go on stage when he was still down from sleeping medication and he'd be virtually still asleep through his performance. He'd come off hardly knowing he had been on stage and say he was only just waking up. Other times, he was too up on dexedrine or whatever, so that he was too highly strung, giggling on stage and being silly, sometimes hostile. It was a big worry. I talked to Dr Nick about it, and to Joe Esposito. I remember Dr Nick telling me that frankly I was not the kind of girl who should be around; I was straight. He advised me to leave. He said no one could ever change Elvis, and he was right, one person cannot change another person . . .

Linda said she knew that Dr Nick had difficulty determining what doctor was giving him which drugs. Over the years that she was with him, Elvis had all kinds of different drugs. He was very well versed in their effects. She talked to Vernon Presley periodically about Elvis's drugs. He was becoming increasingly worried. She continued:

At this time in his life, I suppose Elvis was closer to me than anyone. At one point we had planned to marry, but not after a while. That was primarily because of his drug use, but also, though, because of his whole lifestyle. There was no way he was going to change. He was a very strong-willed person, and he got whatever he wanted. I suppose for whatever reason, Dr Nick continued to prescribe the drugs, and in some ways, I suppose it was so that he could remain Elvis's physician. Elvis would often complain of being in pain; he'd say he was in pain all over, or that he had pulled a hamstring or something on stage. I always assumed it was a very convenient pain because he enjoyed the effects of the painkilling medication. I've been on the tours, I was the closest anyone could be. I think most of the guys tried to keep Dr Nick informed of what was coming in from other sources, the packages that were coming in the mail. Elvis was a pill-aholic. He also injected a lot; sometimes I had to help him inject. He had a psychological dependence. He thought he could not get up or keep going or go to sleep without medication.

As regards the effects on the rest of his life, it is probably true that sometimes his generosity was drug-enhanced. He was generous to a fault, anyway, but I think it was possible some people took advantage when they saw what kind of state he was in.

Larry Hutchinson questioned Linda about Dr Nichopoulos. Was she aware of the financial arrangements between them? Linda replied:

I know that at the beginning he was being paid a personal fee, but then when the medical partnership he was involved with built their centre, Elvis had to pay the practice for the privilege of taking Dr Nick on tours. I knew that Nichopoulos had asked for a personal loan from Elvis. I was there when Dr Nick brought up the plans to his new house, and I was there when Elvis agreed to give him a construction loan. The house was going to cost around 300,000 dollars, and Elvis was going to lend him about two-thirds of that amount.

I viewed the whole thing objectively at the time, but I look back now and think, My God, how did I tolerate all that was going on?

$$\star \quad \star \quad \star \quad \star \quad \star$$

The year of 1974 was as bad as any had been. Elvis collapsed when the tour reached Louisiana. Colonel Parker was forced to cancel the rest of the dates and put out a press statement that Elvis was suffering from exhaustion. It was the first time Elvis had ever cancelled. In spite of his comatose condition, he was flown back to Memphis for admission to the Baptist Memorial Hospital where, in addition to the treatment for exhaustion, hospital records showed that he was placed on a detoxification programme. Vernon Presley persuaded Elvis to undergo therapy to get him off some of the drugs. The doctors were astounded, however, that when they began to wind him down from the sleeping medication, he simply could not go to sleep. They assumed that, at some time or other he would simply nod off. After four days, according to Jerry Schilling, he was still awake and they had to give him a shot to knock him out.

It was Elvis's third admission to hospital within a relatively short space of time; the last occasion had involved traumatic therapy following treatment for his twisted colon, when he temporarily lost the control of his body functions.

Elvis remained in hospital for two weeks, and in the meantime, Vernon Presley was anxious to try to halt the uncontrolled supply of chemicals to Elvis. Soon afterwards, John O Grady, the former drug-busting Los Angeles policeman, received a telephone call from E. Gregory Hookstratten, Elvis's lawyer in Los Angeles, who explained that he was calling on Vernon's behalf and that he wished to discuss a highly sensitive and confidential matter.

O'Grady, in his statement to the district attorney's investigator, said he was formally hired as a private detective to look into 'any and all the use of narcotics used by Elvis Presley.' The investigation lasted approximately six weeks, for which he also engaged the services of Jack Kelly, the former regional director of the Federal Bureau of Narcotics, and then a licensed private investigator. He was to investigate the supply of drugs to Elvis from Los Angeles and Las Vegas medical practitioners. Hookstratten also said Vernon Presley was tremendously upset by the large medical bills submitted by Dr Nichopoulos.

O'Grady discovered the names of three doctors and the Palm Springs dentist who were supplying drugs on prescription to Elvis. These prescriptions were cashed at a pharmacy on Sunset Boulevard. Most were in the names of Charles Hodge and others who were working with Elvis. There was only one prescription in more than 100 examined in the name of Elvis. It was for 100 Percodan.

Vernon had asked him specifically if he could also get into Dr Nichopoulos's bag, which he took on tour with Elvis, to see what drugs it contained. He never did manage to do that. However, during his season in Las Vegas that year, a hotel employee had found a narcotic needle in Elvis's bed and had turned it in. 'There was an extraordinary scene,' said O'Grady:

It was the strangest thing. I was sitting there at the performance and Elvis got up, on the stage, in front of everyone, and told the entire staff they were rotten bastards and should never use narcotics. He was doing his drugs–cop bit. I watched the show and then went backstage and his aide, Lamar Fike, said it was ridiculous. Elvis was out there with 190-degree blood pressure. I couldn't understand why the doctors had let him work. Another thing was his sweating; I look at people coming down from drugs and covered with perspiration, but I had never seen anyone sweat like that. He would lose seven or eight pounds in a performance. He was such a strong character, that he came through it, but I could never understand how any doctor at that point could allow him to work.

After submitting his report to Vernon, O'Grady kept in touch with Joe Esposito to enquire about Elvis's condition. He admitted to Larry Hutchinson that he was 'mortally afraid that some young narcotics officer would knock Elvis off'. O'Grady said that he personally had remained silent because he was hired to produce a confidential report for a client, and that was as far as he could go. He had no idea what Vernon was able to do about his report on Elvis's drug habits. He presumed that he could do nothing, because in spite of everything, Elvis ruled the roost. On a personal level, O'Grady tried other means to get Elvis to reduce his intake:

As a professional drug–enforcement officer, I had long known of his drug problems, and I started to get him interested in law enforcement to try a reversal procedure [around the time he took off to see the president]. The only time I spoke to him about getting off medication was a year after the investigation for Vernon, in 1975. I joined him on a tour that year and had long conversations. When I suggested a detox, his reaction was, 'Absolutely not, you sonovabitch.' Slowly but surely, I observed the debilitating activity of the chemicals, especially watching the show when I, more than most, could recognise his inability to articulate; he had a peculiar walking gait, he would ramble, he would tell stories that didn't make sense.

He would call me in the middle of the night, many times, and I do not regret these calls. He called me one night and said he had just buried Jesse [his twin brother who died at birth] there in Memphis. It was meaningless. His brain would wander; he would repeat and repeat things a thousand times. He would call, perhaps at four in the morning, and just ramble for forty or fifty minutes. I felt in my own way I was just doing some good by listening to him. It was a condition brought on by these narcotics.

The deterioration began in the early Seventies and, by 1974, he was in a bad way; it was obvious. From then on to when he died he was not Elvis Presley. He was a human being under the influence of drugs, suffering a deep debilitation caused by the use of narcotics. I found that southern people accept people as family, and Presley seemed to accept Dr Nick as family. When I would see him on trips, he had that bag and I could never get in it. In my few conversations with him, I did not think he was particularly bright. Over the years I asked him a couple of times how Elvis was doing. He would say that Elvis was doing just fine. Of all the cases I've worked on, hundreds of them, I have never seen so many drugs prescribed for one person ever before, and I have been involved in drug enforcement for thirty-two years...

8

Money Worries

'I suppose I really began to get concerned at the beginning of 1974 when he came to my house. I got worried. He'd gained too much weight and he looked terrible. Now, I spoke out, but I could not get involved. When I told him he did not look well, he said, "No disrespect, colonel, but I know what I'm doing. Stay out of my personal life." I was aware, of course, that he was being treated by various physicians, but I could only speak out when he did a bad show. There were a couple of complaints sometimes when he didn't do a show too good. But every performer has good days and bad days. He had some bad days; other times he was outstanding. I was concerned sometimes, but I just could not talk to him about it . . .'

Colonel Tom Parker, 1980

Those who were close to Elvis never rubbished the image, even after his death. Tom Parker, like Joe Esposito, was economical with his recollections. Neither was he prepared to elaborate in any great detail for Larry Hutchinson, the district attorney's investigator, on his financial dealings on Elvis's behalf. He would later be called to account for some of his own actions when the Memphis probate court began to examine Elvis's financial affairs in the Eighties, a matter which we will examine in a later chapter. One of the court's main concerns would be an extraordinary manoeuvre made by Colonel Parker during those trying times, after Elvis's divorce from Priscilla, and his headlong lurch into precarious experiments with narcotics. Parker decided to sell all the copyrights to his past work.

Vernon Presley, who was charged with running his son's financial affairs, was worried on two fronts. The drugs were a major concern, but matters of finance were worrying, too. Vernon kept telling him that there was a limit to what they could spend. At some point there would be a crossover, and their outgoings would exceed the income. Elvis, as always, said it did not matter. He could go to Las Vegas or do a tour and earn a million dollars in a month. That was quite true. But there was no getting away from the fact that he was all but broke.

Reserves of ready cash were clearly dwindling after Elvis paid out his million-dollar divorce settlement for Priscilla in 1973, and put other money into a trust fund for Lisa Marie. He had never taken professional advice over his money, or stored away cash in investments. Everything he owned was visible – Graceland and eleven acres of land in Memphis, a house in Los Angeles and one in Palm Springs. He did not even have a pension fund.

The colonel was apparently no better. When the *Nashville Banner* published a story about Parker's need for cash to pay off gambling debts in Las Vegas, he threatened to sue for defamation unless the newspaper published a retraction. The paper's editor refused, and said that if they went to court they would naturally expect Elvis's manager to produce a summary of his gambling activities. Parker did not pursue it.

Money shortage was surely the only explanation of why Elvis agreed to the one-sided financial arrangement negotiated by Parker in concert with his record company, RCA, in 1973. In exchange for a one-off payment of 5.4 million dollars, Elvis surrendered the rights to all future royalties on an estimated 650 recordings.

It was a remarkably shortsighted arrangement from Elvis's point of view, especially considering that the long-standing management contract between the two men provided Colonel Parker with fifty per cent of Elvis's earnings. Thus, from the 5.4 million-dollar payment from RCA, Elvis received only 1.35 million dollars after tax, in exchange for the most valuable collection of records made by any singer in history.

The deal would be challenged long after Elvis's death, but for the time being, it demonstrated one thing, and one thing only – that in spite of the millions he had earned over the years, the money had been spent and he was no longer blessed with the great wealth that his lifestyle now needed in order to continue.

He was, at times, running perilously close to spend-out when all expenses were considered, with a household running at up to twenty permanent staff. His income from tours and appearances in Las Vegas had to fund such costs as promotion, the orchestra, the singers, the road crews, the equipment, the sound, the lights and his personal expenses. The tours now carried a workforce – including Elvis's bodyguards and security people – of more than 100. His income alone funded the running of two planes, a four-engined Lockheed Jetstar, which he personally used, and a Dassault-Falcon. He also leased a BAC 111 jet, which ferried around the orchestra, the road crews and all the equipment to the tour venues. Then there was the fleet of cars, the additional security guards hired in for each show, the medical costs, the assorted sundry expenses.

And there were gifts, on-going and ever more costly. Cars for friends and doctors. Elvis brushed aside the warnings and continued to spend as if there would be no tomorrow. But even accounting for his extravagances, his whole financial well-being seemed to be undermined by a black hole through which the surplus was draining away. Everything hung on his continued ability to draw in large cash injections from his tours. It was still possible, but becoming a massive strain on him, and he could never again repeat his workload of 1974, when he went hell for leather, playing more than 150 concerts and shows, mostly one-night stands, which meant he was on the road for more than half the year and confined to life in hotel rooms.

The pattern was always the same. He would arrive in the town, check into the hotel, and take pills to go to sleep. He would be roused two hours before the show was due to start and take more pills to wake him up. An hour later, a limousine would arrive to take him to the show, and often he only just made it before he was due to go on. It was a horrendous period, but at the end of it, he had earned in total more than seven million dollars.

It sounded a wonderful sum, and Elvis boasted how there was no other entertainer in the world who could attract such money. The reality was devastating. Almost half went in taxes, Colonel Parker took 1.7 million dollars in management fees, and the remainder was more than eaten up by the touring costs and staff payments. By the end of 1975, he was still no better off financially and had to dip into reserves and borrow from the National Bank of Memphis to meet all the bills.

The physical cost was appalling. As we have already learned from the graphic descriptions provided by Linda Thompson, one of the most reliable of all the witnesses Larry Hutchinson interviewed, Elvis was at breaking point. He collapsed three times during 1974. One stay in the Memphis Baptist Hospital lasted two weeks. There were other 'secret' admissions for detoxification, as Larry Hutchinson discovered when he interviewed Elvis's constant companion, Charlie Hodge. Was it true, asked Hutchinson, that he, Charlie Hodge, had been admitted to the Las Vegas Sunrise Hospital in 1975 for a drugs problem, for which a bill of 880 dollars was tendered for treatment? No, said Hodge, he had never had a drugs problem and he had never been admitted to the Sunrise Hospital, not ever.

Was it true, asked Hutchinson, that he had been admitted to the Baptist Memorial Hospital, also in 1975, for a detoxification programme? No, said Hodge, it was not true and he could not explain why the records of that hospital showed he had been admitted.

'Was it customary for Elvis to check into hospital and use another name?' asked Hutchinson.

'I'm sure it was,' Hodge replied.

The plain truth was that nothing could be allowed to hinder Elvis's career at that point. He lived constantly on the knife-edge of scandalous exposure. Prescribed drugs were coming in from doctors in various parts of America, made out in other names, mostly of those close to him. Charlie Hodge, Sonny West, Joe Esposito and Jerry Schilling, all discovered their names were being used by Elvis. He could not allow the possibility of some pharmacy clerk leaking information to the newspapers, just as he had to keep secret his detoxification visits to hospital. Dr Ghanem in Las Vegas, who was also a close personal friend, even provided Elvis with private facilities at his own home, where he could go and get a 'sleep' cure. This entailed being knocked out for thirty-six hours at a time.

The cause, apart from the emotional stress of his private life, was the need to go on working non-stop, with tour after tour becoming just as necessary as his own need for uppers and downers. There is no doubt at all that Elvis was now finding the sheer volume of work a great burden. Jerry Schilling observed:

I noticed the sustained change in the last three years of his life. He wasn't having any fun any more. His health was suffering badly. I know for a fact that he was still suffering from a twisted colon, he had an enlarged liver and high blood pressure. His eye condition, glaucoma, was also giving him a great deal of bother. He was a man who had been healthy all his life, and suddenly everything started to happen to him. He was working with a psychiatrist for a time, and for Elvis that was a very big statement to make. It was a very hard thing to let his pride go.

These difficulties were to be confirmed by the sworn testimony of Dr Lawrence Wruble, a Memphis gastro-enterologist, who said he had treated Elvis for his colon condition, which he attributed to the use of large amounts of cortisone, a steroid hormone which was then commonly used in the treatment of rheumatoid arthritis. He was given the cortisone by a doctor who was not among his usual suppliers of medication. Over-use of the drug could have certain side-effects, one of which was a tendency towards obesity. His colon illness and his intake of cortisone was such that he lost control of his bladder function for a time and required padding for incontinence.

This, as Jerry Schilling rightly observed, was a tremendous blow to Elvis's pride. Apart from the curative therapy, the sheer trauma of such a condition for a man of forty, a worldwide sex symbol and showbusiness icon, having to be treated like a senile senior citizen naturally required counselling. Dr Wruble said he understood Elvis's need for drugs to keep him going during hefty work commitment, getting him excited for a show and to relax him afterwards, but he warned Elvis that unless he slowed down, his problems could only increase, and, in particular, the lack of control of his body functions would be exacerbated.

For a time, Elvis cut back. Dr Nichopoulos warned everyone in Graceland to be on the alert for packages of medication coming in from outside, but the respite was brief. Vernon continued to worry about Elvis's medical bills, a constant source of agitation which came to him monthly, when he was required to settle the charges.

He would never admit his son had a drug problem, merely a need for medication because of the life he led. The cost was becoming enormous. Vernon had long ago become resigned to the fact that he was signing cheques to supply uppers and downers for the entourage during the tours. While on the road, it cost 800 dollars a day for the attendance of Elvis's personal physician, Dr George Nichopoulos. Vernon also believed that some of the drugs prescribed for Elvis were being diverted. Once purchased, they were being stolen and sold on the streets or elsewhere, but he could never prove it. The medical costs were just part of the cash that went in the direction of Nichopoulos. Between 1970 and 1977, Presley had made personal loans to the doctor totalling 275,000 dollars, to help him buy a house and finance other projects. In the same period, he paid the doctor 74,000 dollars for medical services and another 147,000 dollars to his medical group practice for cover while Elvis was on tour.

Elvis's external supplies were also often costly to obtain. If he needed some medication quickly and it was not available locally, he might send a courier by plane to collect it. He might even take off himself in search of a chemical adventure. There were some strange and unexplained events and journeys in the planes, which were themselves a drain on funds, with a four-man crew on permanent duty to answer Presley's every call.

Some were journeys which seemed specifically planned as a special liaison for a jolt of medication, as Presley called it. David Stanley related one such expedition to Las Vegas. It was three in the morning and Elvis was supposed to be resting between tours; he was bored and had pulled everyone out at short notice for a trip to the casino city. No one knew why they were going and assumed it was just another jaunt; they had been a thousand times and often just stayed a few hours and returned. They just piled aboard the plane and took off.

Elvis was in high spirits all the way there, and on landing the plane taxied down the runway and parked. Soon afterwards, a dark-coloured Mercedes glided across the tarmac to the bottom of the steps of the plane. Two men got out, carrying black medical bags. They were physicians who Elvis dealt with on a regular basis, and who he had contacted before they left Memphis. They saw Elvis in his private cabin, where they remained for no more than five minutes, and eventually emerged, saying to Stanley that Elvis might need some assistance getting off the plane. When they went to see him, his entourage was shocked. In the space of time it took for the two Las Vegas doctors to leave the plane, Elvis was already unable to sit up or walk.

By the time the entourage was ready to leave for the house where he would be staying, he was unconscious. They all carried him off the plane, put him in the back of a car, and drove him to the house. He did not come round for more than forty-eight hours. It was a sleep cure, devised by the Las Vegas doctor. Stanley said, 'I had no idea what they had given him, or why ...' When he woke up, Elvis

131

took his amphetamines and announced he had never felt better.

This incident and others were the matters that John O'Grady was designated to investigate secretly on Vernon's behalf. Only by monitoring his son's movements did he begin to understand and finally accept the extent of the drug usage and why it had become such a drain on finances. All of these factors through the months of 1976, along with the mounting financial pressures, were compounding Vernon Presley's inability to make sense of what was happening; at the root of it was undoubtedly the great weight of responsibility bearing down upon Elvis. The drugs were a problem, sure enough, but perhaps on average no worse than many others in the same business. Medical opinion of those dependent on chemical aids – as opposed to hard drugs – is that recovery, once attained, is easier to maintain. The general health of the body can quickly recuperate, once the constant attack on the nervous system and the body's organs through these chemicals is halted. It was actually probably true what all of his aides eventually told Larry Hutchinson, that too much was made of the importance of the drugs. Elvis undoubtedly felt they were a necessary crutch to support him during this time of heavy pressure, but without them and with a period of rehabilitation, he could have recovered.

The problem was that Elvis needed to work to keep up the cash flow. He might well have had a million or two in the bank, but net of debts it was no more than a handful of small change.

This single most important factor prompted the colonel to look at ways of maintaining the income, while at the same time cutting the workload. He negotiated a cut-back of the tortuous month of twice-nightly shows in Las Vegas to a more manageable fifteen. He also discovered a way of raising the stakes, increasing the income from venue appearances. He negotiated for major one-off 'hits' – concerts in the largest arenas available, such the massive Silver Dome sports centre in Michigan, which had an audience capacity of 80,000. The concert was a sell-out and Elvis flew into Michigan and gave a rattling performance in the cavernous building. He was received in a rapturous manner and the gig went down in history as producing the largest single gross take for a one-night stand – 840,000 dollars.

Even so, Elvis's share barely patched the hole in his bank account, and Vernon was deeply troubled. He was a conscientious man who still did his best to run the family business in the face of his own mounting ill-health and lack of business acumen; it was all just too much for him. Elvis was, after all, the breadwinner for this whole extended family group. As numerous in that group have since testified, he did not understand the word 'no'.

As long as the money kept coming in, he continued to spend it. In 1975, for example, Elvis had decided to buy a new plane, a huge jetliner and an altogether bigger model than his current executive jet. He wanted a big plane like the Boeing 707 aboard which he had seen Led Zeppelin arrive for a gig. It was also necessary to have some comfort on the many journeys he was having to undertake for the tours.

And here began a tale that was to have remarkable, barely believable and ultimately, perhaps, even fatal consequences.

Life on the road, this continuous circle of venues to keep some sort of career alive in the Seventies, meant that a good aircraft was essential. It was the only way to travel around the United States for the one-nighters. The latest aircraft was a second-hand Corvair 880, until that time in service with Delta Airlines and capable of carrying 112 passengers and crew. He paid almost 300,000 dollars for it, without even seeing it, sending Joe Esposito to purchase it from a dealer in Arizona. David Stanley recalled that Elvis called it the best toy he had ever bought himself. When his pilots flew it in to Memphis from Tucson, Elvis was elated and waiting on the tarmac.

As the giant plane glided towards the runway and landed, he sank to the ground on his knees in front of Corvair as it taxied to a halt. Then he went aboard, and like a boy with a new bike, wanted to try it out. He ran up and down the aisle and sat in different seats, and then sat in the pilot's seat. He had the whole interior ripped out, and spent another 300,000 dollars converting it to his own requirements, with a bed and cinema in the rear, and seating for the entourage at the front in the plush club room. Here he installed a bar and card tables, leather lounging chairs and a 15,000-dollar quadraphonic sound system. There was a dining room with oval table covered in green leather, and a galley, with meals to be served on monogrammed crockery and silverware.

The bedroom was a replica of his own in Graceland, decorated in varying shades of blue, and with a large bathroom running off. The accommodation was almost as sumptuous as the presidential air force craft. He was so pleased with it after the refit was completed that he named the aircraft after his daughter, *Lisa Marie*, and soon the plane became a familiar sight all over the country, as he began arriving on his tour dates in the style of royalty. His quick trips by plane also became legendary, if only for their enormous extravagance – a flight from Memphis to Denver to pick up a peanut-butter sandwich, or off to Las Vegas at a minute's notice and back again when he became bored.

Meanwhile, the Lockheed Jetstar executive jet which was his first expensive plane, and which cost over a million dollars was parked at Memphis airport, now surplus to his requirements. Though he had paid out close to 600,000 dollars for the Corvair, for its purchase and refurbishment, Elvis still owed 600,000 dollars to the American National Bank of Morristown, who had financed the purchase of the Jetstar. The balance was more than the plane was worth in its present state. Elvis had told Vernon to get rid of it, but disposal of the Jetstar was easier said than done. Vernon was at his wits' end. It was costing 10,060 dollars a month in repayments.

$$\star \quad \star \quad \star \quad \star \quad \star$$

There were other unexpected incidentals looming on the horizon, not least of which was the expense of keeping members of the entourage out of trouble. As the security aspect of Elvis's tours had increased over the years, so had Red and Sonny West's propensity to resort to strong-arm tactics to clear away any potentially threatening situations, which more often than not were no more harmful than over-zealous fans. It was a well-known fact that they tended to hit first and talk later. One such case had just been settled out of court and cost Elvis a hefty sum. A Los Angeles property man claimed to have paid one of Presley's aides sixty dollars to get into a party Elvis was attending. When he was refused admission, the man kicked up a fuss and Elvis and one of his bodyguards came over and gave the man a good punching, before kicking him out.

The victim sued for six million dollars in damages, and settled for an undisclosed amount. And after that fracas, Elvis's father called in three of his longest-serving bodyguards and aides – original members of the renowned Memphis Mafia, cousins Red and Sonny West, and Dave Hebler – and fired them on a week's notice. Vernon said there was nothing else to be done. The three men were bitter and aggravated; they walked out of Graceland vowing to get even, and they would.

Matters of the heart also accounted for some additional expense. Vernon's own marriage was ending. He had been away on tour with Elvis and returned in the company of a young nurse named Sandy Miller, who eventually moved in; Dee Stanley moved out amid angry scenes. Dee was bitter on several fronts, not the least of which was that her life of plenty, which she had enjoyed since she returned from Germany as Vernon's intended, was about to cease. She reached for the telephone and called her lawyers. Ultimately, it would be Elvis who would have to pay.

Meanwhile, Elvis's long-standing relationship with Linda Thompson was also ending. She could stand the life no longer and finally concluded that she had to break free if she wanted any kind of future. There was no formal financial settlement, but Linda kept an assortment of jewellery he had bought her over the years, reportedly worth a quarter of a million dollars. She did not feel angry or hard-done-by. She had done her stint.

In terms of what modern live-in lovers seek from broken relationships with the rich and famous, Elvis got off very lightly indeed. Linda, who had saved Elvis's life on several occasions, had been the best thing that could have happened to him. They patched up their differences after the immediate discomfort of a separation, and remained friends.

*   *   *   *   *

All in all, Vernon was fighting a losing battle. By 1976 it was all beginning to come apart at the seams, and he knew it. Elvis's career was as perilous as his son's mental state in times of anguish – hanging by a slender thread which could break at any moment. Despite the sell-out concerts, as the colonel said, there had been a good many complaints. 'I think there was a limit to how long the tours could go on,' said Parker. Elvis was a physical shambles and even some of his friends in the music business were suggesting that it was time he took a break, slimmed down his bloated body, and reconsidered his material.

The fact was, he couldn't afford to.

9

The Incredible Sting

'*To the Director, Federal Bureau of Investigation; Re: Elvis A. Presley (Victim); Investigation into this case predicated upon a request from the United States Attorney's office, Western District of Tennessee, Memphis, wherein they had been contacted by attorney for Elvis A. Presley, an entertainer, indicating they felt a violation of federal law had occurred ... their client was the victim, losing approximately 950,000 dollars.*'
Memo from FBI, Memphis division, to headquarters, 1977

A bleak internal memo, circulated through the channels of the FBI to the hierarchy in Washington and to several interested strike forces throughout the United States, signalled the beginning of one more incredible, alarming episode in the life, and perhaps death, of Elvis Presley. It came at that time of turmoil, when Elvis himself was suffering and his father Vernon was also weak from a heart condition. Neither could have imagined, even contemplated, that they had been selected as the target for a group of Mafia-linked fraudsters, who now moved in with a deliberate and premeditated plan which was intended for one purpose only, to steal from the Presleys.

Worse, the whole business was to embroil the Presleys in a far deeper, dangerous investigation, one that was enveloped by a worldwide securities fraud involving 'billions of dollars'. They walked into it with all the innocence of children. Vernon's belief that their finances were desperate led him to become caught in the events now about to unfold ...

★　　★　　★　　★　　★

136

In June 1976, the Lockheed Jetstar had been standing idle for months, being used only infrequently for short trips by Elvis or the entourage. The large plane, the Corvair, had a crew of four, while the Jetstar had a team of two, who were also on permanent call, costing in total 250,000 dollars a year in staff payments alone, even before the running expenses.

Vernon Presley had tried in vain to sell the Jetstar. Not only was it losing value as each week passed, but the unused aircraft was the cause of a haemorrhage of money in leasing rentals. Unbeknown to him, the plane had already been earmarked as the key to an incredible sting.

In the first half of June, Vernon was contacted by a third party who knew of his keenness to dispose of the plane. He was introduced to a man named Frederick Pro, who described himself as president of Air Cargo Express Inc., of Miami, Florida. To the FBI, Pro was also known as Alfredo Proc, president of a New York financial and investment company known as Trident Consortium, and associated with Seven Oaks Finance Ltd, in Kent, England. Both companies were being mentioned in a major international investigation involving worthless letters of credit and certificates of deposit, which were being presented at banks around the world, and particularly throughout the United States. Millions of dollars in losses had already been reported in dozens of cities.

Pro was a confident, smart man of just over six feet, who carried an authoritative air. Vernon Presley, in spite of the opulence of his surroundings and twenty years in the entertainment business, was still basically a naïve and unworldly man, no match for the wheeler-dealers. Frederick Pro boasted international connections and suggested that they should meet and discuss an idea as to how he, Pro, could turn Elvis's unused plane into a profitable investment.

Had Vernon taken the trouble to run a company check, he would have discovered that Pro's recent financial history in Florida indicated that he had taken over an asset-wealthy company, stripped out the valuables, and put the company into bankruptcy. His Air Cargo Express Company had been incorporated only five weeks earlier with share values of nothing whatsoever.

Elvis Presley became a target for fraud and, later, the unwitting pawn in a major FBI investigation. At that point it was controlled by an order from the FBI directorate requiring strictest secrecy and confidentiality to protect the two agents who were working under cover on the international securities scam.

Frederick Pro arrived in Memphis for a meeting with Vernon Presley on the morning of 25 June 1976. With him came a group of associates purporting to be officers of two other companies, one an aircraft brokerage and the other a leasing company. Pro outlined to Vernon how he could effectively release Elvis from the expense of keeping the Lockheed Jetstar – and show a monthly profit.

Vernon was naturally very interested. Pro said that it was his intention to sub-lease the aircraft from Presley, but first it would be necessary to upgrade the plane with new fittings and modern electronics so that it would qualify for the Federal Aviation Regulation's 121 maintenance programme. Pro said that his associates could arrange leasing finance with a New York bank, which would allow Vernon to pay off the 600,000-dollar loan still owing on the plane and provide for the costs of upgrading the Jetstar for an estimated 350,000 dollars.

This would entail taking out a new mortgage on the plane for 950,000 dollars, with monthly repayments of 16,755 dollars to be met by Presley. Pro would then sub-lease the aircraft for 17,755 dollars a month, giving Elvis a thousand dollars a month profit for doing absolutely nothing. And, at the end of the lease period, Presley would still own the plane, which would remain a valuable asset. To Vernon Presley, such an arrangement was barely believable. Here was a deal which was for once making them money, or so it seemed.

Further, Pro offered an additional carrot. He was prepared to pay Vernon and Elvis an up-front premium of 40,000 dollars upon signature of the leasing arrangement and exchange of cheques.

Vernon agreed to all that Pro set before him and signed the documents there and then. He gave one of Pro's associates, who claimed to represent a finance company, a cheque for 33,500 dollars to cover the first and last rentals, while Pro on his part provided Vernon with reciprocal cheques for 35,500 dollars to cover his rental payments to Elvis, plus one for 40,000 dollars as a premium for the sub-lease, which on the face of it provided Elvis Presley's bank account with an instant injection of 42,000 dollars, net. Contracts were exchanged and Vernon handed over the keys of the Lockheed Jetstar to Pro, who promptly flew off in the plane to Miami promising to arrange a second meeting when the balance of the transaction was finally completed.

Barely had he taken off, when Pro telephoned his friend and associate Philip Karl Kitzer at his home to say, 'I got Elvis's plane. I told you I'd get it. Like stealing candy . . .' Kitzer was a key figure in the securities investigation, the man whose organisation had been infiltrated by the two FBI undercover agents.

Presley's cheques were duly cashed, but when Vernon presented those from Pro to his own bank, they were returned as invalid. No funds available. Vernon immediately telephoned Pro, who explained that there had been an error in the transfer of funds from an overseas account and that it would be sorted out very quickly. He should re-present the cheques in a few days. This was done, and once again they were returned.

Pro continued to offer his explanation of the anticipated arrival of these funds, and Vernon continued to trust him. Always, Pro reminded Vernon of the forthcoming profit; that would overcome these difficulties very quickly. During the next two weeks, Vernon, who clung desperately to the hope that all would yet be resolved and his 40,000-dollar fee would be safe, accepted Pro's excuses that the money would arrive shortly. To Frederick Pro, it was a knife-edge situation.

The final stage of the sting had yet to be achieved.

In the second of week of July, Vernon's fears seemed to be allayed when he received the reassurance that the deal was on the verge of completion. Pro and his associates had arranged for a new mortgage on the plane, to be taken out in Elvis's name. The Chemical Bank of New York had jumped at the chance of funding a leasing deal with such a famous personage and completed the financial arrangements on 16 July 1976.

On that day, Vernon Presley, Pro and two associates met in the office of Cecil Carter, vice-president of the National Bank of Commerce in Memphis, where papers setting out terms of the new mortgage on the plane for the amount of 950,000 dollars were delivered along with two cheques drawn on the Chemical Bank of New York, one for 611,951.67 dollars to pay off the previous finance agreement, and the balance of 338,048.33 dollars made out to Elvis Presley. It was paid into his personal account for the specific purpose of funding improvements to the plane. This agreement had been achieved by the production of phoney invoices and an enhanced valuation of the aircraft, produced by Frederick Pro.

At the same time, Pro and his associates presented Vernon with invoices totalling 341,000 dollars to meet the cost of federal aviation inspections and work to upgrade the Jetstar to meet federal aviation requirements. Cecil Carter made out several personal cheques drawn on Elvis Presley's account, which were signed by Vernon Presley on behalf of his son and then converted into cashiers' cheques, which were cashed by Pro and his colleagues. Pro in turn settled all the outstanding money due from the bounced cheques – effectively with Elvis's own money.

At that point in time, Frederick Pro's concert party achieved their aim – to take possession of the Presley plane, and the funds for upgrading it. Among those invoices delivered to the bank that day was one from Trans World Industries, Inc., for work carried out on the plane. A cheque for 129,500 dollars was received by the representative of that company, Laurence Wolfson.

Had anyone been suspicious enough of the whole business at that time to check the credentials of any of the principles brought into it by Pro, they might have discovered some interesting facts. Wolfson, for instance, had a long history of association with leading Mafia figures, and organised crime investigators knew very well that he was still in touch. In the FBI files, there were reports of recent meetings between Wolfson and Sam 'The Plumber' DeCavalcante, the then reputed head of a New Jersey Mafia crime family, and Sebastian 'Buster' Aloi, a leading member of the Joseph Columbo crime family from Hollywood, Florida.

Wolfson and DeCavalcante were former partners in New Jersey before they both sought more favourable climes in Florida. For four years during the Sixties, the FBI tapped both men's telephones and generated thousands of pages of transcripts of conversations that gave the authorities an incredible insight into the daily lives of Mafia figures. The tap on Wolfson's telephone confirmed his association with the most senior members of the crime family, although in later court proceedings, the FBI was forced to admit that the phone-taps were illegal.

In that June of 1976, DeCavalcante was subpoenaed to attend a New Jersey state commission of investigation into criminal activities. At the same time, the federal authorities were attempting to interview him regarding seven million dollars in back taxes from gambling and kickbacks. DeCavalcante, reluctant to discuss such matters publicly, declared himself unfit to attend any hearings because of heart problems and loss of memory.

But these past and present connections with the Mafia were unknown to Vernon and he was simply gullible enough not to check. In fact, no one on the Presley side apparently mistrusted Pro and his colleagues sufficiently to look into their backgrounds. He was a smooth-talking man who had, like all good conmen, eased away their fears over the bouncing cheques with seemingly cast-iron excuses.

Now, as the matters concerning Elvis's Lockheed Jetstar were completed, yet another deal was suggested by Pro. He was interested in purchasing another unwanted aircraft, the smaller Dassault–Falcon aircraft from Elvis, on similar terms. He introduced another associate who would be involved in providing the lease finance. They talked Vernon Presley into writing out a cheque for 53,000 dollars for the deposit on a sale and lease-back arrangement, while Pro gave him cheques amounting to 95,000 dollars for his commitment under the sub-lease.

As before, Presley's cheque was presented and paid. Pro's cheques were returned by the bank unpaid and so Elvis was, on that day, minus yet another 53,000 dollars, though fortunately Pro had not yet taken delivery of the Dassault–Falcon.

Vernon at last became suspicious. He contacted the family lawyer, D. Beecher Smith, in downtown Memphis, and related all that had happened. Beecher Smith in turn had various conversations with Pro, who continued to promise that all the cheques would be honoured. He was awaiting funds from elsewhere and, subsequently, a telex arrived at the offices of Elvis's Memphis Bank from Seven Oaks Finance Ltd, Kent, England, which read:

WITH REGARDS TO ELVIS PRESLEY/AIR CARGO EXPRESS [Pro's company] TRANSACTION, BY THE REQUEST OF MR FREDERICK PRO, SEVEN OAKS FINANCE LTD HAS BANK CONFIRMATION THAT AIR CARGO EXPRESS HAS AN ACCOUNT IN EXCESS OF 500,000 US DOLLARS. REGARDS, SEVEN OAKS FINANCE.

This was intended to pacify Elvis's lawyers and bankers, and to explain that funds were ultimately available for all that was promised. In the meantime, Elvis's plane was being used by Pro. His movements were logged by FBI in connection with other matters and he was known to have flown by commercial airline to the Caribbean, New York, and Switzerland.

By mid-October no money had been received for the rentals due to Elvis under the sub-lease on the aircraft. Elvis himself telephoned Beecher Smith in a frantic rage, demanding to know what the hell was going on and who were these guys who had done this to his daddy. The lawyer could only advise Vernon Presley to issue default notices to Pro's companies demanding immediate payment of the outstanding money. Elvis wanted more urgent action. He sent his personal pilot, Milo High, to Miami at the end of the month to repossess the plane. The worst news had not yet been broken.

On its return, Vernon discovered that none of the upgrading work – for which he had already paid – had been carried out. The plane was in virtually the same condition as it had been when Pro took possession, except for more hours on the clock.

At that point, Elvis was out of pocket by 400,000 dollars in cash – and was left committed to a mortgage of 950,000 dollars on a plane worth less than half that figure. The total net loss suffered by Elvis would be in excess of a million dollars. As all of this drama was unfolding, more alarm bells began to ring in the Presley camp, and subsequently at the national headquarters of the FBI in Washington. On the morning of 19 October 1976, Elvis Presley's lawyer, Beecher Smith, was reading his copy of the *Wall Street Journal* (*WSJ*) when his eyes fell upon an article headed: 'UNCOLLECTIBLE DRAFTS ON WEST INDIAN BANK FLOOD US AND TOTAL MILLIONS OF DOLLARS'.

The article, written by a *WSJ* staff writer, gave a long and detailed account: 'Reports of millions of dollars in uncollectible cashier's cheques and certificates of deposit drawn on a tiny West Indian bank are flooding Federal Bureau of Investigation offices throughout the US. Securities were issued by Mercantile Bank and Trust Co. which was formed two years ago in Kingstown on the Island of St Vincent in the British West Indies.'

The report quoted Raboteau Wilder, the Department of Justice attorney handling the case, as saying, 'We already have twelve volumes of FBI case reports. It's enough to make you throw up your hands. A lot of Mercantile Bank paper is still in the hands of unscrupulous people trying to pledge it.'

Other, later, reports would be more specific. In London, the

Evening Standard named top Mafia figures, including the gambling supremo, Meyer Lansky, another resident of Florida, as having been identified in a massive operation to shift worthless bonds, letters of credit and certificates of deposit around the world. Losses to major international banks were being counted in billions.

The *WSJ* article identified as a registered officer of the phoney bank, Philip Karl Kitzer, former president of a small stock insurance company that went into receivership a few years earlier, a good friend of Frederick Pro, whose New York company Trident, dealt in financial securities. Although Frederick Pro was not mentioned in the report, Beecher Smith remembered that one of the cheques issued by Pro's associates for insurance cover on the plane was drawn on the Mercantile Bank.

He telephoned the Glen Garland Reid, Jr, assistant US attorney, who in turn contacted the Memphis field office of the FBI.

FBI agents were sent immediately to Beecher Smith's offices. The information which Elvis's lawyer wished to impart did not come as a complete surprise to the leaders of the four separate FBI strike forces investigating the securities fraud mentioned in the *Wall Street Journal*. The investigation, codenamed 'Operation Fountain Pen' involved dozens of agents of the FBI throughout the US and in virtually every major city in Europe.

It was little wonder that the FBI was alarmed at the details from Memphis. Though the suspected fraud on Elvis was small fry by comparison, it had fallen in the path of this massive international operation, and the publicity that such a famous personality might attract could jeopardise months of work.

The two undercover special agents from Louisville, Kentucky, with whom the FBI had managed to infiltrate the organisation, were actually travelling with a key suspect, Philip Karl Kitzer, Jr. And the last thing the FBI needed was for their cover to be blown.

In the Elvis Presley file kept by the FBI is a single sheet of a nine-page report (the remaining pages remain classified), part of which reads as follows:

As a brief background ... beginning on 12 December 1974, Philip Karl Kitzer and other individuals operated an offshore bank identified as the First National City Bank and Trust Company Ltd., Grenada, West Indies. Kitzer was the leading figure of a second offshore bank, the Mercantile Bank and Trust Company, St Vincent and Chicago, Ill. With increasing law enforcement interest in each of the banks, Kitzer and his associates moved to create another vehicle for fraud . . . Seven Oaks Finance Ltd., in Kent, England. Kitzer and his associates . . . are a loosely knit group of 30 – 40 of the world's leading specialists . . . it is reasonable to estimate that the total amount of fraudulent negotiable instruments written is approximately $2.5 billion . . .

Those leading the FBI enquiry faced a major problem and a conference was hastily called in Washington to discuss it. If the investigation of the fraud perpetrated against Elvis was revealed, it would attract so much publicity that the massive investigation of the securities fraud might be placed at risk. The FBI knew in the autumn of 1976 that two of the men involved in a spectacular sting against Elvis were also linked to the wider enquiry, but they had to tread with caution so as not to reveal undercover work on the bond scam.

Looking back through the files relating to both investigations, it is apparent today that the FBI strike force leaders who attended the conference on the Elvis sting took a calculated decision that might actually have put Elvis and his father at risk if, as was undoubtedly the case, important Mafia figures were lurking in the background.

During the third week in October, FBI agents interviewed D. Beecher Smith and then went to see Elvis and Vernon, who were to be kept blissfully unaware that the enquiry concerned anything other than the Presley plane. Although Beecher Smith had his suspicions, none was told of the wider implications. To the Presleys, this was merely a fraud against themselves by a group of men who had been intent, from the outset, on taking them for a ride.

Oddly enough, Elvis was ecstatic about this development, taken as he was by a curious mixture of rage and excitement. He was enraged by the fact that someone had conned him and his father out of so much money, and excited about the dealings with the FBI. He showed the agents his badge and offered them his personal assistance; he confirmed solemnly that he would be happy to join in any investigation, should he be required. The FBI men thanked him politely and said they did not think this would be necessary for the moment.

Meanwhile, Operation Fountain Pen was gathering momentum. All through that winter of 1976 to 1977, the FBI continued their investigation over Elvis's plane, and to anyone not fully aware of the wider implications, progress on the case might appear to have been painfully slow. It was an apparently straightforward investigation – a plot to obtain the plane and money from Elvis Presley by false pretences. The documentation was all available, the perpetrators were all identified, their locations known and all to hand for interview, the evidence lay around in abundance.

But the FBI proceeded with deliberate caution.

Instead of being speedily disposed of and the known culprits arrested, the investigation into the Presley affair dragged on for months. The reason was spelled out in a classified memo to the director of the FBI on 16 May 1977. By that time, the four separate strike forces of the FBI had been joined by agents from field offices all over the country, working on reports and cases linked to Operation Fountain Pen. The vast and wide-ranging implications are made abundantly clear in the memo which was marked with a 'Priority' stamp, and sent to fifteen field offices of the bureau throughout America, and to agents in Berne, Bonn, Caracas, Hong Kong, London, Manila, Mexico City, Paris, Rome and Tokyo. Extracts from the sixteen-page resume, are as follows:

As general info for all offices receiving this communication, the following is set forth re: the highly confidential undercover operation conducted by Indianapolis division ... wherein undercover special agents [names deleted] were introduced to Philip Karl Kitzer Jr, gained his confidence and travelled extensively with him in the United States, the Caribbean, Hawaii, Germany ... and have since returned to the US.

Since the inception of this operation the Indianapolis division has attempted to furnish all info of both intelligence and evidential nature to interested field divisions as well as agents abroad. Due to the immense volume of info, it has been necessary to furnish the details by teletype [instead of coded bureau-grams]. As pointed out in [previous] communications ... numerous fraudulent business transactions have been discussed within the US, Europe, the Caribbean and the Far East. The individuals who planned these schemes have been previously identified. This teletype will identify the known banks and the financial institutions who have been involved in these fraudulent schemes; in many cases, the banks listed will have been victim banks throughout the issuing of fraudulent letters of credit and certificates of deposit ...

The memo goes on to list three dozen major banks throughout America and the rest of the world who were known to have been victim to the fraud through the fake securities. Other banks were believed to have kept their losses quiet to avoid publicity. Cases known to involve the fraudulent papers were springing up all over the American continent – Atlanta, Boston, Chicago, Cleveland, Houston, Los Angeles, Louisville, New Haven, Minneapolis, St Louis, San Francisco, New York; and then in Europe, London, Zurich, Frankfurt, Rome and onwards to the Far East.

There was also a list of phoney banks, usually located in one-room offices in some tax-haven shell building which had been used to carry out the scam, including the Seven Oaks Finance Ltd, Kent, which was involved in the Elvis case. There was a long list of individuals who were known to have been involved in carrying it through; they included a number with Mafia connections.

The memo continued:

From the above listing of individuals, banks and cases being worked on by separate divisions within the FBI, it is obvious that this is a highly complicated investigation. UCSAs [undercover special agents] have advised that the principals in this matter have noted on numerous occasions that one of the primary reasons why they have never been prosecuted is because it is difficult for law enforcement agencies to correlate the info gathered. The principals have indicated to UCSAs that billions of dollars in fraudulent financial transactions have occurred throughout the world. It is therefore necessary to advise ... UNDER NO CIRCUMSTANCES IS ANY OFFICE OR AGENT TO RELEASE INFO RELATING TO THE INDIANAPOLIS UNDERCOVER OPERATIONS. IT IS FELT THAT THIS OPERATION SHOULD BE APPROPRIATELY CONCEALED AS IT HAS CONTINUING VALUE ...

There were continual case reviews and inter-divisional conferences over the progress of Operation Fountain Pen, and a major review exactly one month after the above memo was sent; again on that date, the director of the FBI approved the recommendation of his task-force leaders to maintain the absolute confidentiality of the enquiry.

The FBI, it was well known, leaked like a sieve. It was believed that leaders of organised crime could get to know the contents of any FBI report within twenty-four hours of it being filed within the system, if not sooner. The instruction continued to affect the secondary matters, like the Presley case, because two of the principals in Operation Fountain Pen were also at the top of the list of those to be charged with defrauding Presley.

The date of this last memo was almost a year after Frederick Pro turned up in Memphis with his money-making scheme for Elvis. Yet the wraps were still being kept on the case and no arrests were in sight. The saga of Elvis's plane, a tiny part of the whole mess, trundled on.

Elvis and his father had no way of knowing that their plane had flown into a hornet's nest from which, at the end of the day, there would be no escape.

10

An Image to Preserve

'I would not have put it down entirely to the drugs. They obviously led to the personality changes, but there also were things about the man. We talked about the male menopause when a man reaches forty. And for Elvis, who was a superstar, the fact that his hair was going grey and he was putting on weight, it was troubling him. The image was everything to a man like Elvis. He really had no peers. No one in showbusiness had done what he had done. The King of rock 'n' roll was going grey, getting a little heavy, a few bags under his eyes. His ego was very big, as with most entertainers. Then, he began going with a very young girl, Ginger Alden. There seemed to be a strain in keeping up that relationship, which is natural with an older man and a young girl . . .'
Judge Sam Thompson, former Elvis bodyguard, 1980

The King of rock 'n' roll, who had proved such an easy target for the exploiters and the con artists, the parasites and the limpets, crashed on with his chemically controlled daily routine, largely unaware of the threat to his world and, indeed, to his life. The personalities around him each had a part to play in the drama that would beset him as the weeks passed, and before proceeding with the examination of the Presley files relating specifically to this period, it is as well to remind ourselves of those within the inner circle during these last crucial months.

As we have seen, the key departures of 1976 had been Linda Thompson, his lover and carer for the past four or more years, and the three bodyguards Red and Sonny West, and Dave Hebler, who were now engaged in writing a book on their life with Elvis, ghosted by Steve Dunleavy, one of the sharpest exponents of tabloid journalism from the Rupert Murdoch stable. The book, a mass–market paperback entitled *Elvis: What Happened?* promised sensational disclosures, the first exposé of Presley's eccentric lifestyle, his drugs, his women and his passion for guns. They were stories which were to be repeated and drawn upon so often over the years.

The book was scheduled for publication in the summer of 1977 and leaks about the contents were coming in from Elvis's contacts. He worried that it would totally demolish him and his career. When news of it first reached him, he was on tour in Mobile, Alabama. He had obtained through a contact a copy of the book outline. He cried, 'Those bastards. Those fucking bastards. They're going to finish me.' Tom Parker was also angry and was reported to be on the verge of extricating himself from the Presley connection and salvaging what he could by selling Elvis's management contract to the highest bidder, a fact which he later denied.

The remaining entourage was headed, still, by Vernon Presley, who was growing weaker. Sandy Miller, who moved in after Dee Stanley Presley's departure, was a professional nurse and was seldom from Vernon's side. Sandy was a warm and well-liked addition to the household. Vernon's heart condition was such that sometimes he could barely walk fifty paces without assistance and the stairs of Graceland represented a task akin to the north face of the Eiger. In spite of his medical state, he still ran the Presley household, signed the cheques and managed the finances.

Sam Thompson's arrival strengthened a workforce flagging with low morale. His recollections are particularly relevant to the story of Elvis's final days. Sam, who today sits as a judge in Memphis, is one of the most reliable of all the witnesses to the last days of Elvis. He was Linda's brother and a deputy with the Shelby county sheriff's department. He was offered a job as a security guard and was alongside Elvis as he entered the last year of his life. He was also among the last to see him alive.

What he found in those last twelve months was a man surrounded by a mass of problems, unable to turn back the tide of pressure coming at him from all sides, and not least from within himself. Thompson, who returned to his law studies after Elvis died, and obtained another major on his degree in police administration and criminal justice, gave a dispassionate account of those last months.

He was approached by Elvis several times after Red and Sonny West had been fired. Finally, he accepted a job at 350 dollars a week, working with Elvis's chief of security, Dick Grob, a former police sergeant in Palm Springs, and Al Strada, once a security officer in Los Angeles. Another of Elvis's old friends, John O'Grady, the Los Angeles drugs cop, was a part-time adviser and aide, and his presence added the final touch of irony to the Presley situation – for at that time, when his consumption of drugs was reaching its peak, he was surrounded almost entirely by former policemen. None was able to stop him.

Thompson did not come to the job unaware of the problems involved in looking after Elvis. Linda had warned him of the star's erratic behaviour, his need for a daily delivery of pills and injections, and the night-is-day syndrome that was Elvis's life. In the months to come, he operated as a duty officer at Graceland, guarded Elvis on any of his excursions or jaunts to Las Vegas or Los Angeles, and went on fourteen tours which involved visiting 130 cities in less than a year. That statistic alone demonstrated the clamour for work and money that Parker had assigned to his King. It was, by any standards, an immense workload, representing considerable pressure on Elvis and those around him.

In accordance with the tradition set by the previous minders, all of Elvis's bodyguards carried guns under their shoulders. He still feared the possibility of assassination and that fear was only heightened now by his involuntary involvement in the FBI investigation, about which none of the entourage had the faintest notion. All they knew was that there had been some fraud attempt concerning the plane; all other details were withheld on the instruction of the FBI.

Sam said he understood there was turmoil in the Presley organisation when he joined in June 1976. In addition to the salary, they were paid their living expenses on tour, and in Las Vegas they received a set twenty dollars a day. Anything over that would be paid by cheque at the end of the season.

'The reason for this,' said Sam, 'was that some members of the entourage had in the past gambled heavily in the casinos and lost it, and they would go to Elvis and tell them, and he'd pay off the debts by cheque. Vernon apparently told Joe to make sure this was stopped, because it was costing too much. When I got there, if anyone gambled and lost it, it was their responsibility.'

Sam Thompson listed the remaining entourage that existed when he joined. There was Joe Esposito, head of the command structure and through whom all contact was made with either Elvis or Vernon. Then, there was Lamar Fike, who had been around since the beginning and was listed on the staff sheet as a travelling companion. There was Larry Geller, Elvis's hairdresser, who occasionally came on the tours as a 'kind of a confidante'. There was also Billy Smith, Elvis's first cousin, who was also off to one side in this structure. He was a very staunch friend; if there was a best friend, it was Billy. Another important part of the entourage was Charlie Hodge, who was at Elvis's side on stage. He used to hand Elvis the scarves or a glass of water while performing. Then there were the three security men, Thompson, plus Dick Grob and Al Strada. The two Stanley brothers, Ricky and David, were the duty aides who looked after Elvis on a rota, along with Dean Nichopoulos, the doctor's son, and Billy Smith, who was at Elvis's side wherever they went. In addition, there was a reserve hairdresser and other occasional employees who were counted among the personal entourage.

On tour, they all travelled with Elvis in the big aircraft, the *Lisa Marie*, which had two pilots, a third officer, a flight assistant and a stewardess. They were on standby all the time; they were the only ones who ever flew that aircraft.

There was the Lockheed Jetstar which Elvis was now saddled with, along with a million-dollar mortgage, and so it was pressed back into service, being used by all and sundry. Milo High always flew that one and Colonel Parker used it for going on ahead of the main tour group. The Jetstar was also being used as a 'hopping plane', said Thompson. When they were in Florida, his grandmother died while they were on tour and Elvis sent the Jetstar to pick up Sam and his sister for the funeral. Another time, he had had a fight with Ginger Alden, his new girlfriend, and she didn't come on the tour. They reconciled on the telephone and he sent the Jetstar to pick her up. There was another aircraft, a BAC 111, which was used for the musicians. It could seat about sixty people, and carried all the band instruments and sound systems.

Thompson picks up the story in his taped testimony:

I was thinking of leaving Elvis's employ before he died. I had always been in some phase of law enforcement. Even when I went to him I didn't see it as a career move, and we were travelling at least two weeks a month. You travelled without your spouse and I had two children, so it was difficult at home. Another area of concern was his strong medication. His personality was changing and my sister was no longer involved, which was my initial reason for joining, to look after her as well. In the latter part, it was a real concern that Elvis was addicted to drugs. When I first went to work for him, it seemed to me – and perhaps I had stars in my eyes – that all the shows were good and he always looked well. But the closer I got to the man, the more time I spent with him, I began to realise that some shows were a lot better than others and some were terrible.

I saw how much weight he was putting on, and at different times his personality, his mood, would be altered drastically in a matter of hours. He would be extremely excitable, hopped-up and erratic, and a few hours later he would be completely lethargic and almost unable to budge out of the chair or out of bed.

Thompson, having been involved in law enforcement, felt that it was a most unstable situation. After he had been in it for a while and saw what was going on, he did make enquiries, especially of Dick Grob, the head of security, who had been there seven or eight years. He was concerned that Elvis should have a personal physician with him. It was quite obvious from Elvis's demeanour that he was under the influence of something for a lot of the time. Thompson and Grob even began to make contingency plans to deal with any situation that might occur.

'We also felt that Elvis was highly irrational,' said Thompson:

He always carried weapons on him. I'm not going to go as far as to say we were in fear of our lives, but we did feel that some due caution was needed. We also needed to look at the possibility of collapse. When Elvis went on stage for a couple of hours it would be physically shattering. You do that night after night, there has got to be an effect on the man. All of that contributed to the fact that his personality was so changeable.

It came as a shock. When I went to work for him, no one said he was a drug addict. The very term conjures up all kinds of thoughts of lying in the gutters, buying nickel bags and fixes, and living day to day. We knew drug addicts live in all sections of society, but we just knew that Elvis consumed certain amounts of drugs, and I was given to understand that they were prodigious amounts. He had various health problems. I was never told he was a junkie, and that you had to watch him. I was told that he was on maintenance medication which would change his personality.

He imposed his total will on members of the group and if anyone said to Elvis, 'You don't need that', he would become pretty irrational. He was always the master at turning the tables and making out that you did not care anything about him, and tried to explain that he had these medical problems that he knew he had but you didn't.

Thompson described the absolute irony of the situation of working for a man whose use of chemicals was nothing short of scandalous, but who at the same time was adamant that no member of the entourage should cause him any embarrassment. Never should anyone attract harmful publicity and, more definitely, become involved in the use of street drugs of any kind.

They were all schooled to the thought of never embarrassing Elvis, never embarrassing the group. They were told to deny any use of drugs if approached by the media. Elvis always carried the Drug Enforcement Administration (DEA) badge and he was totally against street drugs. The entourage was always aware that he needed to be shielded from any bad publicity. They were certain that if there was any publicity it was most likely to come from Elvis collapsing from an overdose somewhere public. Grob and the security team devised a plan that if anything went wrong, Elvis would be brought back to Memphis, if it was at all possible. If something happened in-flight, they were to have the flight turned back to Memphis. At all times, they were to ensure that anything that went wrong did not reflect upon him as a star.

They worked out contingency plans for other possibilities, to guard against anyone taking a shot at him while he was on stage, or to ensure Lisa Marie was never in a position where she might be kidnapped. All of those eventualities were ever-present in their minds, said Thompson.

Meanwhile, there was an understanding within the group that if anyone required any medical treatment, they could go to Dr Nichopoulos for pills or treatment. Charlie Hodge, who 'drank a great deal', had a lot of trouble sleeping, and he used to get Placidyls from Nichopoulos. They were available to anyone who asked. Charlie was not dependent on drugs, more likely alcohol, said

Thompson. He was always the personality of the group, the centre of attention, telling jokes. Sam went on:

The Stanley brothers had a propensity for drugs and it is pretty evident that their taking of the drugs was so well known that Nick wouldn't let them have them. There was talk of Nick keeping his bag locked up for fear of them getting into it. By and large, no one administered drugs to Elvis except Nick or his nurse, Tish Henley, who lived at Graceland. They could not be on duty twenty-four hours a day, so Dr Nick left packages of drugs, which his personal aides would give to Elvis at appointed times. The Stanley brothers, the youngest members of the entourage, seemed to me to demonstrate less than good judgement as to what they did and how they behaved on tour. We were aware that they smoked marijuana in their rooms, and that they would take pills. I had seen them spaced out. Elvis would get upset about it, and talk to Dick Grob. He worried that these things would come to light, that people in the Elvis group were taking drugs.

It was important to Elvis not to have that kind of reputation. So from time to time we would stage little fake raids on the boys and advise them the police were on their way up with a search warrant. It would scare them to death and they would end up throwing all this stuff down the toilet. We used that as a leverage, they both knew we were ex-cops. TCB – Taking Care of Business – meant not just taking care of Elvis, it meant taking care of any extraneous situations which would bring embarrassment to him. Joe Esposito would complain a lot that the Stanley brothers were a nuisance, that they would get into Dr Nick's bag, and get medication which was meant for Elvis.

Colonel Parker did not get involved in these domestic things, not at all. He was well known in Vegas, he gambled a lot. I understood he had a fifty- or sixty-thousand-dollar marker; in other words, he would owe that to the casino all the time. He had a suite of rooms at the Hilton in Vegas and we certainly stayed in the Hilton chain wherever we could.

Thompson said that in early 1977, he heard a rumour that Elvis's contract was going to be sold, that the colonel was getting tired of him and all the problems. The colonel would always ask him about Elvis. It was never so much about how he was feeling – he wanted to know how his show was going. Was he able to complete it? Sam Thompson added:

Colonel Parker seemed to have a particular animosity for Dr Nick, and for any other doctor, for that matter. Sam noticed that he was very vocal in cursing the medics who treated Elvis. The colonel told me he felt that some of these people were responsible for getting Elvis in the position he was in with his medicines. He was concerned about Elvis and his consumption of drugs, but I felt he was more financially motivated, like that was his meal ticket. The colonel did say to me that Elvis was a lot of trouble, and said that he was more trouble than he was worth. Then, later, when I asked him if he was still considering selling Elvis, he would deny everything, and say he'd never sell.

★   ★   ★   ★   ★

Two other members of the group who were important to the final act of the Elvis drama were the Stanley brothers, Ricky and David, who stayed on after their mother and Vernon Presley split up. The third Stanley brother, Billy, had already left and continued to hold his stepbrother in contempt, after his marriage broke up when he discovered Elvis had seduced his wife.

In many ways, Elvis's treatment of the brothers was alarming. Instead of guarding them against the life he knew was ruinous, and was the cause of so much anguish within his own sphere, he brought them into it. They, it must be said, were willing and eager participants, who were also pushed along by their mother, Dee, with the intention of establishing them as closely to Elvis as anyone could be. Ricky, the second eldest, joined the entourage first, at the age of sixteen, and had become the messenger and courier. He often made the connections and the pick-ups for Elvis's drug supplies, and, by 1976, had long been entwined in the drugs himself, as was his brother David.

Both were eventually taking a scaled-down version of their stepbrother's chemical intake while on tour, to which they added their own hits of marijuana and other more fashionable drugs. Elvis introduced them both to uppers and downers when they were still in their teens. They were often required to inject him before he went on stage. When they were on duty, they had to deliver the allotted packages of medication, prescribed by Dr Nick, to get him off to sleep.

Rick's own adventures with a bad drugs crowd led him to a close call with an overdose, and later to being arrested for forging a prescription and attempting to get it filled at the Memphis Baptist Hospital pharmacy. Elvis received a call one night to say that Ricky had been arrested. He went down to Memphis city jail, where he was as well known as any cop, showed his own DEA badge, and managed to get Ricky released into his custody. The boy eventually admitted a lesser charge of malicious mischief and accepted a fifty-dollar fine with some alacrity.

His brother David, also a self-confessed user of various chemical substances and hash, had assumed the 'heavy' role – the close protector and constant shadow of his stepbrother whenever they moved out of Graceland, be it for pleasure trips or working tours.

Also in the entourage was Billy Smith, Elvis's cousin and long-time aide, and another of the surviving old stagers, Charlie Hodge. Now, past forty, he chain-smoked, drank heavily, and had jangling nerves. He lived in a converted building behind the mansion, which had for years been known as 'Charlie's Room'. An Elvis man, through and through, he also kept Colonel Parker well informed of events. All of this team reported to Joe Esposito, who remained the road manager and minder-in-chief.

There were other ancillary staff – the cooks, the maids, and the house cleaners – who came under the charge of Elvis's housekeeper, his Aunt Delta Mae, a big, bold southern woman who was a permanent resident in Graceland. Other remaining relatives occupied a string of mobile homes up on an incline at the back of the house.

Elvis's Uncle Vester, Vernon's brother, ran the gatehouse staff, where enough men were employed to keep a twenty-four-hour vigil on the music gates entrance, where fans gathered daily. Also living on the estate, in one of the mobile homes, was Graceland's resident nurse, Tish Henley, who was employed by Dr Nick, but had lived at Graceland with her husband Tommy, a local deputy sheriff, since 1975, to handle the local medication requirements of this motley group of residents. Not least among her duties was to ensure that Elvis's supply of medication, his sleeping pills, his amphetamines and his syringes were readily available, as prescribed by her boss, and handed out from a doctor's black bag, which she kept locked away in the mobile home.

Into this curious mix of personalities came Ginger Alden, who would have the distinction of being the last girlfriend, the one in bed with Elvis on 16 August 1977. They had met in the autumn of 1976, when she was barely out of her teens. She was stunningly attractive, a natural beauty, slender and lithe. Elvis was exactly twice her age, paunchy and heavy, in spite of recent attempts to shed weight for his next tour. She was brought to Graceland to meet Elvis by George Klein in November 1976. She was in total awe of him and half-expected his arrival to receive them to be heralded by the sound of golden trumpets. When he spoke to her, she replied in a shy whisper, and was so overcome that she could never remember what he first said to her.

Ginger and her two sisters had been seen at the mansion, by the gates, many times. Since they were children, their mother, an ardent Elvis fan and front-gate groupie, used to bring them in the hope of catching sight of Memphis's most famous resident. Ginger was approaching her fifth birthday when her mother took the girls to the fairground one night when Elvis had taken over the whole park for his friends after hours. It was almost fifteen years since Elvis patted that small child on the head as she was going aboard the roller coaster, and there she was with her sisters, finally entering Graceland. There was a small bet among the entourage that he would choose Ginger's sister Terry, who had just been elected Miss Tennessee. But Elvis, moved as usual by his penchant for naïvety and innocence in a woman, selected Ginger to succeed Linda Thompson as mistress of his house.

The pattern was much as before, in Elvis's serious courtships. He took her for a ride in his sportscar, the Stutz-Blackhawk, and drove around Memphis. He played the part of the perfect gentleman, using chaperones the first time he took her aboard one of the jetliners for a trip to Las Vegas. There they checked into the Hilton at dawn and suddenly Ginger found herself alone with Elvis, in the great star's room, wondering whether she would be expected to go to bed with him.

She was.

She clambered between the sheets before him, and nervously waited as he joined her. He clasped her hand . . . and promptly fell sound asleep, having taken his downers to knock him out for most of that day. When he awoke, they got up, dressed and showered, and went back to the airport and returned to Memphis, Elvis having done nothing more than sleep. She had not seen the inside of a Las Vegas casino, or a restaurant, or anything.

The whole adventure had been a bizarre and costly trip which amounted to nothing but travelling there and travelling back, with no activity in between. Ginger was still in awe, and when they returned to Graceland, and moved finally to the inner sanctum which was his bedroom, she marvelled at the decor; the walls padded with buttoned-back artificial suede, the floor covered in a deep carpet, the drapes to two huge windows overlooking the lawns were colour-matched. The windows themselves were blacked out so that no light shone through. Like Las Vegas, Elvis's bedroom was a time-free zone, unaffected by the hours of daylight, or the climate, since he always had the air-conditioning turned up high.

The central feature was the enormous bed, double king-sized, measuring nine by ten feet, with black and gold trimmings and, at its head, on either side, were balancing portraits of his mother and Jesus Christ. There was also a curious aroma, a smell that Ginger would have noticed, which was a mix of perfumed spray overlaying a fustiness which she could not identify – though soon would liken to that which pervades the bedroom of an ageing relative.

Within nine weeks of that first encounter with Ginger, Elvis proposed to her, on 26 January 1977, in his bathroom of all places, going down on bended knee and slipping a 70,000-dollar, eleven-and-a-half-carat diamond on to her engagement finger. The location of this ceremony was perhaps not unusual. The bathroom was very personal to Elvis. This was the room into which no one could enter without his permission. It was in similar proportions to the huge bedroom. The toilet was padded and comfortable. There were armchairs spread around the room because he liked to congregate in there and hold conferences with his closest companions. A circular shower cubicle dominated. It was about eight feet in diameter and contained a black vinyl chair, which appeared to serve the purpose of providing a comfortable position from which to take a shower while still drowsy.

Elvis, as always, inundated his new possession with gifts and promises. He presented her with the customary car, a Cadillac Seville, and according to her mother, promised to pay off the mortgage on the family home in Memphis. To Ginger Alden, it was an awesome, crazy world into which she had been initiated, about to participate in the final months of the Elvis drama, the last act of which would be played out in that very bathroom where he proposed.

But was Ginger Alden really the girl of his dreams? There were rumours among the entourage that he was about to ditch her when he died. Billy Smith said that Elvis was becoming increasingly disenchanted with Ginger, and she with him. For most of the time they were together, he was heavy and sleepy. Sam Thompson said they rowed often because Ginger did not like going on the tours, and Elvis always needed the companionship. They usually made up, but it was certainly not the love match it was made out to be in the wake of Elvis's death. This was already apparent in April 1977, when he was at the point of replacing Miss Alden with another.

One evening that April, when Elvis was just back from a tour, he telephoned his friendly arranger of female companionship, George Klein, who, sure enough, delivered once again. There was talk of this switch of affections after Elvis's death, but none of the media was able to track down the mystery girl. Larry Hutchinson, the district attorney's investigator, did find her and now we are able to glean a first-hand account from her full tape-recorded testimony, never previously published. Her name was Alicia Kirwin, and she was a twenty-year-old teller at the United Bank of America, in Memphis:

I had lived there all my life. I went to the Central High School and graduated in 1974. I had known George Klein since I was about eighteen. In April he just called me up out of the blue and asked me if I would like to meet Elvis Presley. It was a spur-of-the-moment call. I was shocked. He said Elvis and his girlfriend, Ginger Alden, had had a fight and Elvis was upset. He said he just wanted me to go up there and talk to him. I agreed and I went up to Graceland in my car around ten p.m., and I met Jo Smith, Billy's wife. She was a real good friend of mine. I met Elvis's daughter, Lisa Marie, and we talked for a while. Then, Jo took me up to the sitting room, which was full of people. They were talking about the forthcoming tour. Elvis was in the centre. Later on, he and I talked. I had never met him before. We just talked about things, what I did for a living and so on. It was all very relaxed and comfortable. It wasn't strained. He seemed to be in very

159

good spirits. His physical appearance surprised me. He was very heavy. His voice was slow, but not slurred. The room was crowded. The phones were ringing a lot. There were papers everywhere; it was hectic. We talked about Ginger in between times, after I'd been there a while when I was more relaxed.

Elvis told Alicia that he and Ginger had had an argument and he didn't think he was going to see her any more. He said he thought she was after his money. Alicia left after about two hours; nothing had happened except conversation. As she was leaving, Elvis asked for her telephone number and, two days later, she got home from work to discover that he had called and left a number to ring back. She telephoned, and it was Elvis. He wanted her to go over to Graceland. Alicia wasn't sure about whether or not she should go, and pondered for a long time; in the end, she decided she would. She recalled:

Several hours later, I went over to the mansion. I was late so I was shown into the kitchen, and he kept me waiting for about an hour before I was shown upstairs. In the meantime I was talking to the maids. Upstairs, I was taken into his daughter's room, where Elvis was sitting. Lisa Marie had left to return to her mother's that day and he was despondent. He just sat there, drinking iced water. He introduced me to Tish Henley, who I learned later was his nurse. He had just given her a bracelet and she showed it to me. It was obviously very expensive. She stayed the whole time I was in the bedroom. David Stanley also came in, and then one of Ginger's sisters came in. She was obnoxious. She wanted to know what I was doing there, very inquisitive. I talked with Elvis for about an hour and we went for a stroll around the grounds for about an hour and he showed me some of his cars. He was calm and natural, no different than the time I met him before, and I left around eleven-thirty p.m. I think they were all planning to go out to the cinema after midnight.

The next day, Alicia received another telephone call from Elvis, asking her if she would go to the mansion. She told him that she already had a date, so he slammed the telephone down. Seconds later, he called back, and said, 'What about tomorrow?' She agreed and then he asked her if she could get a few days off work. He said he wanted to take her to Las Vegas in his plane. She had never been to Vegas. First getting permission for the time off work, she called him back and agreed to go. They fixed a date for the following Wednesday. Alicia continued:

I drove over to Graceland on the day of the trip. We took off for the airport with Jo and Billy Smith, Charlie Hodge and Dick Grob at about eleven p.m., and flew out on one of the smaller planes. We didn't take any luggage, except that one of them carried Elvis's little leather bag. I fell asleep on the plane and I didn't wake up until we were there. We had a car to the Hilton Hotel and that night I stayed with Elvis for the first time. There were a few bottles of pills beside his bed. I assumed they were sleeping pills. He told me they were mostly muscle-relaxing pills, Valium and stuff. He told me if I couldn't sleep, he could solve it. It was the middle of the night by then and I just fell straight to sleep. I wasn't used to those kind of hours. Elvis woke me for breakfast.

Elvis telephoned his Las Vegas doctor, Dr Ghanem. He said why didn't he come over, because he had someone he wanted him to meet. I went shopping with Billy and Jo Smith, and I met the doctor later on. David Stanley and his wife came in during the day; they flew in on Elvis's big plane. I saw Dr Ghanem several times during the three days we were there. Elvis complained of having pulled a muscle in his leg, so the doctor gave him some pills and prescribed some additional medication, and Billy Smith went out to the store to fill the prescription. He did not prescribe very many, and Elvis was a bit upset.

Otherwise, he was in good spirits all the time, except he got a bit angry when someone in the group teased him. He never went out of the room the whole time we were there, just watched television and smoked cigars. We talked quite a bit. But I noticed everybody just bowed to his wishes; they laughed when he laughed and got him everything he needed, even if it was just a glass of water. Then he announced we were leaving, and we took off for Palm Springs, where we stayed until Sunday. It was much the same procedure. He stayed in the house and he had one visitor, the dentist, Max Shapiro, I think. That was after Elvis got very upset. He had called his father, who was angry because we weren't supposed to be there. He hadn't told his father or Tom Parker we were going to Las Vegas. He said we were going to Nashville. Vernon was real mad. We stayed until Sunday and went back to Memphis.

Alicia next heard from Elvis a couple of weeks later. He was on tour and called her several times. In June, she decided to telephone Billy Smith and tell him she did not want to see Elvis again. 'It was just too much,' Alicia said. 'I couldn't handle it, because he was Elvis Presley. I had never been used to this kind of thing, staying up all hours of the night and all.'

That night, Elvis telephoned and pleaded with Alicia to go to Graceland and talk. He said he was very depressed, and said he wished he could go out on a Saturday night like other people. Alicia drove over, and they just talked and talked until about three in the morning, when she left to go home. He asked her to stay the night, but she refused. He had taken some of his pills and seemed ready to sleep. He said he just wanted to make sure there was someone close by. Alicia next heard from him a few weeks later. He had just returned from filming a CBS television special which had not gone at all well:

He called me in the middle of the night, it must have been about three a.m. He was terribly depressed about the show and asked me to go up to Graceland. I said I had to go to work the next morning, but he persisted, and said come anyway. He was going to send someone over for me, Dr Nick's son, Dean, who was working for him. But I said, No, I'd drive over and bring some things and go straight to work from there. He just looked so sad. I stayed with him for a few hours, and then he fell asleep. He had taken some medication, sleeping pills, though I hadn't seen him take a lot. I felt like he took the pills when he shouldn't, but I wouldn't have said he was addicted. I left for work around eight a.m., and that was the last time I saw him. My overriding impression of him was that he was so very, very sad ...

Alicia's story is also a sad one. Having been shown the bright lights of Las Vegas by Elvis, she threw up her comfortable and respectable job as a bank teller in her home town of Memphis, and headed back to Las Vegas where she trained as a croupier. She too suffered an untimely end. She died from an overdose a few years later.

11

Death by Coincidence

'*August 8, 1977. Subject: Presley, Elvis A. (Victim): Bureau case, entitled Operation Fountain Pen, involving travel with suspects by undercover special agents, has generated a great volume of information concerning a group dealing in fraudulent securities drawn on offshore banks. While the covert operation is still intact, coverage of leads should continue to protect the Indianapolis operation. Successful prosecution is heavily dependent upon a co-ordinated effort in the bureau and the various strike forces involved . . .*'

Memo from FBI directorate to all field offices in
Operation Fountain Pen

The FBI investigation into the men who had defrauded Elvis to the tune of a million dollars rumbled on at a controlled pace. The pages and pages of FBI reports relating specifically to the enquiry display an apprehension, on the part of the investigators, about upturning too many stones, for fear of damaging progress on their main enquiry – Operation Fountain Pen. Agents were warned against action which would ultimately reveal the presence of the two undercover special agents from the Indianapolis Division, who were supplying the FBI strike forces with a voluminous amount of information from their position with one of the main suspects in the securities fraud.

The files documenting the investigation during the early months of 1977 contained numerous references and instructions which insisted, 'This individual is not to be interviewed at this time.'

By the end of May, all of those involved in the Presley Jetstar case were known and their whereabouts logged and monitored. But still no arrests were made, and on the instructions of the FBI directorate, none was to be arrested for the time being. They were not to be interviewed, or even approached. Only the most discreet observation and surveillance was permitted.

Furthermore, no one in the Presley entourage was aware of these developments. Only Vernon and Elvis themselves knew that two of the recent hirelings among the roadies were undercover FBI men travelling with the tour for Elvis's additional protection. They also kept a watch at Graceland, though Vernon himself had said internal assistance was not necessary since the house and the grounds were covered by the Presleys' own security men.

The protection squads laid on in abundance for any of Elvis's public appearances were much in evidence at his last concert at Rapid City, South Dakota, on 21 June 1977.

Lines of uniformed and armed guards awaited his arrival and covered his every move, as if they were attending the incumbent president of the United States. It was all the more fever pitched because Colonel Parker had negotiated a lucrative television deal, allowing CBS to film moments of the tour for a princely 750,000 dollars. Albert Goldman poured scorn on Parker for allowing it to happen. In his biography of Elvis, he claimed that when the producers of the show, Garry Smith and Dwight Hemion, got a glimpse of Presley they were appalled at the sight of him, weighing in at around 250 pounds. 'Elvis looked grotesque,' Goldman wrote. 'His voice was shot. His speech was slurred. His memory was so bad that he had trouble recalling the words of songs he had been singing for twenty years ... the only consistent feature of his performance was the droopy-eyed smile which plainly said, "I'm stoned."'

The roadshow completed its tour and broke up until the next concert, scheduled for 17 August. Elvis and the entourage went back to Memphis. He was in a dark mood, vowing once again to go on a fasting diet to shed some weight. 'I didn't look good,' he kept saying to Rick Stanley. The reality was different. He became even more reclusive than before, seldom venturing out of the house and spending most days in bed. The impending publication of the book by his three former guards merely added to his discomfort. He raged about it. David Stanley said that he once woke in the middle of the night to find Elvis – high on liquid cocaine from cotton-wool balls stuffed in his nose – in his bedroom, looking like a guerrilla soldier. He was carrying a Thompson sub-machine gun and had two Colt .45s sticking in his belt. They were going huntin', he said, for the sonsovbitches who had done this to him. He was going to kill them. David Stanley related that he had humoured him for a time, but eventually persuaded Elvis that for the sake of Lisa Marie, it would be better not to go down in history as a killer.

Ginger Alden was concerned by these violent mood changes. He wanted to know her every move, often prohibited her from going out of the house, and once, when she defied him, he came out of his bedroom brandishing a Colt .45. When she refused to come back, he fired a warning shot over her head as she walked down the stairs.

In part, he was concerned about the imminent appearance in the bookstalls and supermarkets of the paperback by the West cousins and Dave Hebler. Those around him could feel the tension reaching explosion point.

No one knew, either, that in the background was another explanation for his edginess, and the true reason why he had taken to his rooms and was refusing to come out. The FBI's investigation into the plane fraud and the securities scam was reaching a climax, certainly as far his own involvement was concerned. Investigators had been in touch with Vernon, and had made fresh contact with Elvis's lawyer, D. Beecher Smith. All evidence had been collated against the suspects in the Presley case and on 26 July 1977, a complete review of the case was filed by the Memphis division of the FBI to the Department of Justice headquarters in Washington.

Numerous pages of documents relating to both the JetStar enquiry and Operation Fountain Pen around the latter part of July have been retained in the Department of Justice as classified material, and in 1992 were still unavailable under the Freedom of Information Act. However, among the available pages released to me is a document under the reference ME S-16997, relating to an enquiry the FBI made with respect to developments on the Elvis plane case. It stated:

On August 1, Assistant US Attorney Glen Garland Reid, Jr, Memphis, Tennessee was contacted relative to prosecutive action in connection with this case. He advised he is prepared to present these facts to a Federal Grand Jury convening in Memphis on or about August 15, 1977.

Copies of this note were wired to the directorate of the FBI, and to the fraud section, criminal division, US Department of Justice and the heads of the FBI strike forces and field offices throughout the United States. Later documents stated that the FBI anticipated arrests of identified suspects at addresses in Miami, Boston, New York and Indianapolis. Sealed indictments would be presented to the grand jury, thus ensuring continued secrecy concerning the case.

On 8 August 1977, a further substantial review of the proceedings was filed by Memphis office, with copies to all other interested FBI divisions; fourteen specific offices of the FBI were named to receive the review. It was a long and detailed summary of the case involving those who would be charged on seventeen counts relating to the fraud of Elvis Presley, to be presented before the grand jury. Among those to be charged were Philip Karl Kitzer, Frederick Pro, and Laurence Wolfson, the man whose records carried a prefix of 'LCN Associate', denoting his connections with La Cosa Nostra (the Mafia).

There then followed a review of the case relating to those suspects who they planned to arrest in connection with Elvis's plane, and after outlining the manner in which Frederick Pro and his associates had gained possession of the Jetstar, went on to reveal for the first time conversations recorded by the Indianapolis undercover agents in a New York hotel earlier that year. The agents had travelled with Philip Kitzer from Miami to New York.

Kitzer, it will be recalled, was at that time the key figure in the investigations of fraudulent securities. When they checked into the Mayflower Hotel, New York, Kitzer telephoned Frederick Pro, who by then had returned to the city. Another man at the meeting whose name has been deleted from FBI documents, since he was not connected with criminal charges, was, according to Kitzer, a 'good man to know if ever they had any trouble with "the outfit". He can arrange a sit-down conference in New York and iron out any problems.'

Pro subsequently arrived and, according to the undercover men's notes, began to boast how he had 'conned Elvis Presley out his JetStar'. He went into a detailed explanation of how he had done it, and then the discussion switched to the operation of dealing in securities, for which he acted as a broker – dealing with 150 telephone enquiries every day.

The FBI documents indicate that the FBI was moving into a state of readiness for the arrest after the presentation of the sealed indictments to the grand jury hearing in Memphis 'on or about 15 August'; it was therefore likely that Elvis and Vernon Presley, who had both made statements to FBI agents, would be required to give testimony at the eventual trial.

A memo putting all agents involved in the case on arrest alert was sent to all relevant FBI divisions. It read:

Re: Memphis Report . . . Captioned Frederick Pro, et al; the bureau has designated case entitled 'Philip Karl Kitzer, Jr, Indianapolis' as a bureau special . . . concerning group of international brokers dealing in fraudulent securities . . . bureau has advised all leads set out in this matter to be covered immediately . . .

The bureau was preparing for the arrest of seven men. Agents in five cities were readying themselves to apprehend their suspects. All were known and located. The date stamp recorded at the bottom of the wire was 16 August 1977. But, suddenly, it was all put on hold. Events at Graceland had overtaken the FBI plans. At the very point that the FBI's top-secret investigation, which had been in progress for many months, was about to take a dramatic turn, a paramedical crew at the Memphis fire department received the call, soon after two o'clock that afternoon, which sent them racing to 3764 Elvis Presley Boulevard. There they attempted to revive the lifeless body of a man lying in the bathroom, who they then sped at eighty miles an hour to the Baptist Memorial Hospital and admitted under the name of Mr John Doe. Later that afternoon, another coded telex had been flashed to the FBI directorate in Washington, and to the heads of all strike forces, revealing that Elvis Presley was dead.

The circumstances which had warranted the attention of so many agents of the FBI for so long – in which volumes of paperwork a couple of yards high had been accumulated – could at least be regarded as being of sufficient significance on that day to be taken into account in the subsequent enquiry into the events surrounding the death of Elvis Presley. But it was not. The death of Elvis was to be classed, officially, at least, as being devoid of any suspicious circumstances.

Before proceeding with the chronological order of events, let us turn back the clock a few hours and re-examine the known facts leading up to the point at which the paramedics were called to Graceland.

*   *   *   *   *

The last recorded twenty-four hours were no different to any other day, except that it was supposed to be Elvis's last day at home before he was due to begin a twelve-day tour of mostly one-night stands, which were scheduled to begin in Portland, Maine, and carry on to a string of dates through the south and eastern states. He was to end up back in Memphis for two shows at the end of the month.

Elvis had been agitated in the past few days, and those in the entourage put it down to the prospect of another tour which, though only twelve days in duration, was so packed with appearances that it allowed him virtually no time for anything other than work and sleep. Sleep was what he had spend most of his time doing in recent days, in spite of the fact that Lisa Marie was staying for one of her summer visits. He was due in Portland on the morning of 17 August for a concert that evening, and another the following day.

Billy Smith was with Elvis for most of the final hours. He recalled that his cousin rose at around four p.m. on the afternoon of the fifteenth, for the start of a fairly typical day. Outside, it was hot and humid; a thunderstorm threatened. Elvis telephoned downstairs to announce that he had surfaced, as he always did. Thick black coffee was to be delivered immediately, and he did not want 'breakfast', normally a large portion of bacon and eggs, because he was still dieting. His voice was thick and groggy, but there was nothing unusual in that; it always was when he finally awakened from the deep, artificially induced sleep.

Billy said that everything was as normal as it ever was, except that Elvis and Ginger were in the midst of yet another running row, which had continued that night when she had refused to go on tour with him. She had, like Priscilla and Linda Thompson before her, grown to hate the tours and she had no intention of joining him. When Ginger wasn't around, Elvis was complaining to Billy Smith about her, and he said, as he had on a number of occasions, that he wasn't sure if he would ever marry her.

It took a couple of hours to arrive at the point where he had shaken off the effects of the sleeping narcotics, which he had counter-acted with his usual late-afternoon dose of uppers, small golden heart-shaped tablets of dexedrine, which he consumed in daunting quantities. He spent some time in the bathroom attending to his daily ablutions and eventually came downstairs in the early evening in as near a normal state as he ever reached during any twenty-

Priscilla and Lisa Marie, a glamorous shot taken after the marriage ended (*Camera Press*). *Inset*: Lisa Marie had been an unexpected addition but brought unexpected happiness to Elvis (*Elvis Presley Fan Club*).

Above: Graceland, home of the King (*Camera Press*). *Left*: Elvis greets fans at the music gates (*Elvisly Yours*). *Below*: Graceland's billiard room (*Elvisly Yours*).

Above: The pop star and the president: Nixon and Elvis join forces in the battle against drugs (*Elvis Presley Fan Club*). *Left*: J. Edgar Hoover and Richard Nixon (*National Archives*). *Below*: The 'Memphis Mafia' receiving honorary sheriff's badges. Elvis is flanked by Dr 'Nick' (left) and Red West (right) (*Elvisly Yours*).

Elvis in his prime – signed by the King himself (*Elvis Presley Fan Club*).

Right: Elvis in his karate robe – the
TCB logo conspicuous on his chest
(*Elvisly Yours*). *Below*: Linda
Thompson, Elvis's girlfriend of many
years (*Camera Press*). *Bottom left*: An
older, heavier Elvis greets the New
York press in the early Seventies, at a
pre-concert conference (*Elvis Presley
Fan Club*).

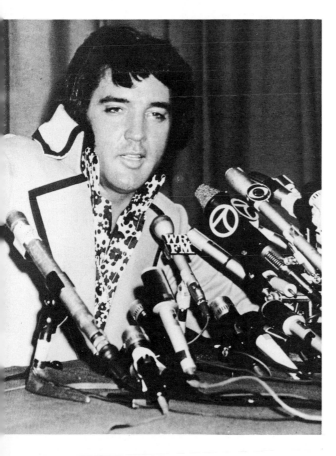

Ginger Alden, Elvis's last girlfriend,
was asleep in the next room when he
died (*National Archives*).

Left and Centre: A sequin-studded, stout Elvis performing live in 1975. He was already addicted to the drugs that were thought to have killed him. He is assisted by Charlie Hodge. *Bottom*: Charlie Hodge offers Elvis one of his celebrated scarves – a ritual part of his concert initiated by Priscilla (*All pictures Elvis Presley Fan Club*).

Right: Always the King. Elvis held audiences across America in rapture until the day he died. Despite his weight problem, to many he was the sexiest man alive. *Centre*: Elvis tussles playfully with Jo Smith, Billy's wife, on the last vacation Elvis would ever take. *Bottom*: Ginger Alden is embraced by Elvis on that same Hawaiian holiday; several weeks later he was dead (*All pictures Elvisly Yours*).

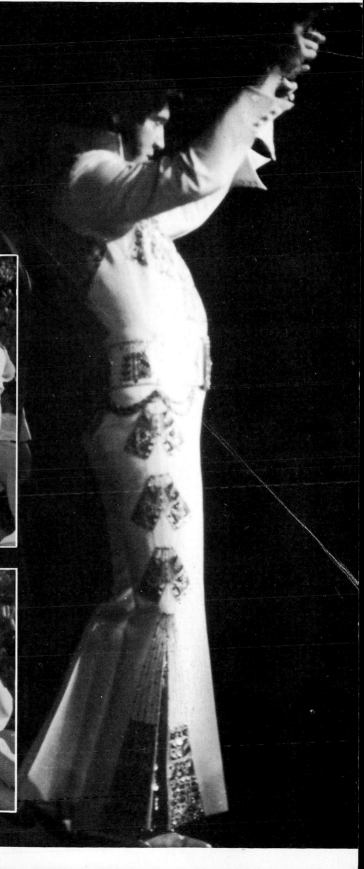

TV special claims Elvis really is alive

By CHRIS FULLER

Elvis Presley is alive — and hiding in the federal Witness Protection Program, claims a new TV documentary that says the rock star's death was faked to shield him from Mob hit men!

But the notion that Elvis is still alive is sheer nonsense, counters an outraged family member.

"That TV show is being done just for the big ratings and for no other reason," Elvis' aunt Lorene "Nash" Pritchett told The ENQUIRER.

"The National ENQUIRER's photo of Elvis lying in his coffin is genuine and proves beyond a shadow of a doubt The King is dead."

Yet even that photo hasn't convinced Monte Nicholson, a Los Angeles Sheriff's Department forgery-fraud investigator. He appears on the TV special "The Elvis Files" to discuss what he's uncovered after a 12-year probe.

"Elvis' death may have been the biggest fraud in the entire world," he declared.

"Being a policeman, I am really a skeptic. But we are relatively sure that on Aug. 16, 1977, (the date Elvis supposedly died), that was not Elvis lying in the mansion."

The two-hour syndicated special is set to air August 14 and will be seen in 135 cities. It will present FBI documents and experts — including police investigators and a relative — to support its shocking claims, says producer Melvin Bergman.

"We will actually show how Elvis was inducted into the FBI, how the government infiltrated two agents into his band and how during a three-year period Elvis and his father helped indict six Mafia figures.

"We are saying Elvis was a patriot. He did more for this country than anybody ever realized."

The FBI's files on Elvis — more than 600 pages long — show that he was the victim of an organized crime ring called "The Fraternity," which conned him out of hundreds of thousands of dollars for work that was never done to his private jet. Nicholson and other experts on the show are convinced that Elvis cooperated with the FBI in a sting targeting The Fraternity and was put into the Witness Protection Program until the crooks could be brought to justice. After that, the singer was supposed to be brought out of hiding to a hero's welcome, say sources close to the production.

But the plan backfired and only six of the mobsters ended up behind bars.

As a result, Elvis was left in the program for his safety, said Nicholson.

The police expert added that he interviewed Elvis' cousin Gene Smith, who said the man in the singer's coffin was definitely not Elvis.

"They may have used a lot of wax makeup to make the face look like Elvis," Nicholson declared. "Gene also said the sideburns kept coming unglued as though they were pasted on."

But Elvis' Aunt Nash told The ENQUIRER:

"This claim is idiotic. It's the most bizarre thing I have ever heard!

"I saw Elvis myself in the casket. There is no question in my mind that it was him.

"I wish it were true that Elvis is still alive — but he's dead!"

Rubbish! says his family — 'Enquirer photo proves that The King is dead'

SECRET AGENT? President Nixon shakes hands with Elvis in 1970. TV program claims it will show how Nixon inducted him into the FBI.

LIFE AND DEATH: Elvis shown wearing a Drug Enforcement Administration badge as he poses with a fan (above) shortly before his death in 1977. At left, The King lies in his coffin in famous Enquirer photograph. A cop says the body in the coffin is not Elvis, but Elvis' aunt insists: "That's idiotic. There's no question in my mind that it was him."

The *National Enquirer* story that broke following Elvis's death, and the much-publicised photograph of Elvis's coffin. A freelance journalist for the paper was tipped about events at Graceland two hours before the emergency services were summoned.

four-hour period. He ventured briefly into the garden where Lisa Marie, then nine years old, was playing on a golf cart. She was to be returned to her mother's home after he left on the tour the following day.

The evening passed uneventfully, with Elvis watching some television between rows with Ginger. She went out and returned to Graceland about nine-thirty p.m.

Meanwhile, Elvis wanted to go to the cinema and, as usual, one of the entourage had telephoned the Ridgeway Theatre in Memphis, to have the place opened up for Elvis and party immediately after the last show had finished. Elvis had asked for the showing of the film *MacArthur, The Rebel General*, starring Gregory Peck, which had been released a few weeks earlier. In fact, the Ridgeway manager phoned back some time later, full of apologies. The projectionist would not be able to stay on that night, and there was no one else to do it.

Elvis was bored, and quite suddenly he announced he was going to the dentist to get some work done on his teeth before the tour. Sam Thompson, in his testimony to Larry Hutchinson, remembers Elvis and his ensemble trooping down the back stairs while he played cards at the kitchen table. There was Elvis, Ginger, Billy Smith and now Charlie Hodge, and they all piled into the Stutz-Blackhawk with Elvis at the wheel; the low-slung car swung off down the drive and out of the music gates, where a small crowd was still gathered. Knowledgeable fans knew very well that they were more likely to see Elvis by night than by day. They just caught his face, with the customary dark glasses, and the hood of a track suit, with DEA embroidered on the back, pulled over his head.

Dr Lester Hofman, who lived half an hour away in east Memphis, was relaxing drowsily at his home when the telephone rang with the request to open up his surgery at eleven p.m. to treat Presley. Dr Hofman did not bat an eyelid at such a request. It had happened often in the past; he might mumble a mild complaint to his receptionist the following day, but then the rewards were better than for treating his average patient. He drove a Cadillac he had received as a gift from Presley.

According to Hofman, the only work he carried out on Presley was to give him two fillings, and his teeth a scrape and clean. He also examined Ginger Alden's teeth, and suggested she came back at a later date for some minor dental work. They chatted for some time, small talk, about a new Ferrari Elvis was thinking of buying, and how the dentist would like to hitch a ride in the *Lisa Marie* next time he flew up to Los Angeles. He wanted to surprise his daughter. Hofman gave Elvis two painkillers, codeine, one when he was in the chair and the second before he left.

They arrived back at Graceland soon after two a.m. There was still a small crowd outside the gates as the Stutz turned into the driveway and Robert Call, a tourist with his wife and four-year-old son from Pierceton, Indiana, took the last known picture of Elvis alive. Elvis waved as they passed by. Inside, Sam Thompson was still in the kitchen. Elvis passed without a word and went to his room, followed by Ginger Alden. Billy Smith said they were still arguing. Billy and Charlie went off to their respective apartments to get some sleep.

Elvis went to his office. Ginger went to the bedroom. He picked up the internal telephone and rang down to the kitchen and instructed Sam Thompson to book two seats on an American Airlines flight to Los Angeles on the afternoon of the sixteenth, to take Lisa Marie back to her mother. Then, he should take a flight to join Elvis up at Portland, Maine, just as soon as possible after that. Thompson groaned, silently confirming to himself that he intended to quit this job before long. He stayed around for another hour and then went home to pack his bags. By then, Rick Stanley had come on duty, to act as Elvis's through-the-night guard and gofer.

At two-fifteen a.m., the bedside telephone of Dr George Nichopoulos rang, startling the sleeping doctor. He knew the identity of the caller before he even picked up the receiver, and complained often that he hadn't had a good night's sleep since he took on Elvis as a patient. It was Elvis all right. He said that he had just had dental treatment for an abscessed tooth, which had left him in severe pain. Dr Nick offered to write a prescription for six strong painkillers, Dilaudid, a narcotic drug normally reserved for cancer patients in extreme pain, but which Elvis took frequently. The doctor would say later that there was no point in giving Presley normal painkillers. He was immune to them.

Elvis called Rick Stanley on the internal telephone and instructed him to go down to the all-night pharmacy at the Baptist Memorial Hospital and pick up the prescribed tablets. He then telephoned the resident nurse, Tish Henley, also fast asleep in her mobile home. He told her Ginger was suffering from menstrual pains, which Ginger later denied, and suggested that the nurse give her a Dilaudid tablet. Henley released just one of the tiny white pills and sent it over to the house. Ginger said she took no Dilaudid that night, so it can be assumed that Elvis took the pill himself.

While Rick was away, Dick Grob, head of security, came to the office and talked about arrangements for the tour. When he left, Elvis called Ginger into the office, where she found him watching television. His mood had swung again. She would later state to the newsmen who interviewed her that Elvis began speaking excitedly about their relationship, pacing around as he talked. He wanted to discuss the wedding and amazed her as he spelled out grandiose plans that seemed, in hindsight, said Ginger, aimed at providing some distraction from the sensational material which had been published about him following the release of the book, *Elvis: What Happened?* It was going to be a royal wedding, and she would have a fabulous dress and it would be a magnificent ceremony. He had never been so much in love, he told her, and then added, 'D'you know what my daddy said. He said he'd never seen me so happy as a man. I looked so happy to him.' This story did not ring altogether true, bearing in mind the revelations of Alicia Kirwin.

By now it was past four a.m., and Rick had arrived back at Graceland bearing the six small Dilaudid tablets. He brought them up to Elvis's room, along with the first of three yellow envelopes of drugs, prescribed by Dr Nick and released by Tish Henley for Elvis to take when he was ready to go to sleep. The first consignment consisted of Placidyl, Quaalude, Valium and Valmid tablets, all measured doses designed to calm the central nervous system hyped by his earlier intake of amphetamines. Also in the envelope would be a syringe of Demerol, another sedative and painkiller, which he or an aide would inject into his hip or back, below the shoulders. This package of drugs might be repeated three times before he finally went to sleep, because of the lingering effects of the uppers and his own increasing immunity.

Elvis took only the Dilaudid for the time being. He was not ready to go to sleep. He told Ginger he wanted a game of racquetball. He picked up the phone again and rang Billy Smith, at his mobile home, and told him and his wife Jo – who had long ago taken to her bed – to join him and Ginger on court for a game. They were always on call, whatever the hour.

The racquetball court was one of the most recent additions to the Graceland estate. The building was modern in design and contained a smart court, plus a play area with a piano, pinball machines, jukebox, steamroom, Jacuzzi and exercise room. Elvis came down in a new striped sweatsuit and started bouncing around. Ginger and Jo Smith sat in the observation pit while Elvis and Billy smashed the ball around the court. Then Ginger and Jo had a game; Elvis fooled around again and accidentally hit his leg with his racket. He was showing off to Ginger, according to Billy, and then they all sat around the piano while Elvis played and sang some songs.

Jo went back to the mobile home while Billy joined Elvis in his bedroom. Ginger went to her own dressing room for a time, and then came into Elvis's room, where she laid on the bed, still in her sweatsuit, and fell asleep. Billy dried Elvis's sweat-wet hair and then left. Elvis had already taken some of his sleeping medication, but the exact amount is unclear. Rick Stanley's recollections over the years have been inconsistent and contradictory, largely because, by his own admission, he was 'zonking out' himself on Demerol.

Ginger, whose recollections were also unreliable, said she heard Elvis call for more medication around eight o'clock in the morning, which Rick brought to the bedroom; another envelope containing eight tablets. Less than half an hour later, Tish Henley, by then at work in Dr Nick's surgery, received a call from Elvis. Apparently he had failed to raise Rick and he still could not sleep. He needed more medication because he had a hard day (or night) ahead of him.

She said she would arrange to send up some more sleeping pills. She telephoned her husband, Tommy, and asked him to take two Valmid tablets and a Placidyl over to the house. Both were standard prescription drugs for insomniacs, and Dr Nick dispensed them for Elvis every day of his life. Rick, by then, could not be found, so Tommy Henley gave the tablets to Elvis's Aunt Delta Mae, who took them upstairs and gave them to him.

Ginger, by her account of these last hours, was then asleep and heard nothing of this exchange. She remained asleep until around one-thirty p.m., when she awoke and discovered that Elvis was not by her side. Like the preceding events in this strange night, this was not especially unusual, either. She did not go looking; instead, she casually picked up the telephone to call a friend, had a brief conversation and then called her mother.

Her account to the coroner's investigator, Dan Warlick, was scant and lacking in detail; she did not mention the drug packages until she was questioned again two years later, and seemed persistently unclear of the timing of events, and even the number of times Rick had come to the room bearing pills. Rick seemed equally confused. But now, for certain, there was a five-hour gap in everyone's version of events – between the time Aunt Delta handed Elvis the sleeping pills from Tish Henley, to around two p.m., when Ginger Alden, having made two telephone calls, decided to knock on Elvis's bathroom door – a gap which was later explained away by the reasoning that Elvis had asked not to be disturbed.

Receiving no response, she said she cautiously opened the door and found Elvis lying in a foetal position on the floor, with his face downwards in the shag-pile carpet. Again, the initial sight of him laying unconscious was not new; he might fall asleep anywhere after taking his pills. She called his name and he did not stir. She touched his body and felt it was cold; she looked at his face and he was barely recognisable. His cheeks were puffed and purple, his tongue hung from the side of his mouth and there was blood where he had bitten into it. Paramedics who find comatose bodies in this state say this is a regular occurrence, especially in cases where a stiffening of the joints through rigor mortis has already begun.

Ginger went back into the bedroom and telephoned downstairs to the kitchen. She screamed into the mouthpiece to tell whoever was on duty to get upstairs. *There was something wrong with Elvis.* Al Strada reached the bedroom in double quick time. He took one look and reached for the phone near the toilet; he asked for Joe Esposito to get upstairs right away.

The clock was ticking away. Joe arrived, took one look, turned the body over, and a gasp of air was expelled from Elvis's lungs. Joe tried mouth-to-mouth resuscitation, but had difficulty getting Elvis's mouth open. The efforts were in vain, and Esposito grabbed the telephone again, punching out the number of Dr Nick's bleeper. The operator said he was at the Doctors' Hospital, almost six miles from Graceland. Esposito left a message for him to get to the Presley house straightaway. Joe tried another local doctor, but he was not there, either. Finally he called the emergency number which sent the paramedics from unit six of the Memphis fire department racing towards the house. Not long ago, the same team had saved Vernon's life when he collapsed from a heart attack, but they had no idea that this time the call related to Elvis Presley.

By now, word had spread through the household. Vernon Presley had made his way upstairs from his office and was moaning over his son's body, already convinced that he was dead, but crying, 'Son, don't die . . . don't leave.' Lisa Marie came to the bedroom door and asked if there was something wrong with her daddy. Al Strada hustled her away.

David Stanley said he was playing pool with a friend when he heard the news. His first thought was to get his friend, who he later admitted should not have been in the house, out of the gates as quickly as he could. It was a curious thing to do, at such a vital time, when his beloved stepbrother and provider was lying dead on the floor. He put the friend in his car, and drove towards the music gates, just as the ambulance swung into the drive. Stanley came back a few minutes later, entering the house through the rear, and bounded up the service stairs to Elvis's bedroom. Vernon was at the point of collapse. Sandy Miller attended to him, in between taking turns with Joe Esposito to pump Elvis's chest.

Charlie Crosby skidded to a halt in his fire-department wagon outside the front door of Graceland, and he and his partner Ulysses S. Jones, Jr, unloaded their medical gear and were shown upstairs. They found six or seven people in the room, men and women. Jones would later record that the patient was lying on the bathroom floor, naked except for a pair of gold-coloured pyjama trousers. His face and the back of his body was so coloured up – a sign that Elvis was already dead – that Jones thought it was a black man lying there. He was shocked to be told it was Elvis Presley.

When Jones asked what had happened, David Stanley replied that Elvis had probably OD'd. The medics could not find a pulse or a flicker of life, but did not declare him dead. They inserted a tube in his throat and began pumping air into his lungs through a squeeze bag. Vernon was still wailing as they moved him on to the stretcher. It took five men to lift him and get him downstairs to the ambulance; Elvis weighed 250 pounds at the time. The entourage went, too. Esposito, Charlie Hodge, Al Strada and now Dick Grob jumped into the back of the ambulance.

As they were closing the doors, Dr Nick arrived in his gold Mercedes and clambered aboard the moving vehicle. He immediately began pumping, with his now famous chant of, 'Breathe Presley, breathe.' Ulysses Jones noted that the doctor showed total disbelief that Elvis could be dead.

Billy Smith was just about to chase the ambulance on his motorbike when David Stanley jumped into his Datsun 240Z and shouted, 'Get in.' They raced after the emergency vehicle. As the ambulance sped away at eighty miles an hour, Crosby, driving, headed for the nearest hospital, the Methodist Hospital South. Dr Nick shouted alternative instructions. They should go to the Baptist Memorial, seven miles away. They had Elvis's records of previous admissions. They arrived four minutes before three p.m. The hospital's Harvey emergency team was ready to receive their patient in the trauma room. Eighteen resuscitation technicians were assembled. The body was laid out on a stainless-steel table and a surgeon went straight to work. Tubes were inserted to pump out the stomach and the contents were thrown down the sink.

They probably knew their battle was lost before they started, because rigor mortis had already begun to set in; but they went through the motions. At three-thirty p.m., Elvis Presley was formally declared dead. Looking pale, Dr Nick came out of the trauma room and told the entourage, warning them to say nothing. Joe Esposito said they would have to call a press conference.

What was the cause of death? An official autopsy would be carried out by a team from the hospital under the supervision of the county medical examiner. A full statement would be issued later. By four p.m., a crowd had begun gathering at the music gates. Radio and television stations reported Elvis's death.

The news was flashed to FBI offices in Memphis, and elsewhere, and was received with a mixture of shock, disbelief and even suspicion. A serving FBI agent working on the Presley case, and the associated Operation Fountain Pen at the time, said in 1992 that it was not unnatural that the first thought to cross the minds of those investigating officers involved in the case, was foul play. He said:

You have to understand that we were party to a vast amount of information that was not in the public domain. We knew the extent of the enquiry that was going on behind the scenes, and any one of us could testify there and then that it would not be beyond some of the personalities named to take some kind of action to halt the enquiry – scare off the witnesses, pull off some spectacular stunt to thwart the FBI investigation. Indeed, we were half-expecting it. The FBI directorate had already warned us that it would be very difficult to get some of these people into court.

I am not saying that those men who were eventually arrested were involved in any way with events at Graceland that day . . . but there were plenty of people around who were not only very capable of murder but who were quite likely to resort to it. And, quite frankly, murder was immediately being discussed. It had to be. I would go as far as saying that it was our first thought, certainly mine, when I heard. We definitely could not dismiss it, whatever reasons might be given for the cause of death . . .

Such thoughts were not far away from the minds of others close to Elvis. 'They've killed my son . . . they've killed my son,' Vernon Presley kept saying, later that day at Graceland. Those around him took it to mean that those who had supplied Elvis with his drugs were indirectly responsible for his death. Vernon would pursue the possibility of foul play himself, in the days ahead, but for the time being any possibility of an open enquiry into the death of Elvis Presley was already being blocked.

12

Natural Causes, Murder ... or What?

'The results of the autopsy are that the cause of death is cardiac arrhythmia,
due to undetermined heartbeat ... there are several cardiovascular diseases
that are known to be present. One is a mild degree of hypertension that had
been under treatment for some time, and there was hardening of the arteries,
known as coronary atherosclerosis ... he was using medication to control
blood pressure and for a colon problem, but there is no evidence of chronic use
of drugs whatsoever ... the most likely conclusion after all tests are complete is
natural causes ...'

Dr Jerry Francisco, chief medical examiner for
Shelby county, 16 August 1977

The body of Elvis Aaron Presley, hero of a generation, lay ignominiously, naked and bulbous, barely recognisable, on a dissection table, in the centre of the autopsy room of the pathological suite on the second floor of the hospital. It was ready for examination.

Under normal circumstances, a corpse in any hospital death would have been removed to the county morgue, but this prospect had been discounted because of the large crowd gathering by the minute all around the hospital. Two Memphis policemen, armed and alert, stood guard outside the room while two hospital security guards remained inside. There were already wild rumours about Elvis's death, and reporters and photographers disguised in white coats, dressed as doctors, had been discovered wandering the hospital corridors.

By the time the news that Elvis was dead had been confirmed to the press with a simple statement that he had died from heart failure, – to which Joe Esposito had added erroneously and somewhat

185

mysteriously that Elvis had died peacefully in his bed – the hospital became the gathering point for representatives of the world's media. The official statement was short and said that no other details could be released until after the autopsy, which would take place later that day. A press conference would be called in the evening.

The importance of this tragic event was mirrored by the attention it was receiving from the most senior medical staff and pathologists who had begun to assemble at the hospital late that afternoon. A team of ten of these most senior people had been earmarked to conduct the post-mortem examination, to discover the cause of death. Soon after four p.m., Dan Warlick, the investigator for the Shelby county medical examiner's office, who normally spent his days looking into rather mundane sudden deaths and suicides, was dispatched to Graceland to begin an enquiry, the results of which he would report to his boss, the county medical examiner, Dr Jerry Francisco.

Neither Francisco nor Warlick would be informed of 'external events' to do with the case, which were not thought to concern them. Yet with the benefit of total background knowledge, they may well have believed it was crucially important to have received at least some clue of the extent and range of the FBI investigation, which had been going on for months. None was volunteered.

So now, the *only* official enquiry into Presley's death was to be placed in the hands of a medical investigator.

After a routine visit to Graceland by policemen, no other detailed enquiry either by local or federal police was publicly instituted. Yet Memphis police and the Shelby county sheriff's department, where Elvis Presley was an honorary deputy, were certainly aware of their most famous resident's habits and lifestyle. They knew he had been the subject of numerous assassination threats and they knew of the incidence of past drug-related enquiries concerning members of the Presley entourage. Certain senior officers must also have had an intimate knowledge of Presley and his known history of drug abuse. Even a suspected accidental drug overdose, or even the possibility of suicide, could, on the face of it, have been sufficient for a more detailed examination, not withstanding the knowledge of the FBI's interest.

The fact that Elvis Presley had been the victim of fraud was no secret among the hierarchy of authority in Memphis, Tennessee, and elsewhere in the US federal judiciary system, where investigations into Operation Fountain Pen were reaching startling proportions. It must be said, however, that full details of that investigation were not common knowledge even in the US attorney's office, which would eventually prosecute in the case of fraud against Elvis. In 1992, Glen Reid, then an assistant US attorney, who left soon afterwards to go into private practice, told me, 'I have a memory of the case concerning Elvis's plane, but I cannot recall being made aware of any wider implications. Certainly, the US attorney's office was in touch with the FBI constantly on this matter, but if there were documents floating around relating to an international fraud of the nature you are now describing, I have no recollection of having seen them.'

Reid suggested that perhaps these documents were retained within the hierarchy of the US attorney, or even within the office of the district attorney-general. Even so, anyone in the legal offices of the US federal prosecution service were aware that Elvis was named as a victim in the sealed indictments which were to have been presented to a federal grand jury 'on or about 15 August 1977'. The Memphis field office of the FBI knew it, and a lot more besides. Presley's own family lawyer knew of the FBI's operation. So did Vernon Presley.

And yet, here was the investigation into the death of one of the most famous personalities in modern history being more or less delegated to the one-man show of Dan Warlick, who might, at the end of the day, conclude that the whole purpose of his task was to support the eventual conclusions – that death was due to natural causes, a theory that was by no means unanimous among the eminent medical people involved.

The police went to Graceland with Warlick. The most senior officer was Lieutenant Sam McCachren, a veteran of the Memphis police homicide division, who was on the verge of retirement. McCachren in turn was accompanied by Jerry Stauffer, a young and inexperienced prosecutor with the Memphis district attorney's office. By the time Warlick, McCachren and Stauffer arrived at Graceland, two other officers, Sergeant John Peel and Detective Roy Millican, were already there – four policemen and a medical county investigator in all.

Warlick and McCachren, with Stauffer trailing behind, entered Graceland and found a scene of bewilderment and grief. Vernon Presley was weeping and wailing that his son was dead. Lisa Marie, whose mother Priscilla had been informed and was already on her way from Los Angeles to Memphis, was crying and confused, and being cared for by a nurse. Other members of the household were in a similar state.

The policemen and Warlick were shown up to Elvis's quarters, first to his office and den, in which the dominant feature was the largest collection of teddy bears they had seen outside of a toy shop. There was a placard on a desk which read ELVIS PRESLEY: THE BOSS. In front of it, Warlick noticed a hypodermic syringe, empty. They moved on into his bedroom. Warlick had brought a Polaroid camera to take instant shots of the scene. They all stood, quietly amazed at the garish decor, the paintings and the huge bed. Their attention was immediately drawn to the number of guns, various weapons laying on top of the furniture. There were three television sets, side by side, and one suspended from the ceiling. On a bookcase, the policemen found a second syringe.

The bed had been made and Warlick complained to Joe Esposito, who had by now joined them, that the place appeared to have been cleaned up. Sam Thompson confirmed that a maid had been in. Had she cleaned the bathroom, too? Unfortunately she had, and Warlick would later discover from the paramedics, Ulysses Jones and Charlie Crosby, that when they arrived at Graceland, the bedroom and the bathroom were in a state of chaos. The bed was unmade; there were papers strewn about, and the bathroom was even worse – a book appeared to have been flung across the room, knocking bottles and aerosols off the top of the vanity unit. A black bag, which belonged to Elvis, was open and upturned. When they returned later in the day to pick up some of their equipment, left behind in the dash to get Elvis to hospital, both rooms had been cleaned. A patch of vomit had been scrubbed from the carpet, and their gear was stacked neatly, ready for them to collect. It was obvious to Warlick and the policemen that the two rooms had been given a pretty thorough clean-up. Later, no one in the house could recall who gave the instruction for the clean-up, and it was suggested that the maid did it of her own accord.

In spite of this, the police did not pursue any vigorous search or examination of the scene of death; they looked no further than what was immediately apparent to the human eye, in a cursory survey of the rooms. They took no fingerprints, no photographs, other than those taken by Dan Warlick with his hand-held black-and-white Polaroid. They made no searches in and around furniture; they moved nothing and they questioned only those party to the discovery of the body for their account of events surrounding his death. They discovered a general reluctance on the part of most of those they interviewed to give any detailed answers to the question of what medication Elvis might have taken on the night he died, and they failed to press the matter beyond this polite enquiry.

The police and Warlick concluded their examination of the scene and left after about forty-five minutes. As they went, the county sheriff, Eugene Barksdale, arrived and was expressing his condolences to Vernon Presley. As the police cruisers drove off, the scene in Elvis Presley Boulevard was incredible. Already, two or three thousand people had gathered outside and the police had begun a crowd-control operation.

Lieutenant McCachren returned to his office and reported back to his chief. They would do nothing more until the autopsy report was available. As it turned out, apart from writing up his report, it was the last contact McCachren would have with the case before retiring the following year. Years later, and by then working as a plumbing contractor, he admitted that had he known then of the undercurrent of suspicion, he would have pursued the case more vigorously. But, in the end, he was never given the opportunity . . .

★   ★   ★   ★   ★

Dr Jerry Francisco was no stranger to controversy, nor to dealing with VIP autopsies. He had been medical examiner of Shelby county since 1961, and had been in charge of the autopsy on Dr Martin Luther King, following his assassination in Memphis on 4 April 1968. His report on the wound that killed Dr King was later to be questioned in a medical report to a House of Representatives select committee on assassinations, because his team had failed to dissect the entire wound to define the trajectory of the bullet, which was said to have been fired from a boarding house 100 yards away. At the time, when James Earl Ray pleaded guilty to the killing, Francisco's autopsy assessments would not be challenged. Only later, when new evidence suggested that a second shot might have been fired from a movement in some bushes, did the trajectory analysis of the wound become vital. Francisco had to explain that he had chosen not to conduct more extensive surgery on the body to save distress to Dr King's family.

But, in 1977, autopsies on famous people had become a regular topic of controversy (the Kennedys, Monroe and King, to name but four), and if the qualifications and expertise of the team which gathered around the body of Elvis Presley that evening was any indication, the intention was clear – to reach conclusions supported by knowledgeable men, loaded with respectability, integrity and professionalism, so that the result would be beyond question.

If this was the aim, it was never achieved.

There would be eventual disagreement among the team members about the outcome; a great blanket of secrecy was pulled up and over their findings, and to this day Dr Jerry Francisco finds it necessary, from time to time, to defend the conclusions which were contained in an unpublished report that bears his signature. Although he was indeed Shelby county medical examiner, in supervision of the autopsy, he had taken no actual part in the dissection of the body.

The events of that night are as remarkable as the crowd scenes that were gathering momentum outside. Rumours spread like wildfire. The world was waiting to know what (or even who) killed Elvis Presley, and the media was surging forth, demanding information.

Before commencing the autopsy, a hospital spokesperson, presumably with Francisco's approval, stated that there would be a press conference at eight p.m. that evening. The medical team began surveying the body at around seven-fifteen p.m., but the first incision, the opening of the chest to examine the main organs and arteries was not made until around seven-thirty. The scalpel was drawn in the customary Y-shape cut, cutting through the tissue and muscle over the stomach and the rib cage, before the pathology surgeon opens the chest with his electric bone-saw. This done, the breastplate is lifted, exposing the organs contained in the chasm from neck to pubis – the heart, lungs, liver, spleen, stomach and intestines – which are then visible and available for initial examination. For a total examination and possible dissection, each is removed. Samples are taken for analysis, some on the spot, others to be sent away to more specialised laboratories.

Samples for analysis should have included contents of the stomach. There were none. These had been pumped out and thrown away during the vain efforts of the Harvey team to establish some sign of life remaining when Elvis was first admitted. This was a disappointment to the pathologists, since it immediately eliminated a valuable clue about what drugs Presley may have taken orally, immediately before his death. Only tissue from the stomach lining could be examined.

One of the specialists examined the heart and held it up to show the rest how enlarged it was; another inspected the liver and kidneys. The liver showed signs of damage through alcohol or drug abuse, but it was not sufficient to have caused death. The kidneys were in fair condition and the spleen was enlarged, but otherwise disease-free.

There was an on-going undercurrent of conjecture. Possibilities were being discussed, signs of infected or damaged organs noted, and often being rejected as insignificant. As yet, the pathologists were ignorant of Elvis's drug intake during the previous twenty-four hours. Only Dr Nichopoulos was aware of the extent of Elvis's drug regime and he also knew that his patient topped this up with supplies from other sources. The total intake in any single day might represent a cocktail of drugs that would floor a normal man. No one had apparently suggested that an accidental or even deliberately applied overdose might be the cause of death.

Only the results of later tests would show that he had traces of fourteen identifiable chemical substances in his body at the time of death, and although Dr Nichopoulos could have enlightened the pathology team on his patient's long-standing use of sedatives, narcotics and amphetamines, such matters were *also* contained in records at the Baptist Hospital, to which Elvis had been admitted on five occasions since 1973, for a distended colon, fatigue, detoxification and drug-related problems.

One of the team members who specialised in cardiac pathology virtually ruled out a heart attack. There were all the usual signs of hypertension, blood pressure and the onset of atherosclerosis – the hardening of the arteries. There were problems, true enough, but in his view none was bad enough, singly or even cumulatively, to have been a cause of death. The arteries were no more congested than they would be in many men of Elvis's age.

With the body still laying back-down, the dissecting surgeon now moved to open up the skull for examination of the brain, for indications, perhaps, of a blood clot or stroke. Initial examination showed no immediately identifiable abnormalities. Still no firm cause of death could be pinpointed and the time had reached two minutes to eight. Dr Jerry Francisco looked at his watch, and spoke to the team leader, Dr Eric Muirhead, head of pathology at the Baptist and an eminent man in his field; he nodded and together they announced that they would now meet the press as previously arranged.

Francisco, Muirhead, Dr Nichopoulos and others in the team trooped out of the room, leaving three of their number to complete the work of taking samples and examining the body. At that point, the autopsy was far from complete. Furthermore, the microscopic slides of samples would take several days to prepare and examine, while the results of toxicology tests would take much longer. As they left the autopsy room after less than an hour examining the body, it was a definite fact that the team had reached no unanimously agreed conclusion about the cause of death. This has been stated and re-stated by doctors who were present.

Dr Jerry Francisco took his seat in front of the world's press and the mass of microphones that would broadcast his statement to the waiting nation, and, indeed, world. He took a positive view of the outcome of the autopsy, despite the fact that nothing had been confirmed. 'The cause of death is cardiac arrhythmia,' he said after a short preamble, 'due to undetermined heartbeat.' Eyebrows were raised, not least among members of the medical team who had just come from the hospital autopsy suite. To utter such a firm conclusion before the completion of the autopsy and the tests came as a shock to the medical team.

If he had asked for a vote of the doctors on the most probable cause of death, it is unlikely that this particular explanation would have received widespread support. However, he did cover himself by stating that further tests were still being carried out and it was unlikely that the cause of death could be positively established for some weeks, if ever.

He went on to announce that there were several cardiovascular diseases identified by the cardiac specialist, such as atherosclerosis. Mr Presley was also known to be using medication for blood pressure and a colon problem, but, *'there is no evidence of chronic drug abuse whatsoever'*.

For such a statement to be made, for such vital facts to be discarded and disregarded was barely believable. The county medical examiner's own investigator had sounded alarm bells about the empty syringes at Graceland, and the clean-up of disorder at the scene of death. There existed records of Elvis's 'secret' history of detoxification at the Baptist. Elvis had even befriended one of the hospital nurses, Marian Cocke, during one of his stays, and she went to work for him. (After his death, she wrote a small book entitled *I Called Him Babe: Elvis's Nurse Remembers*.)

There was to be no apparent notation which recorded more obvious signs of Elvis's drug habits, such as the needle holes in the skin around his thighs, buttocks and shoulder blades. As any of his entourage knew, they were the most usual sites for his injections of Demerol for sedation purposes or for the daily programme of Dr Feelgood shots, which he received while on tour. On any normal day, he might have two shots; on tour, he might have four or five. No mention was made at the conference of the pin-cushion effect on his body, but Francisco repeated when questioned that there was no evidence of a drug-related death.

Any observer monitoring the unfolding drama in the aftermath of Elvis's death might well have begun to question the reliability of such comments at such an early stage of the autopsy. None of the other doctors present spoke against Dr Francisco's assessment of heart failure, though some later wished they had.

Dr Nichopoulos was also questioned at the press conference and he pointedly denied that Elvis was taking hard drugs, street drugs like cocaine or heroin, which was true. He wasn't. He merely consumed unbelievable amounts of prescription chemicals, but that wasn't the question and therefore it was never answered. Only Dr Nick and his nurse knew that on the day before Elvis died, the doctor had written prescriptions in readiness for the forthcoming tour so that he could stock up on the drugs he would need for the ten days they would be on the road. It was a remarkable shopping list:

Amytal: 100 three-gram capsules and twelve half-gram ampules; it is a powerful drug which has a hypnotic effect when taken in large quantities. Its most potent form is amytal sodium, which is used for the treatment of meningitis or tetanus.

Dilaudid: 50 four-milligram tablets and twenty cc of two-milligram solution. Said to be Elvis's favourite drug, it is a strong painkiller.

Quaalude: 150 300-milligram tablets. Another sedative drug, most widely used and a fashionable pill among the showbiz set of the Seventies; usually taken after cocaine.

Percodan: 100 tablets. Another fashionable narcotic drug which has a similar effect on the central nervous system as morphine.

Dexedrine: 100 five-milligram tablets; this was and still is the most common form of speed.

Biphetamine: 100 twenty-milligram spansules of another popular and powerful amphetamine.

Dr Nichopoulos, as he sat in front of the world's press that night, knew very well that this prescription had already been filled before Elvis died, so that it would be available for the duration of the tour. The cache of pills was sitting in his office. It was normal practice to stockpile the drugs, since he would have difficulty filling the prescriptions in other states. He would say later that the drug supply was to fill the requirements of the Presley entourage during the tour.

Even so, he knew that Elvis was a heavy user of chemical aids and yet he went further in his denials that Elvis ever had a drugs problem – at least 'not in recent years'. He had given Elvis a complete physical five days earlier, and apart from an eye infection and a sore throat, he was a healthy man.

If he was so healthy, why had he died?

And were there any suspicious circumstances?

There were plenty, but no one was talking.

Not Dr Nichopoulos, who knew the true extent of Elvis's chemical intake. Not the Memphis police, who had every reason to show *some* interest. Not the US attorney's office, who knew of the FBI investigation – no one in authority in Memphis that night raised even a glimmer of public dissent to the official verdict now being broadcast to the world, that Elvis Presley, the King of rock 'n' roll, died of natural causes.

$$\star \quad \star \quad \star \quad \star \quad \star$$

The autopsy from which this conclusion would be drawn was completed by the three doctors left to finalise the dissection work at around eight-fifty p.m., soon after the press conference ended. The body was sewn up, minus certain organs, which were retained for tests, and was prepared for removal to the funeral home to be repaired – suitably dressed in a white suit and made up for the official public viewing of the body, set for the following day.

Dan Warlick, who had been a formal observer throughout, returned to his own office and telephoned Lieutenant McCachren in the homicide squad, as arranged. McCachren had not even bothered to hang around. He had gone off duty, and the call was taken by a colleague, who noted the official autopsy verdict of natural causes. This was duly entered on a single sheet of paper. The following day, the police formally closed the slender file and it was locked away, marked secret, and not seen again for several years.

A lot could have been investigated, but it never was. Apart from medical discrepancies, which would be debated for years afterwards, there was a formidable list of unresolved mysteries existing even then:

- How long had Elvis lain in the bathroom – three, four, or possibly five hours?
- Why had no one discovered him earlier?
- Where was his duty valet, who should have been sleeping in a bed at the rear of the bathroom?
- Was it true that a freelance journalist had been warned to stand by, almost two hours before the emergency team was called?
- What caused the disarray in the bathroom, and why had the rooms been cleaned so rapidly?
- Were there any signs of violence?
- Who was in the house at the time?
- Was there someone known to have been inside who should not have been?
- Was there anyone who might have wanted Elvis dead? If so, what were the circumstances?
- Had there been any recent threats to his life?
- Could he have been injected deliberately with a drugs cocktail that would kill him?
- Or even injected accidentally?
- Or was it suicide?
- And how many pills was he taking each day? How many injections was Elvis having?

A truthful answer to any one of those questions would have rendered the case worthy of investigation in the immediate aftermath of Elvis's death, even apart from the medical matters which arose during the autopsy. They were all being swept conveniently under the carpet, by one Memphis department after another, presumably, in the hope that interest would quickly die down.

It never would.

In the short term, there was limited acceptance of the official findings, incomplete though they were. Yet, even on the night of the death, nationwide television stations were wheeling out personalities who had known Elvis for years. Not least among them were Red and Sonny West, whose book, *Elvis: What Happened?* had been on the bookstands for two and a half weeks, and suddenly became an overnight bestseller. Talk of a cover-up was already stirring among the media. They focused on things they knew, and those matters related to Elvis's lifestyle and his chemical dependence.

What no one knew, and nor would they for many years to come, was the behind-the-scenes FBI interest in Elvis's death. The background of intrigue that had been building for months went silent. Federal agents at Memphis had been alerted to keep a watching brief. The US attorney's office was to be kept fully informed, but the official files at the bureau headquarters suddenly went quiet. Nothing appeared in the files in documented form until the narrative picked up again in October.

★   ★   ★   ★   ★

Meanwhile, at Graceland on 17 August, there began the procession of homage for which there is no modern comparison; Rudolph Valentino's funeral is the only one that can be called to mind. That day, just after noon, the big music gates were swung open for Elvis, as his body was driven home in a gleaming white hearse for the pre-burial ceremonies. By that afternoon, when the gates were to be opened to allow mourners to file past the body of their idol, there were 20,000 or more fans crowded outside the gates. Others were arriving from near and far by the minute.

At Memphis airport, every plane that landed brought newsmen and women from throughout America and the rest of the world. Fans, too, flew in; every aircraft seat on every arriving aircraft was full. All roads into Memphis were bumper-to-bumper, and by six-thirty p.m. that evening, when the music gates were closed once more, 80,000 people had passed through to pay their respects. The fans were kept well away from the body. Photographs were banned, though one of Elvis's cousins had already been equipped with a tiny spy camera by the *National Enquirer* newspaper, and took his famous picture of Elvis, with only the profile of his head visible above the casket walls.

Security guards were very much in evidence; 150 uniformed policemen surrounded the estate. A unit of the National Guard also stood by, and military sentries were placed at the music gates. The great crowd of weeping fans seemed gripped by a mounting hysteria. Dozens fainted and there were cries for doctors. All kinds of rumours were flashing around, and already there was talk that the body wasn't really that of Elvis, just what they said when James Dean died, and Marilyn Monroe, and Jim Morrison ... Many were still not convinced the following day when the funeral cortège arrived. After a private service inside Graceland, eight pallbearers, including Elvis's most faithful aides and Dr Nichopoulos, shouldered the heavy seamless copper casket from the house and loaded it aboard the gleaming white Cadillac hearse.

Then, a brilliantly shining silver Cadillac limousine led the procession, with the hearse followed by sixteen white Cadillac limousines carrying the mourners of Elvis's inner circle through the music gates for burial at the Memphis cemetery, half a mile away. There was a certain aptness in the lines of one of his earliest hits, 'Mystery Train', which describes a train sixteen coaches long.

Slowly, this white mystery train, flanked by police outriders, and with helicopters circling overhead, made its journey at walking pace to the cemetery through the thousands who lined the streets. The cortège halted at the granite mausoleum, where family and guests stood with their heads bowed and the coffin was placed inside. They dispersed, leaving Vernon alone to watch the five workmen seal up the tomb, with double layers of concrete covered by a marble slab that would protect his son's body from the ghouls.

And then he left the scene to allow another remarkable demonstration of fan worship to take place, when more than fifty thousand people, kept moving by police with loud hailers, walked passed the King's final resting place, each one being handed a token flower stripped from the thousands of floral tributes which had been delivered in a fleet of vans that morning to the cemetery.

Vernon returned to Graceland to be comforted in the grief that his family believed might kill him. He had been as anxious as anyone to keep the events surrounding his son's death from public knowledge, naturally concerned that the secrets of Elvis's drug consumption during the last years of his life would remain within the household. Vernon could still pull strings in Memphis, and there were many who shared his view that the name of the city's most famous son should not be blackened in death.

Even so, as Vernon's grief turned to anger, he began to make dark insinuations. 'Who killed my son?' he kept saying, more and more loudly. And, gradually, the word murder crept into conversations.

13

Suspicion

'I think Vernon Presley quite seriously considered the possibility that Elvis had been murdered. He was asking all around what happened. He asked me if I had seen anybody who I didn't recognise going upstairs on the morning Elvis died. I told Vernon that I was sound asleep and had seen nothing. He asked me if it was possible that someone had come into the bedroom while Elvis and I were asleep. He was talking about foul play . . . I could not rule it out.'

Ginger Alden, 1979

Even as Memphis officialdom was attempting to remove public doubt that Elvis's death could have been anything other than from natural causes, a certain unease remained within the Presley household in the days and weeks that followed. Vernon Presley seemed intent on establishing a clearer picture of what actually happened the day his son died, and he began questioning members of the entourage about the possibility of foul play. It could be said, of course, that sick and tired, and under the most severe strain from recent events, he could not bear the thought that his son might have died of causes brought about by his own excesses – therefore, really, death at his own hand. Even if he had, Vernon would be looking to blame others – the doctors and suppliers of the substances – rather than Elvis himself.

Yet his thoughts were far more wide-ranging than drugs; even though, at the time, there was no real pressure from any quarter, either from investigators or the media, to show that Elvis's death was caused by anything other than a natural complaint. Newspapers had revealed Elvis's use of drugs in the immediate aftermath and there was plenty of information to draw on from the book by Red and Sonny

West. But there was insufficient knowledge, then, to make it an issue of major concern.

However, Vernon knew things that the others were not aware of, such as the FBI investigation, and this perhaps explains to some degree the scenario which developed at Graceland as he progressed with attempts to resolve the nagging doubts in his mind. He seemed intent on exploring the question: Could Elvis have been murdered? And, if so, who would have wanted him dead? There were plenty of possibilities. No one, except Vernon, Elvis and the lawyers, was aware, for example, that his will would name one single heir, his daughter, and that no other member of the entourage would benefit financially.

This was clearly a disappointment to several in the Presley sphere when it became known, and some went so far as to suggest that the will was a fake, and there was talk of court action to challenge it. There were business deals which had gone sour, in which he had gathered enemies. There was a shady underbelly of hangers-on for the drug connections, and there were many dubious characters in the background of the FBI investigation – a thought that had already occurred to FBI agents working on the case. To anyone unaware of the full facts, the possibility of murder seemed too fantastic for words, and perhaps still does. Vernon knew differently and, before long, a sequence of events would support his suspicions.

Once the shock of Elvis's death had subsided, he began to raise the question of death by foul means, in conversation with members of the household, apparently intent on establishing a clearer picture of what exactly happened between the hours of eight a.m., when he was last seen alive, and after two p.m., when Ginger Alden raised the alarm. He went through the sequence of events with Ginger. He asked if it was possible that someone had come into the room that morning, someone she did not recognise, perhaps, and had slipped past her unnoticed into the bathroom. She said it was possible. She said she slept soundly from six-thirty a.m. to after one-thirty p.m., because she had had no sleep the day before. She said she stirred only once, around eight a.m., when she heard Elvis telephoning downstairs for some more medication.

Although in her early interviews after the death, she denied having taken drugs herself, she did later admit that she had taken a Quaalude. She repeated her suspicion of foul play publicly two years later, when she was interviewed by Geraldo Rivera for ABC television's '20/20' programme, and said anyone could have come into the room and she would probably not have heard them. Vernon, she said, obviously believed that murder could not be ruled out.

Ginger's story became something of a focus within the household. Dick Grob, as head of security, had already started his own investigation* and was interested particularly in the telephone calls that Ginger made when she woke up – and before she raised the alarm. One had been to her mother, who was at work in the Memphis Internal Revenue offices, around two p.m. A second was to a friend. And why was it, Grob wanted to know, that by the time that everyone began crowding into the bedroom, Ginger was already dressed and made up, looking as if she was ready for a mannequin parade? Ginger said that she had spent some time in the bedroom before going to the bathroom. She said it was not unusual for Elvis to be in the bathroom for a long period of time and it was only after making the calls that she eventually tapped on the door and looked inside.

One other thing troubled Grob and Elvis's cousin, Billy Smith. There was definite evidence that someone had telephoned Jim Kirk, a local freelance journalist and stringer for the *National Enquirer*, at least an hour, possibly two, before Elvis was rushed to the Baptist Hospital; the call was made long before the alarm was raised by Ginger.

A week or so after the death, the two of them devised a scheme to try and sort out the exact timing. Grob invited Kirk, and then two staff men from the *Enquirer* to Graceland on the pretext of giving an interview. While Billy Smith hid in a roof space and dangled a microphone to a tape-recorder through the ceiling, Grob chatted to the men and established that someone definitely had called Kirk at least two hours before the time Elvis's body was reported by Ginger Alden. Kirk reckoned he was telephoned by an unidentified caller, a high-pitched voice that could have been a man or a woman, alerting him to stand by for some news from Graceland, big news. It was a fact that Kirk and the *National Enquirer* were well ahead of their rivals by the time the death was announced.

Thus, when Ginger Alden later signed a contract with the *Enquirer*,

---

*Later to be outlined in a synopsis for a book which he had registered for copyright, entitled *The Elvis Conspiracy*.

for which they paid her 35,000 dollars for an interview in the week after the death, there were members of the household who suggested it was she who had telephoned Kirk. Ginger furiously denied ever making the call and though some aspects of her story have been inconsistent over the years – in particular, in recalling exact times of events that morning – on this one part of her story she has remained firm and positive.

Ginger's mother, Jo LaVern Alden, confirmed that her daughter had telephoned her at work around two p.m. She even said that Ginger had told her Elvis was in the bathroom and was going in to check on him. Ginger, she said, called back thirty minutes later, hysterical and crying there was something wrong with Elvis.

Jo LaVern would say later that in the following weeks, she too had a number of conversations with Vernon Presley in which he raised the question of foul play. She said Vernon kept going over possibilities and theories, including one that his son might have been poisoned, that he could have been deliberately injected with an overdose of drugs, and even suggested the possibility of him being given a poison that would not show up in the bloodstream.

A subsidiary matter that Jo LaVern spoke to Vernon about was Elvis's promise that he would clear off the mortgage on her house when she became his mother-in-law. This had not been done by the time of Elvis's death, and she was anxious that the promise should be fulfilled. Vernon replied bluntly that there was nothing he could do; if she wanted to pursue it, she would have to sue the estate. This she did.

Vernon also questioned Ricky Stanley, who should have been on duty in the valet's quarters immediately behind the bathroom. The whole point of a duty aide was to help Elvis if he got into difficulties, as he had in the past, with his breathing or because he could not sleep. There was always speculation about Ricky's state of mind at the time, and whether he was using drugs that had been earmarked for Elvis.

He has made no secret of the fact that at the time he had a drugs problem. It was not until 1989, in an interview with *People* magazine, that Ricky publicly admitted that after delivering Elvis a package of sleeping pills sometime around six-thirty a.m., Ricky took Demerol and 'zonked out' until noon. Elvis had been unable to raise him when he called for another batch of sleeping medication, which was subsequently taken to the house by nurse Tish Henley's husband, and brought to Elvis's room by Aunt Delta Mae.

Rick's recollections were hazy, anyway. His brother David wrote in his book, *Life with Elvis*, that Rick 'had been an emaciated, wild-eyed druggie – a man who would shoot anything into his veins if he could melt it down.' Rick would not have been a good witness, either on his own behalf or for anyone attempting to discover the truth of what happened. He could never be clear about the amount of medication he had supplied to Elvis that morning, nor about the manner in which it was taken – orally or through injections. He has been consistent in one element of his story – that he was out cold at the time Elvis was thought to have died.

David Stanley's recollections of events have also been somewhat varied. Over the years he has given many interviews, appeared on television, and gone on the speakers' circuit, talking to Elvis fan clubs. He was co-author with his mother and brothers of an earlier book, published in 1980, called *Elvis: We Love You Tender*, whose title gives a good indication of the content. He and Ricky also put together an outline for another book in 1985, which suggested that Elvis committed suicide. It was never published.

The following year, David wrote *Life with Elvis*, in which he documented the sheer horror of the declining years of his stepbrother, and wrapped it all in a sugary, semi-religious coating, best summed up by his acknowledgement to 'Elvis Aaron Presley for loving me when no one else seemed to and for allowing me to be part of his life for seventeen years.' In spite of his switch to clean living, he was not averse to revealing sordid details of Elvis's final years.

In the first book, he said he came on duty late on the morning of the sixteenth, bringing a friend named Mark White to the Graceland to play pool. He admitted Mark should not have been in the house. He said that when Lisa Marie came to the door of the pool room and said her daddy was sick, he took his friend to the car and smuggled him off the estate, and then raced back to discover what was going on. He went up to the bedroom via the service stairs and found everyone crowding around Elvis, who was lying on the floor.

The second book went through much the same detail, though made no mention of the friend named Mark, or of delivering him out of the estate grounds before going up to see what was wrong with Elvis. Members of the entourage have often speculated on the identity of this man, and were even more mystified later still when, in 1990, David Stanley claimed that Elvis committed suicide and he had helped to destroy the evidence that pointed to it. He said that during the commotion in the bathroom after Elvis had been discovered, he saw four empty syringes lying on one of the surfaces and put them in his pocket along with a drugs packet. No one other than David Stanley recalled seeing any syringes, other than the two found by the policemen.

But it did at least confirm the theory of the county medical examiner's investigator, Dan Warlick, that a clean-up operation had taken place, but it also raised another somewhat incredible issue – the possibility that Elvis had injected himself four times that morning. Stanley would have known that there should not have been four syringes present. Nurse Tish Henley carefully controlled and monitored the drugs she gave out to Elvis.

The prescriptions were clearly measured into packages, and the three packages that were delivered on the morning of his death would not have included four syringes. And, with Dan Warlick having found two other syringes, that made six in all. The story did not add up. The only way there could have been six used syringes was if someone had brought in more than the prescribed amount.

David Stanley said he had come back to Graceland on the morning of the sixteenth, close to midday, bringing Mark into the house with him. He later spirited him out when the alarm was raised. He was seen driving out of the gates at high speed, and he came back alone. This, Stanley admitted, was the case when he was again interviewed by Albert Goldman for his book, *Elvis: The Last Twenty-four Hours*, in 1991. David said there was nothing sinister in this. He repeated, it was a friend he'd brought back to play pool.

There was talk of some animosity between David Stanley and Elvis, which David has denied. In his book, David describes how he and his wife Angie had separated, and Elvis had intervened as peacemaker. He credited Elvis with trying to bring them back together, but according to Goldman's book, David was convinced Elvis was really 'up to no good' and harboured desires towards Angie himself, just as he had done with his brother Billy's wife some years before.

On the day of Elvis's death, David had just returned from one last vain attempt at reconciliation. Yet, one day after the funeral, Vernon called David aside for a private conversation. Vernon said he was looking for answers, and he talked vaguely about his suspicions that

Elvis might have been murdered. He said that the last thing Elvis had said to him was that he was afraid that David and Ginger were having an affair. David said it was a crazy idea. Even Ginger would have been angered by the suggestion. Vernon led his attack with the allegation of an affair, and followed it up with questions about David's movements that morning. David replied with restrained anger that he could see what was being suggested and he certainly did not kill Elvis. He said it was an outrageous thought.

David Stanley did not stay long in the Presley household after that, moving out to stay with friends. He went on the road, in a haze of drugs, and barely saw Vernon again before he died in June 1979. Rick also cleared out. He went to Florida, where soon he straightened himself out and became an clean-cut, clean-living evangelist.

David took longer to come to terms with life outside that mad, mad world of Graceland. He said that the whole of 1978 was 'wiped out – I missed it because I was zonked out on one thing or another.' He overdosed on drugs and alcohol several times, had spells in hospital, and he described a remarkable incident when he was under the influence of Valium and Quaaludes and had a very public row with a girlfriend in a Memphis street. Another girl came along and screamed at him: 'You lousy jerk! You probably killed Elvis.' Then she slapped him across the face.

David Stanley responded with a right hook to her mouth and left her lying on the pavement. A police car pulled up and he was arrested and thrown into jail, until a friend bailed him out. 'By that time,' he recalled, 'I was at the point where I hated myself. I was a drugged-out drunk with no money whatsoever.' He went from one job to the next, and for a time hit what must have been rock bottom, working as a flunky for an Elvis impersonator. Towards the end of 1979, he finally pulled himself together and followed his brother Rick into evangelism. He became a preacher.

★   ★   ★   ★   ★

So Vernon had questioned almost every member of the household. The possibility of a stranger in the midst had been thoroughly aired, but there were no firm conclusions. Next, he challenged Dr George Nichopoulos, for whom he'd always felt a deep dislike. There was first a question of outstanding debts to be resolved. In 1975, Elvis had lent Nichopoulos 200,000 dollars on a promissory note, and on 1 April 1977 had advanced a further 55,000 dollars at a time when Nichopoulos's medical partnership had run into financial difficulties and the bank had put their medical centre into receivership. The new loan was consolidated with the first loan at seven per cent.

The repayments were to be 1082.85 dollars a month, until 1 February 2002. As executor of Elvis's estate, Vernon wanted first to establish that nothing had changed, and the estate would expect the agreement to be honoured and the repayments to be made promptly and without the need for any reminders. He had never approved of the arrangement in the first place, and by any reckoning it was a strange relationship to have existed between doctor and patient. Vernon's attitude towards Nichopoulos was decidedly cool, and it was this that largely resulted in Vernon's view that doctors in general had been allowing his son far too much leeway in his quest for medication.

There was another outstanding matter concerning Dr Nick, which troubled Vernon. Long before his death, Elvis had been invited to participate in a business plan to develop a chain of racquetball courts. The partners in the venture were all his friends, a real estate developer named Jim McMahon, who had known Elvis for years, Joe Esposito, Elvis's right-hand man, Dr Nichopoulos and Elvis himself. Elvis was to underwrite the project for 1.3 million dollars in exchange for twenty-five per cent of the company, and the courts would all bear his name – the Presley Center Courts.

It would be a terrific investment for the future, he was told, and it would be good for Elvis's name. All was proceeding with the first building when Colonel Tom Parker heard of the deal and flew into a rage. He said Presley was exclusively tied to his promotion and merchandise licensing company formed in 1975, called Boxcar Inc., in which Parker was the majority shareholder. It would be in breach of contract for Elvis to be associated with the racquetball courts, which the colonel thought was a doubtful and under-capitalised scheme, anyway.

Elvis had no alternative but to pull out, even though he had already put up Graceland as security on a million-dollar loan from the National Bank of Commerce in Memphis. The other three partners, Esposito, Nichopoulos and McMahon, were advised by lawyers to sue Elvis, even if it jeopardised their friendship, and subsequently

Elvis received a writ for damages and compliance with the terms of the original contract.

Joe Esposito distanced himself from the project when it all began to fall apart, and Elvis had a major falling out with Jim McMahon and Nichopoulos. McMahon reckoned Elvis had threatened to kill him, which perhaps explained why he was sufficiently worried to carry a revolver in his car.

Meanwhile, the doctor was banned from Graceland for weeks, although he continued to prescribe Elvis's medication through his nurse, Tish Henley. He only returned to the fold when Colonel Parker intervened, worried that without the regime of medication – controversial, though it was – Elvis was in danger of becoming hopelessly uncontrollable.

When Elvis died, his estate became liable for the commitment Elvis had made on the loan to the racquetball project, which was by then in disarray through lack of funding. The development was eventually taken over by another company, although a dozen or more years later, there was still a liability listed in the books of the Presley estate.

Another curious event, one more unexplained happening in this story of mounting curiosities, occurred a month after the funeral. Nichopoulos was at a football game at the Liberty Bowl Memorial stadium, Memphis, with a friend, Dr Charles Langford, a specialist from the Baptist Hospital.

Suddenly, a shot rang out, just as Nichopoulos leaned to one side. Langford, who was sitting behind him, was struck by a bullet in the shoulder. He was not seriously hurt, but Memphis police believed that it could have been an attempt on Nichopoulos's life and immediately put him under guard. The shooting was never resolved, and the police eventually took away the bodyguards and recorded the explanation that it must have been a stray bullet, not intended for Nichopoulos at all.

★   ★   ★   ★   ★

There was an undercurrent of menace and suspicion running through Graceland and all those who had contact with Elvis at the time of his death, either socially or through business ventures. His former business partner, Jim McMahon, made no secret of the fact that he thought there were determined people about, who would stop at nothing to prevent any major investigation into Elvis's death, and when McMahon's friend, television producer Charles Thompson, began doing just that two years later, McMahon was sufficiently concerned to offer him a .357 Magnum stainless-steel pistol, and a box of fifty shells for protection.

The concern that associates of Elvis were showing for their collective safety, the dark rumours of foul play, the intensive questioning of those around Elvis at the time, was in a way self-feeding, but came from a central and very definite presence of fear.

For the most part, this air of menace remained below the surface. The possibility of murder was seldom discussed openly and, when it was, the suggestion was quickly silenced. Fourteen years later, the possibility was revived from a surprising source – Dr Nichopoulos himself, whose theory will be discussed in the final chapter of this book.

Did he make that suggestion to Vernon at the time? Did he ever raise it with the Shelby county medical examiner, Dr Jerry Francisco? Nichopoulos will not say, but was adamant in 1990 that his theory held water.

Standing somewhat aloof from the Graceland swarm was Colonel Tom Parker, whose own activities at the time were sufficient to give Vernon, as executor of Elvis's estate, cause for some sleepless nights as he pondered how far he should go in exploiting the memory of his dead son. Vernon needed income to keep the financially precarious Presley estate running. He was, in short, saddled with a financial mess. Parker came riding to the rescue with deals and plans to make Elvis live on after death. 'Nothing changes,' he told Vernon, and very quickly totted up the wealth of opportunities that now abounded.

Someone had said, out of earshot, to Vernon, that like James Dean, death was the best career move Elvis ever made. Within two weeks of the death, Parker had negotiated a deal with Factors Inc. for exclusive rights to Presley merchandising, which would go into production immediately, with everything from Elvis T-shirt, posters, toiletries, pens – any saleable commodity – from which the estate would receive guaranteed royalties.

There were other highly marketable items, such as a mass of archive film, for example, that the colonel rightly pointed out was now worth a fortune. There would be re-issues of records, albums, and television specials. He made a list of special events, like Elvis festivals and special concerts using film. He even bought up the stock of a Michigan vineyard and produced Elvis wine with a commemorative poem written by himself. The money began to roll in.

Colonel Parker continued to take his very large management slice and RCA Records was saved from virtual bankruptcy by pumping out re-issues and previously unpublished material, with its presses working round the clock to meet the demand. In death, Elvis was worth far more money to everyone than he would have been as the fading, ageing star who had found it increasingly difficult to keep up his last available source of major income, the endless tours.

There were other side-effects to this windfall that did not benefit the estate, such as the book, *Elvis: What Happened?* by Red and Sonny West, which had caused Elvis so much anguish he had threatened to kill them personally. It was a best-seller, and went on to record sales of almost five million copies. Other books and budding authors reached for their ghost writers and began negotiating valuable contracts.

All these aspects arising from his death, all the theories that Vernon had been considering, all the stories and allegations, and even the facts of the FBI involvement, became the smouldering embers of an incomplete, inept, perhaps even stifled, police investigation which ended the night of Elvis's death. Dan Warlick telephoned the police department and said, 'Natural Causes'. The investigation was over before it had begun.

But, if Lieutenant McCachren, or any other detective had stayed on the case for even a month, turned up a few stones and questioned more thoroughly the individuals in this maelstrom of intrigue, he would have surely have assembled sufficient material to provide reasons for continuing. All the ingredients of a classic thriller were present – drugs, sex, money, crime, fraud, Mafia – along with a colourful and varied list of names and motives, which Vernon had turned up by his own limited prodding, and would have amply populated the final scene of an Agatha Christie novel.

The incredible twists and turns, blind alleys and mysteries that had cropped up in the aftermath of the death of Elvis, would have been fascinating enough for any criminologist to examine more closely.

But that wasn't even half of it.

If intrigue and curiosity was the stuff of any police investigation of this sort, nothing could match the covert operations of officialdom now beginning to unfold . . .

14

FBI Swoop

'VICTIM: *Elvis A. Presley (deceased): On October 13, 1977, the facts of this case were presented to a Federal Grand Jury, Western District, Tennessee, Memphis . . . a sealed indictment was returned [listing twenty-one counts] of fraud and deception devised to obtain money and property from Elvis A. Presley; the indictments and warrants for arrest were sealed under order of the US District Judge Robert McRae . . . to be opened only upon application by the United States Attorney to the District Court . . .'*

Memo from FBI Memphis division to
Washington headquarters, 18 October 1977

The FBI was preparing itself for an imminent flurry of activity in the Elvis plane case, and offices and strike forces in several cities had been alerted to stand by for instruction. In fact, this resurgence of activity was one of two crucial events relating to Elvis Presley, which occurred almost simultaneously in Memphis five days later, on 18 October.

First, a medical team led by Dr Jerry Francisco, the county medical examiner, and Dr Eric Muirhead, who had supervised the post-mortem examination at the Baptist Hospital, drove to Graceland to meet Vernon Presley. Full reports on all tests on the samples taken during the autopsy were now to hand and Francisco said it would be necessary to make a once-and-for-all statement to the press.

The intention of the meeting was to explain to Vernon the results of the tests and to tell him, in advance of the press release, what the official verdict of the cause of death would be. Then, a press conference would be called on 21 October at which the still-clamouring world media would be given a extract from the autopsy report, along with a press release. The full forty-four-page autopsy report would remain secret, and sealed from public view for fifty years, and thus the county coroner's file on the death of Elvis Presley would be formally closed.

Meanwhile, there were coincidental stirrings in the FBI and US attorney's offices across the town on that same day – 18 October – in the case of the fraud involving Elvis's Jetstar and the investigation of the international bond fraud. The FBI files relating to these enquiries were silent for the period from the day of Elvis's death until mid-October 1977, when the FBI and the US attorney's office were ready to activate the case and obtain indictments against the men who had allegedly defrauded Elvis.

The files pick up again with a report by the Memphis FBI, with a document whose headings had been changed to reflect Elvis's death:

Victim: Elvis A. Presley, deceased; and Frederick P. Pro, Philip Karl Kitzer, et al ... Captioned case was initially handled on original complaint of being an Interstate Transportation of Stolen Property matter. It has developed into an international fraud matter ...

On October 13, 1977, the facts of this case were presented to a Federal Grand Jury, Western District of Tennessee, Memphis. Following deliberation, a sealed indictment was returned ... the indictment charged that Frederick P. Pro, J. Laurence Wolfson, Raymond Baszner, Gabriel Robert Caggiano, Roy Everett Smith and Philip Karl Kitzer Jr, devised a scheme to defraud and obtain money and property from Elvis A. Presley knowing that all representations made were false. The indictments and all warrants for arrest were sealed under the order of the US District Judge Robert M. McRae, to be opened only upon application by the United States Attorney to the District Court.

The wider implications of the Elvis case continued to be shrouded with the utmost security and confidentiality because of the agents still working undercover. Timing was vital. The indictments accusing the six men, and later a seventh, of an accumulation of twenty-one charges were to remain sealed until 18 October. Philip Kitzer, by then, was also subject to a separate arrest warrant issued by a federal grand jury in Louisville, Kentucky, in connection with the more serious offences of securities fraud, and the first prosecution resulting from the FBI's two-year investigation under the codename Operation Fountain Pen – intertwined as it was in Memphis with the case concerning Elvis's plane – rested upon the successful apprehension of Kitzer, delayed after Elvis's death.

Until he was taken into custody, the indictments from the Memphis grand jury were to remain sealed. None of the other men was to be approached until word was received confirming Kitzer's arrest. It was a carefully planned and timed operation.

Just after four-thirty p.m., on the afternoon of 18 October, Kitzer, who was still travelling with two FBI undercover agents, landed at Miami international airport on a Braniff International Airlines flight from Panama City. Two bureau agents were waiting and arrested him as he cleared customs. The identities of the undercover agents were revealed and Kitzer virtually threw up his hands in admission. At five p.m., an agent of the Miami division of the FBI telephoned the Memphis division and informed them that Kitzer had been arrested. This information was relayed to the district court where assistant US attorney Joe Dycus was waiting to make a formal application to Judge McRae to unseal the indictments charging Kitzer and the other five men with fraud by wire, in connection with Elvis Presley's Jetstar.

The application was successful and the judge ordered the immediate arrest of the remaining suspects. Attorney Joe Dycus handed the approval documents to the Memphis FBI, and instructions were flashed to waiting FBI field offices to move; with the movements of the men having been monitored throughout, the FBI knew of their exact whereabouts and their arrests followed rapidly.

Laurence Wolfson, the man with past Mafia connections, was taken into custody that night from his home in Miami, as was Caggiano, a lawyer living in Boston. Frederick Pro, mastermind of the con trick on Elvis, was also arrested that night at his New York offices, where he ran a securities and bond sales business under the name of Trident Consortium; the two remaining men were picked up in Miami during the following twenty-four hours.

By 20 October, all the men accused in the Elvis Presley fraud case had been arrested. Pro secured his a substantial bail bond of 100,000 dollars in forty-eight hours, and was released. Kitzer remained in custody to be taken by US Marshal to Louisville, Kentucky, where he would appear on charges concerning the securities fraud. It would be months before the cases involving Kitzer and Pro came to court, and all went quiet again. The arrests received comparatively little publicity and there was to be no public mention at all connecting the Elvis case defendants with the international securities fraud.

Coincidence or not, another story on Elvis Presley's death was breaking in Memphis on the very same day that Pro was arrested. It would completely distract media interest from the arrests of Kitzer, Pro and the rest.

    ★   ★   ★   ★   ★

All day on 18 October, when the arrests were being ordered in the district court, speculation had been mounting that some sensational medical news was about to be revealed. It became known that the medical team had met with Vernon Presley and that an announcement was due at a press conference called for 21 October. Leaks filtered through local news channels and on 19 October, major American international news agencies carried stories that tests commissioned by Dr Eric Muirhead, who led the autopsy team at the Baptist Hospital, suggested that Elvis's death resulted from the ingestion of a multiple combination of prescription drugs.

Dr Jerry Francisco had that day filed a death certificate with the state department of health for Elvis; under Tennessee law, death certificates are not available as a public record. Copies are available only to immediate next of kin.

On the morning of 21 October, the Memphis newspaper, *The Commercial Appeal*, carried a story by one of its reporters, Beth Tamke, suggesting that the Baptist Hospital's privately commissioned tests showed traces of multiple drugs in Elvis's body, some at levels considered toxic. Tamke's unnamed sources accurately provided her with a list of the drugs identified in the report compiled at the Bio–Science Laboratory in Van Nuys, California, and the story, published on the day of Dr Jerry Francisco's press conference, caused an explosion of embarrassment and controversy.

The drugs that Bio–Science had identified included several which Elvis was known to take regularly, or which he had taken in the last hours of his life. These included codeine, which was said to be present at ten times the normal therapeutic dose; Quaalude (at near toxic level); Valium; Valmid, bordering on the toxic level; Placidyl; Nembutal (phenobarbitone); Amytal (amylobarbitone); Demerol and other substances which are largely classed as downers. Even in lay terms, the quantity of drugs in Elvis's body was evidently extraordinarily large.

But were they sufficient to kill a man with such a known level of immunity?

Dr Francisco opened his press conference with a preamble about the exhaustive nature of the autopsy and concluded that the cause of death was 'hypertensive heart disease with coronary artery disease as a contributing factor.' In response to questions, he conceded that his own tests had revealed traces of eight prescription drugs, but only four were in significant amounts. The drugs, he said, were not a contributing factor to Presley's death and had they not been there he would still have died.

Francisco's press release expanded further on the drugs element, seemingly aimed at quelling speculation over the Baptist Hospital's tests, privately conducted by the Bio-Science Laboratory: 'All the toxicologists [that Francisco had consulted] agreed that the decision whether these medications played any role in death causation should be left to the forensic pathologist.'

He also made it clear that the autopsy had been conducted privately at the request of Vernon Presley. It was not a criminal investigation. No such investigation had been ordered. It fell to him to base his conclusions on the available evidence. This he had done.

The news reporters, of course, all wanted a copy of the autopsy report so that they could see for themselves. None would be forthcoming. The autopsy report would not be published, said Dr Francisco. It was a family document and would remain private under the laws of the state of Tennessee. Nor would Dr Eric Muirhead, the respected leader of the Baptist team, be drawn further about his agreement – or otherwise – with the conclusions announced by the medical examiner. He ventured to comment only that he had made his own views known to Vernon Presley and he would not reveal what they were.

Two years later, however, one of his assistants, Dr Noel Florendo, said in a television interview that Elvis Presley's heart tissue was examined under an electron microscope and no evidence was found of a heart attack. Florendo said that he and Muirhead agreed – even as Dr Francisco spoke on that morning of 21 October 1977 – that the cause of death was the cumulative effect of the drugs in Elvis's body;

that individually none might have been seen as being present in a sufficient quantity to kill him, but together, as a drugs cocktail, commonly known as polypharmacy, it was.

And so the death of Elvis was plunged further into controversy. Before long, there was renewed talk of a cover-up, as might be expected when the forty-four pages of a properly prepared medical document, outlining the findings of an autopsy on the world's most famous entertainer, is withheld from public view. Added to that was the apparent disagreement between the county medical examiner and the hospital team leader about the exact cause of death.

Then, there were the unknown facts, still pressed firmly and confidentially in the background, about the extent of the FBI investigations. This would never be revealed to contemporary enquirers into Elvis's death, and only began to filter out in the late Eighties as classified FBI documents were released under the Freedom of Information Act (FOI). Only now, in the Nineties, is there a sufficient collection of those documents to indicate that they could have had a very great bearing on any investigation at that time, in the immediate aftermath of the death, if only to eliminate them from any suspicious circumstances that might have been prevailing.

Even as the press and local commentators argued among themselves about the cause of death, the possibility of a cover-up, and the validity of Dr Francisco's ruling that the autopsy report should remain confidential, a far more fundamental question was going unchallenged through ignorance, secrecy and the blanket press coverage afforded to the formal announcement of the autopsy results.

It was this. With all that was going on by the third week of October – embracing Vernon's suspicions of foul play at Graceland, the varying stories of those around him, the question of the drugs Elvis was taking, the knowledge of the drugs found in his body, the apparent disagreement of the medical men as to the cause of death, the arrests for fraud perpetrated against Elvis, and the still-secret international securities fraud investigation which had touched Elvis through no fault of his own – no one in authority in Memphis or elsewhere in the state of Tennessee felt that there was anything sufficiently untoward to institute a full-scale, if belated, investigation into Elvis's death.

Even if there was no suspicion on the part of the FBI that the men under arrest for defrauding Presley might have had anything to do with his death, there was surely a possibility of foul play engineered by any one of the high-profile names in the world of organised crime, who had cropped up in the two-year investigation of the securities fraud; surely there was a possibility that someone, somewhere, might have ordered the assassination of Elvis Presley in an attempt to halt the wider investigation in its tracks. It may have appeared to outsiders a fantastic possibility, but it was by no means a thought that was easily discounted when the full depth of the FBI activities was known. There were those in the FBI elite who believed it was not only possible, but a serious probability.

The FBI administration was already sufficiently concerned about the safety of some of its informants to set up a witness-protection programme and, by the end of 1977, there were nineteen separate divisional field offices of the FBI along with the fraud section of the US Department of Justice to whom all relevant papers of the case were being dispatched as a matter of course. They were classified under the administrative instruction 'immediate', so that all concerned could be kept fully up to date with each new development.

The sheer number of FBI people involved indicated the size of the investigation – still exceedingly active in the dying months of 1977. There is no better way of demonstrating this than taking a look at the destinations of the classified memo headed 'Victim: Elvis A. Presley (deceased)', sent from the FBI at Memphis at that time. Instructions for the circulation of that document requested that it should be wired immediately to the following: The director, Washington, and then to agents in charge at Boston, Chicago, Charlotte, Cleveland, Houston, Indianapolis, Kansas City, Los Angeles, Louisville, Miami, Milwaukee, Minneapolis, Newark, New Haven, New Orleans, New York, Philadelphia, Pittsburgh and Tampa. A note written by hand in Washington added that it should be relayed to agents in London, Berne, Rome, Paris and the Far East.

Back in Memphis that October, these facts were apparently still known only to the FBI and senior people in the US attorney's office. The first-night findings, on which Dr Francisco had speculatively adjudged the cause of death to be a faulty heart beat, had been accepted as sufficient to justify the statement that death was due to natural causes.

By 21 October, nothing had changed, except that Dr Francisco had backed this up with a much more detailed report. As the door on the vault containing the autopsy report slammed shut, and the death certificate was filed away with all due secrecy, Dr Francisco's work was done. As far as he was concerned, the Elvis file was closed. As it transpired, that was wishful thinking.

*   *   *   *   *

Although the events surrounding the death of Elvis were clouded by the controversy of the autopsy, in the absence of any new information, the story took little time to fade temporarily from the headlines. Media pressure failed to shake the resolve of authority to keep the lid firmly on the real story – whatever that story might be – and so other angles were sought. There was no shortage of head-line-grabbing material and the newsmen were able to keep the Elvis saga very much alive by other revelations pouring forth at each new dawn.

Elvis in death had become far more visible than in the latter stages of his life. As always, the past was trawled and old forgotten material, past scandals and intriguing old photographs were recovered from dusty archives, often revealing Elvis in an unfavourable light.

Far from understanding the needs of the true fans, the media largely followed the normal pattern of crucifixion, while conversely the fanzines continued to portray the King on his pedestal, and presented Elvis the performer as a true icon who had, like Dean, been rewarded with immortality. Soon their efforts were submerged by the clamour for profit, with bootleggers and licensed salesmen clawing in cash. There were some very public rows over the rights to Presley merchandise and memorabilia. Writs and lawsuits flourished.

There was also a running commentary on latest developments regarding the estate when it became known that he had willed everything to Lisa Marie, the sole heir and beneficiary. Many writers endeavoured to show that she was at that point one of the richest young ladies in the world. Grandiose figures were being trotted out, with suggestions that she was then worth between twenty and fifty million dollars, worked out on the basis that Elvis had sold five hundred million records in his lifetime, and had made about a million dollars from each of his thirty-one films.

Only Vernon and the president of the Memphis National Bank of Commerce knew that the estate was in real terms worth very little.

The figures were a fantasy, a total misnomer. Unlike many of the world's multi-million-dollar showbiz stars, Elvis had salted nothing away. There were no fortunes in numbered bank accounts in Switzerland or vast investment projects in the world's tax havens. He just plonked huge sums into non-interest-earning bank accounts and spent it, on his personal extravagances and continuous generosity to others. He also paid his taxes, every penny due on every dollar, without attempting to duck the issue – the greatest beneficiary by far from the lifetime earnings of Elvis Presley had been the US Treasury. Millions upon millions had rolled into the IRS coffers without protest, complaint or devious accounting. Elvis just paid up. Period.

So, Lisa Marie's inheritance was not awash with money and Vernon wrestled with the figures with deepening gloom.

There were some considerable liabilities. The estate was still liable for the lease agreement which Elvis and Vernon had signed when Frederick Pro and his cronies gained possession of the Jetstar aircraft. Repayments were running at 16,000 dollars a month and an attorney for the estate went on record as saying to the FBI that the cumulative effect to the estate was a net loss exceeding a million dollars.

The commitment to guarantee the funding of the ill-fated racquetball scheme, Presley Center Courts, still remained, and there were other leasing agreements, taxes and financial nightmares hidden away in the books. The liabilities at the time of death actually outweighed tangible assets.

A valuation of the assets filed by Vernon to the Memphis probate court on 10 November 1977 listed the following: There were three bank accounts at the Bank of Commerce, one a non-interest-bearing chequing account with a credit balance of 1,055,173 dollars, and two savings accounts, one containing 35,000 dollars, and one with just thirty-nine dollars – a mere pittance compared with his earnings. There were eight cars listed, including his Stutz-Blackhawk, a 1955 Cadillac and a 1962 Jeep, two aircrafts, the mansion plus eleven acres of land, sixteen television sets, four horses, a colt and a pony, plus personal jewellery including a gold and diamond Maltese cross pendant containing 236 round diamonds, weighing about twelve carats, suspended by a gold chain. All in all, it wasn't much to show for the world's highest paid entertainer, who had earned a billion dollars in his lifetime.

Worse, the bills were piling up. Graceland alone cost more than

100,000 dollars a year to maintain, and in the first couple of years, the royalties from the merchandise barely matched the outgoings. There was also a far smaller income than was being speculated upon from royalties on the re-released records being sold in their millions around the world, because Elvis and Tom Parker had, as discussed earlier, secretly sold the rights in perpetuity to his record company RCA, to raise money in 1973, in return for a pittance. The final blow came from the IRS, which was requesting statements of income and valuations of property to assess its dues in back taxes and inheritance tax.

The Presley estate teetered on the brink of bankruptcy.

Meanwhile, unlicensed traders in Presley memorabilia, especially in a row of shops opposite Graceland, were generating an enormous amount of money from tacky, appalling excesses of bad taste – with everything from fake copies of the death certificate to phoney bottles of Elvis sweat. And several so-called friends, relatives and employees were already penning their memoirs of Elvis. Even some of his old medication bottles were appearing, having somehow or other reached the outside world. An advertisement in the local paper offered a genuine Elvis Presley pill bottle for 1000 dollars, which seemed to confirm Vernon's theory that some of Elvis's drugs had been sold on the streets.

Even in death, Elvis was still the body upon which a large number of creatures were feeding.

*   *   *   *   *

Vernon wrestled with the legacy virtually on his own, with the help only of a bookkeeper, an accountant and the family attorney. Tom Parker was no real help in the personal matters. His main concern was ensuring the highest possible cash flow from merchandising. No one knew the true worry that confronted Vernon in that winter of 1977 to 1978 when, on top of all else, the prospect of giving evidence at the trial of the men who had defrauded his son over the plane became a reality. He dreaded the thought.

*   *   *   *   *

It seemed he would soon have to come face to face once more with the men whom he had trusted so implicitly in June 1976 to part with large

219

amounts of cash and hand them the keys to Elvis's plane. In the event, he received news that he might not be called – for the time being. Philip Karl Kitzer had negotiated a plea-bargaining deal and intended to enter a plea of guilty to all charges against him.

Frederick Pro, meanwhile, having been granted bail of 100,000 dollars, had now disappeared. He had failed to report to his bail officer and was apparently on the run.

According to the FBI files, his lawyers had earlier discussed a plea-bargaining deal under which Pro would have admitted all charges again him. In the end he declined to co-operate because 'he felt the period of suggested incarceration was too long.'

Since being charged with the Elvis fraud, he had faced a police enquiry regarding dud cheques in Florida, and his business in New York was also being investigated. FBI agents had obtained a search warrant for his apartment and premises, and had taken possession of a small quantity of drugs, a mass of paperwork and more than 10,000 dollars in low-denomination bills. Pro had also been required to attend a district court hearing in February 1978, but had failed to turn up. He had violated his bail conditions by failing to report to the bail-bond office and on 10 February 1978, he was listed as a fugitive from justice. A warrant for his immediate arrest was subsequently flashed to all FBI offices.

As a precautionary measure, the FBI sent an agent to Graceland to inform Vernon Presley in person of the latest development.

Kitzer, in the meantime, was arraigned before the US district court at Louisville, Kentucky, where, as agreed with the local US attorney working with the FBI, he pleaded guilty to two counts of racketeering relating to obtaining credit and cash through fraudulent securities. He was sentenced to ten years' imprisonment.

On 20 April 1978 he was transported under guard to Memphis to appear in the district court on three counts relating to the fraud of Elvis Presley.

Kitzer was sentenced to a further five years on each of the first two charges of fraud, and was given three years' probation on the third. In all, he was sentenced to twenty years, but under the plea-bargaining deal, he was to serve a maximum of ten years on all charges.

Frederick Pro was subsequently arrested in Los Angeles on 18 May and was to be brought back to New York. His lawyers immediately began new plea-bargaining with the US attorney for New York southern district, where he was also required to answer charges. A memorandum circulated to FBI strike forces on 23 August stated that Pro had entered a 'Rule 20' plea, which meant he was admitting all charges against him in Memphis, and asked for them to be dealt with in his admissions to further offences being brought against him in New York.

On 28 September 1978, the US attorney filed charges against Pro in the US district court of New York. They alleged that Frederick P. Pro, together with co-schemers Paul Chevonac, Silas Guthrie, Philip Karl Kitzer, Dorian Mangiamelli, John Packman, Patrick Amiratti, Andrew D'Amto, Robert Moebius, David Friend, John Santiago (also known as Sonny Santini), William Hicks, Grover McConnell and others known and unknown to the US attorney, unlawfully engaged in racketeering activity and schemes to defraud and obtain money and property from numerous victims by false and fraudulent pretences.

The charges also alleged that 'Pro and his co-schemers falsely promised that Trident Consortium could call upon the resources of financial institutions, including Seven Oaks Finance, Kent, England; Silverpool Bank, Denmark; First National Bank of Grenada; First National City Bank of Haiti; and the Mercantile Bank and Trust Company, knowing that each of them was worthless and not capable of providing credit.'

In addition to the charges he faced in Memphis, relating to Elvis's plane, Pro had also been indicted with others on fraud charges filed in the District of Kansas and still further charges in the District of North Carolina. In the plea bargaining deal negotiated with the US Attorney's office in New York, all these charges were transferred under Rule 20 to the jurisdiction of the New York District court to be dealt with at the same time.

The details of his plea bargaining deal were not revealed in the microfiche records made available to me at the New York district court records office. However, it did state without explanation that eleven of the charges against Pro which had been transferred from Memphis had been 'dismissed with the consent of the US Government'. Further, in the same microfiche records relating to the Memphis charges, the name of Elvis Presley was not mentioned. Thus the link between the charges alleging Pro's racketeering activities and his connection with the Elvis Jetstar case had been curiously expunged from public records.

Elvis: The Secret Files

In all, Pro was fined 20,000 dollars, placed on probation for five years and sentenced to 48 months in prison, a term which was later reduced by ten months on application by his lawyers.

Meanwhile, two more of the remaining five defendants involved in the fraud against Elvis had skipped bail and thus the prosecution was stalled until early 1979, when the runaways were re-arrested. Their trial was initially set for August 1979, and witnesses were alerted at the beginning of June, including Vernon Presley and a female secretary who was to be flown from England to give evidence concerning the operations of the company named Seven Oaks Finance, operating from Kent, and of the Bank of England involvement.

History repeated itself. Just as Elvis had died on the eve of a grand jury hearing two years earlier, tragedy struck before the men could be arraigned. With all the pressure of worry from the events which had rained upon him since 16 August 1977, Vernon's health continued to decline. He suffered another heart attack and was admitted to the Baptist Memorial Hospital where he died on 26 June 1979, at the age of sixty-seven.

With the key witness no longer available to testify, the trial of the remaining men in the Elvis plane case was postponed. In the event, it would be almost three more years before they finally came to trial.

By then, the FBI's Operation Fountain Pen investigation had resulted in many arrests throughout the country. As bureau agents repeatedly noted in their reports, the investigation was hampered by the 'hostile' attitude of many of those interviewed. Some victim banks even refused to press charges for fear of potential damaging publicity. The investigation slowly petered out and, although the securities scam had, by the FBI's own admission, netted billions of dollars worldwide there were no spectacular arrests among the fifty or so men and women eventually taken into custody and charged with racketeering.

The FBI had sought from the outset to keep its involvement with Elvis Presley at the lowest possible profile. This they had achieved most resolutely, and it is only now possible to gauge that throughout the year before and two years after Elvis's death, FBI activity flourished, providing a dark and largely secret backdrop to the events which materialised at Graceland.

The saga had still not ended . . .

15

Enter Geraldo

'[*Elvis's death*] *had been surrounded by mystery and contradiction ... it became apparent to me that there had been a cover-up, generally approved by the county government and others concerned ... it is apparent that there was collusion hiding the facts by the county examiner, the county attorney-general and the county coroner and I resent this very much.*'
Dr Vasco Smith, Memphis politician, 1979

Bold as brass and to the point, Dr Vasco Smith, a Memphis dental practitioner, civil rights leader and a member of local government, was among the first to publicly question the possibility that Elvis had been laid to rest in undue haste, and it took a ratings war between two rival American television news magazine programmes to give an airing to this assault on the secrecy surrounding Elvis's death. It had remained pretty well unchallenged for almost two years. After the first flourish, there had been no questions asked.

Initially, the motives behind this attack by television on the Elvis story were not a lot better than the commercialism surrounding the Elvis legend that had pervaded Memphis since August 1977. ABC had launched their '20/20' programme in 1978 in answer to the established CBS '60 Minutes', and to survive in a prime-time slot, it needed a succession of strong, high-profile topics to keep up its ratings. In the summer of 1979, the future of '20/20' remained uncertain in spite of the success of a recent investigation by one of its most agile young reporters, Geraldo Rivera, on the last days of Howard Hughes. Rivera discovered that Hughes had been addicted to drugs and under the control of his staff before he died. Ratings for the show soared and inspired by this success, Rivera began to examine other possibilities that fell into the same category of famous names whose deaths contained elements of suspicion, intrigue and scandal. Elvis Presley was nominated as the star candidate.

Rivera, a former policeman and law student, is a slightly built man with an imposing personality; a journalistic ferret. At the time, he was a smart man about town, with fashionable long hair and a moustache. He made a point of touting his Hispanic-Jewish background, and was fast making a name for himself. In this, he succeeded, going on to become one of America's top-rated talk-show hosts, continuing to deal in controversial subjects.

In 1979, he was no stranger to controversy. His stories often became headlines through his own involvement and tactics. He once broke into a state-run mental institution with a cameraman to expose a major scandal – a regime which administered appalling conditions and cruelty. Publicity followed him around, as did criticism of his often unorthodox methods.

After an editorial conference at the beginning of July 1979, the '20/20' editors gave the go-ahead for what promised to be an extensive investigation, and one with a degree of urgency, because it was planned to air at least part of the story to coincide with the anniversary of Presley's death. Among the production team was Charles Thompson, a Memphis-born journalist, who had begun his career with the Memphis *Commercial Appeal*. He contacted his brother-in-law and fellow journalist James Cole, another former *Commercial Appeal* reporter, then working freelance in Memphis. Together they began the groundwork in advance of Rivera's own arrival with a camera crew.

Both the Memphis men knew well that they would probably face a hostile reception. Few in Memphis would want to contribute to anything that attacked Elvis's reputation. The television biopics that had been produced so far had mainly drawn on the rather schmaltzy recollections of those who could boast they knew him, but who offered little other than well-worn stories. As in life, Elvis remained in death the prime commercial attraction for the city. Tourists, fans, pilgrims, journalists, writers and souvenir-seekers came in droves. Elvis dominated the city, and still does.

There were other reasons which convinced Rivera and his team that there was much more to the story than had yet been published. Among the early interviews conducted on camera was one with Dr

Vasco Smith, who came straight out with words that were music to the ears of any conspiracy theorist. Smith said that it had long ago been apparent to him that there had been collusion to hide the truth about Elvis's death. He believed that the facts had been suppressed. Rivera wheeled out a couple of other local politicians in front of the camera to voice similar views.

Thompson, Cole and Rivera were hearing similar words of disquiet – usually off the record – at almost every turn, and as they began the task of ploughing through dusty local archive sources and going through their list of interview subjects, the hostility they had anticipated proved to be present. It was during this period of the investigation that Elvis's friend and former business partner, Jim McMahon, offered Thompson a .357 Magnum, and told him it was for his own protection, as there were people who did not want the truth to come out.

The television men received decent co-operation from the Presley entourage. Ginger Alden, David Stanley and others all contributed their recollections of events leading up to Elvis's death but their stories barely varied from the way they had been peddled a thousand times before.

Furthermore, there was virtually no enlightenment gleaned from officialdom. Dr Jerry Francisco would say nothing more than he had said at the time of the press conference in 1977, that Elvis had died of natural causes. The local police had no file on the death which could be made public. The district attorney's office blandly said they had not been involved in any aspects relating to Elvis's death and Elvis's physician, Dr Nichopoulos, was guarded and monosyllabic in his explanations for Elvis's drug intake, stating that patient confidentiality precluded him from being more specific.

What Rivera needed more than anything was evidence of some hidden facts that could throw new light on their task. There was simply no point in repeating all those stories – which came out with the book by Red and Sonny West – of Elvis's eccentric behaviour and his passion for prescription chemicals. That was already an established and pretty well irrefutable fact.

The idea of airing the '20/20' show on the anniversary of Elvis's death was scrapped and a new date was set for the autumn. The investigation became far more complex than they had ever imagined. There were new leads to be followed, concerning Elvis's drug connections and suppliers, predominantly in Memphis and Las Vegas. They had unearthed evidence of a huge number of prescriptions written for Elvis, many in fictitious names. The core of the '20/20' exposé now centred on the amount of drugs in Elvis's body on the day he died. Rivera was more convinced than ever that therein lay the story.

Thompson and Cole had already unearthed the pirated version of the Bio-Science report – which was partly revealed in the *Commercial Appeal* on the morning of Francisco's press conference on 21 October 1977 – that listed traces of all the substances found in the analysis of Elvis's body tissues. Armed with testimony from medical experts who were prepared to go on-camera with the view that Elvis died from a drugs-related death, the '20/20' team began to pursue the drugs aspect as the basis for the programme. What they needed then was a copy of the autopsy report conducted at the Baptist Memorial Hospital to ascertain how the medical team had officially accounted for this discovery in the eventual adjudication of the cause of death.

An official request for a copy was formally refused at every point of call, and so Thompson and Cole put their names to a lawsuit, attempting to force the county medical examiner's office to grant them access to the report on the grounds that it was a matter of public record. But, if they had hopes that they would get a ruling in time to include it in the television programme now under preparation, they were to be sorely disappointed.

The case dragged on for months with banks of lawyers on both sides taking depositions and statements from all concerned. When it finally got to court, there were legal arguments which required separate deliberation. The estate of Elvis Presley, by then under new management following the death of Vernon, let it be known through its lawyers that it would not support the autopsy report being made public.

By the time the case came to court, Geraldo Rivera and '20/20' had long ago moved on to pastures new. Thompson and Cole persevered in vain – the verdict was delayed until February 1981. The court ruled against releasing the report. The case went to appeal at the Tennessee Supreme Court, and the verdict was upheld. The forty-four-page medical report must remain secret. And, apart from piecemeal leaks, that report has to this day remained unavailable for public scrutiny.

★　　★　　★　　★　　★

Back in the autumn of 1979, however, the '20/20' team was still hopeful of achieving its release. The first part of the Elvis story was screened in September, entitled 'The Elvis Cover-up', and basically recreated the night of Elvis's death through witness accounts. It went on to discuss the suppression of the autopsy report and the lack of any kind of investigation. Medical experts were lined up to challenge the conclusion that death was by natural causes and the whole scenario surrounding Elvis's death suddenly had renewed significance. Dr Francisco went on television the following day, angrily denying a cover-up, and reiterated once again that Elvis's death was due to heart disease, and there were *no* contributing factors.

What no one had discussed or even hinted at were the other confidential aspects of FBI involvement. The fraud on Presley had become public knowledge, but was still sub-judice, because five of the men charged had yet to be brought to trial. No link between the international securities fraud and the Elvis case had leaked into the public domain. There was simply no knowledge of it outside of the FBI and the only other man to be aware of the implications – Vernon Presley – was now dead. Certainly Rivera's team had no way of getting to these facts because the first of the archive documents did not begin to filter through the FBI declassification system until the mid-Eighties.

There was one more startling development to occur as Rivera stirred up the hornets' nest and Charles Thompson was offered a pistol by McMahon for protection. As they prepared the first instalment of 'The Elvis Cover-up' for screening, a complaint was filed with the Tennessee board of medical examiners in Nashville, charging Dr Nichopoulos with unprofessional, dishonourable or unethical conduct, gross incompetence and malpractice.

The accusations tabled by the state claimed that he had over-prescribed pharmaceutical drugs to fifteen named individuals. They included Elvis himself, another of Memphis's most famous singers, Jerry Lee Lewis, and Nichopoulos's own daughter, Chrissy. The charges resulted from a cursory audit of the previous six months of prescriptions found to have been written by the doctor, which showed that he had issued Elvis with more than 5000 assorted pills, uppers and downers, including a substantial quantity of narcotic drugs: barbiturates, Quaaludes and Demerol. The prescription search was still proceeding through the months previous to the broadcast to discover the sum total of all medication prescribed to Elvis by the Memphis doctor in the previous eighteen months.

Nichopoulos denied everything. He said he had prescribed drugs which he knew were used by the whole entourage. As far as Elvis was concerned, he had been pursuing a programme of reducing his intake by substituting placebos and sugar pills for the real thing.

He claimed he was being made a scapegoat.

This story of the state action against the doctor broke two days before Rivera's investigation was aired on 13 September 1979, and naturally heightened the interest in the television show. Rivera denied he had leaked the information to send up the ratings on which the future of '20/20' rather depended. The hour-long programme opened with strong criticism of the Memphis officialdom. It was a no-holds-barred assertion that for whatever reason or motive, no real effort was ever truly made to unearth the circumstances of Elvis Presley's death. It was as if the city of Memphis did not care to know the truth.

Rivera attacked the secrecy surrounding the autopsy report which the '20/20' team was attempting to get published. 'We believe there has been a cover-up,' he said. Much was made of the alleged disagreement by members of the Baptist medical team, with Dr Francisco's pronouncement that death was due to heart problems. He brought one of the team, Dr Noel Florendo, on camera to state that there was no evidence that Elvis had suffered a heart attack. His view was that his death was related to drugs.

The focus switched to Elvis's addiction to uppers and downers. Rivera produced the report of the Bio-Science Laboratory, detailing the number of drugs in Elvis's body. Members of the entourage went through their set pieces, describing the last days of his life. Elvis's old friend, retired cop John O'Grady, blamed doctors in Memphis and Las Vegas for the uncontrolled access Elvis had to all kinds of chemicals. Rivera developed the theme they had set out to prove on evidence available in that year of 1979: it was drugs that killed Elvis and not a heart condition.

The stark, often shocking, documentary, watched by seventeen million viewers, put the whole question of the death back into the spotlight, but still no new enquiry was launched, other than that involving of the question of Dr Nichopoulos's medical ethics.

Dr Francisco himself, meantime, had called his own press conference to answer the allegations in the '20/20' programme. He challenged the programme's credibility and said he had never been involved in a cover-up. He attacked the qualifications of the medical experts called upon by the television reporters to speculate on the cause of death, and said he heard nothing that would cause him to alter his opinion: 'Presley died of heart disease and drugs did not cause or contribute to his death.'

It was a sudden death, he said, and this was supported by the way Elvis was found in the bathroom, in an awkward position. Victims of drug deaths were normally found in a 'position of comfort'. If he had taken all of the drugs mentioned at one time, then that might have been sufficient to cause death. But he had not, and a fatal toxic level was not reached.

Asked by reporters whether the investigation of Dr Nichopoulos affected his findings, he insisted there was no medical evidence to support a conclusion of criminal homicide on the part of Nichopoulos.

And so, while the '20/20' broadcast had outlined a powerful case, showing that the Elvis death scene had been carefully cleaned up, there were unexplained happenings – everything pointed to a rush by all concerned to get Elvis buried and out of the way with the minimum of fuss. In the final analysis, no positively conclusive evidence could be offered to prove that Elvis had died of drugs, foul means or – as Albert Goldman was to suggest later – that he committed suicide. It is only possible to speculate now on what effect the knowledge of Mafia personalities lurking in the background might have had on the debate at that time.

Much rested upon the possibility of new evidence emerging during the investigation of Dr Nichopoulos. In the meantime, '20/20' aired a second instalment of 'The Elvis Cover-up' in December, concentrating on the comments from medical experts in an attempt to prove that Elvis died of drugs; they concentrated on a key new fact that Elvis Presley's name had appeared on 196 prescriptions filled in Memphis pharmacies in the previous twelve months, for the supply of over 12,000 pills.

These astounding figures were confirmed when the civil case against Nichopoulos was being prepared for hearing by the Tennessee board of medical examiners. Towards the end of December

Nichopoulos spent three days giving a sworn statement before lawyers for the board; this deposition can now be seen as the source of new and most revealing facts about the life of Elvis – but not his death.

Now, for the first time, the full horror of Elvis's drug problem was to be revealed out of the confines of doctor-patient confidentiality.

Leafing through these depositions today, it's obvious that the doctor did not deny the amounts of pills given in the prescriptions of the previous twelve months before the death, but said they were not intended for Elvis alone.

He named several members of the Presley entourage who regularly took uppers and downers as relief from the life they had to lead, especially while on tour. He recounted how he prepared packets of drugs which were to be given to Elvis four times a day by his duty valets, and how these pills and injections were supervised by the resident nurse. This had been done because Elvis was quite capable of taking large quantities of barbiturates, handfuls, before going to bed. He was virtually incapable of sleep without sedatives.

He tried to control the intake. He told of the placebos and sugar pills that were often substituted for the real thing and admitted that he was unable to control drugs coming in from other sources, identifying a Las Vegas doctor as one of those who regularly prescribed for Elvis.

He told how Elvis's drug problems were exacerbated in 1973 after he had been treated by a doctor in California for a strained back. 'He was given multiple injections of Novocaine, Demerol and steroids,' said Nichopoulos. 'When he came back to Memphis, he was addicted to Demerol. The drugs almost killed him.' He was admitted to the Baptist hospital for detoxification.

This desperate period of addiction was confirmed later by the evidence of another Memphis doctor, Lawrence Wruble, the specialist gastro-enterologist who recalled that he treated Elvis in 1973 after he had taken injections of massive amounts of cortisone to the extent that he had no control over his bladder functions. Elvis agreed to undertake counselling.

Occasionally, after that, Nichopoulos would try to reduce his intake by putting him into a sleep clinic for three days, or by keeping him awake for a similar period. All had limited effect, and eventually Elvis would revert back to his old habits. He was undoubtedly dependent on pills to make him sleep, said the doctor, but he did not think Elvis was hooked on amphetamines.

As the sheer extent of the consumption of chemicals now became obvious, one other revelation caused astonishment among the lawyers listening to Nichopoulos's deposition.

Elvis, said Nichopoulos, was psychologically dependent on a drug which he had sent in packages from Sweden. It was not a physical dependency because the concoction was merely a mixture of herbs. It was supposed to achieve inner cleanliness and Elvis felt that by taking it, he would not need to take a bath. He never liked to bathe at the best of times, said the doctor and he assumed that by taking these pills, he could do without one altogether.

Nichopoulos was finally brought before the medical board amid much media attention on 14 January 1980 for a five-day hearing in the large chamber of Memphis City Council, where every one of the 420 seats was taken by those involved in the case, media reporters and spectators.

As in a criminal hearing, the state produced its evidence to support their charges against the doctor, and the defence countered with its own witnesses. Presley was only one of sixteen patients named in the charges accusing Nichopoulos of over-prescribing, but naturally the great attention was fixed upon his medical history. The county medical examiner also found unexpected support for his own long-held and persistently repeated view that Elvis did not die a drug-related death. The same theme was, not unexpectedly, pursued by Nichopoulos's defence.

The state brought in more than a dozen former patients who testified to the amount of drugs prescribed to them by Nichopoulos. They produced medical specialists who would state that the amounts were excessive and often 'inappropriate' while the defence wheeled in other experts with similar qualifications to support their client and state otherwise.

Nichopoulos himself was largely being portrayed by his patients as a kindly, caring community doctor and when he came to the stand, to explain his actions – the dosages he had prescribed to Presley – he repeated the main thrust of his defence. Though he had prescribed large amounts of drugs to patients, which he admitted, his underlying intention was to achieve a therapeutic reduction. His defence also called Tish Henley, the resident nurse, who told how she tried to sidetrack drugs coming into Graceland from outside sources so that as far as possible Elvis could be kept to the regime prescribed by Nichopoulos.

Billy Smith, Elvis's cousin, who was among the last to see him alive after drying his hair following the racquetball game, on the morning of the death, once again confirmed that Elvis was in good spirits and very alert. There was nothing in his manner that was unusual. And among the final defence witnesses called was Jerry Francisco, repeating for the umpteenth time that drugs were not a contributing factor.

Lawyers squabbled loudly over whether the key issue in the case, the autopsy report, could be brought into evidence, and Nichopoulos's attorney angrily postured that his client was virtually being accused of murdering Elvis Presley.

Lawyers argued the importance of having the report available so that Dr Eric Muirhead, the leader of the pathology team, could be called to give evidence and be questioned upon the contents of the report. It was to no avail. If the report was made public, Muirhead might face contempt of court proceedings and possibly a lawsuit from the Presley estate.

Thus the autopsy report was not produced, and remained secret.

With all evidence and submissions heard, the board of medical examiners considered its verdict and, finally, Nichopoulos stood white-faced before the panel to discover his fate. Dr Howard Foreman, the board's secretary from Nashville, said he did not believe from the evidence that Dr Nichopoulos was a bad doctor nor had he been negligent in the care of his patients, adding that his primary complaint in the Presley case was the way the drugs had been handled. There were absolutely no records kept, he said.

The panel therefore found the doctor not guilty of charges of unprofessional, dishonourable or unethical conduct, and not guilty of gross incompetence.

He was found guilty on ten charges of illegally over-prescribing addictive drugs to nine patients and himself. Dr Howard said it was inexcusable that Nichopoulos prescribed addictive narcotic drugs to anyone who happened to call in. The panel agreed that a period of suspension was required to give the doctor time to reflect upon his past mistakes. They ruled against the prosecution's call for his licence to be revoked and ordered him to be suspended from the medical register for three months, to be followed by a period of three years' probation.

Nichopoulos, drawn and haggard after weeks of media pressure and meetings with his lawyers, breathed a sigh of relief. Suspension was bad, but the verdict could have been worse. In fact, worse was to follow.

★ ★ ★ ★ ★

Throughout much of the hearing sat Larry Hutchinson, chief investigator for Hugh Stanton, Jr, district attorney-general. Ostensibly, Hutchinson had been co-ordinating the security arrangements for the case, marshalling a joint force of sheriff's deputies and local police. There had been a bomb scare at the start of the hearing when an alert was given that a bomb had been planted in the council chamber. There were anonymous threats against others involved in the hearing on both sides, and the Rivera team had also attracted a following of angry fans not wishing to have the name of their idol dragged further through the mire.

But there was another reason why Hutchinson remained on hand, observing the witnesses and noting the evidence. Stanton had just authorised him to take charge of the one and only criminal investigation ever to arise out of the death of Presley. For months, Hutchinson had been straining at the leash to take a look at the case.

It intrigued him beyond measure, although when he was finally given the go-ahead, the brief for his investigation would not include a detailed look at the circumstances of the death. That would merely be an incidental aspect, which Hutchinson would not be required to probe. Indeed, Elvis was not even to be the prime subject of the enquiry.

The brief that his team was set related simply to Dr Nichopoulos, to make a closer examination of the doctor's activities in the preceding years, following his appearance before the board of medical examiners, with a view to indicting him on criminal charges for over-prescribing drugs to patients, which included Elvis Presley, in the area of jurisdiction covered by the Memphis district attorney.

Hutchinson was charged with the mammoth task of sifting through millions of medical prescriptions filled in the Memphis area from as far back as 1975. He assembled a team of detectives drawn

233

from the Shelby county narcotics squad, the federal Drug Enforcement Administration (DEA), the Tennessee Bureau of Identification, plus a deputy and two secretaries from the district attorney's office. Meanwhile, the attorney-general Hugh Stanton, Jr, announced to the press that he was launching a criminal investigation into Nichopoulos with a view to pursuing a prosecution for medical malpractice. No further investigation into Elvis's death was planned and he reiterated what he had said earlier, that he was not prepared to go against the findings of the county medical examiner.

Larry Hutchinson, a tall, laconic and thick-set man, known for his dogged determination and old-fashioned approach to detective work, would follow the rule book to the letter. In his own mind, he was already planning to sink a good deal more effort into the Elvis-related aspects of the case, perhaps more than some would have wished. Before long, as he began to turn up a few stones, issuing subpoenas to some of the central figures in the Elvis affair, and prodding around among the murkier aspects of the Memphis drugs scene, there was talk that a contract had been taken out on his life.

16

The Hutchinson Tapes

*'Larry . . . we've received an anonymous call on the 'Crime Stoppers' hotline
. . . it was a woman. She claims that a group of people have put up 50,000
dollars to hire a hitman from Houston, Texas, to take you out. It looks like
you've struck a nerve somewhere . . . you'd better take care.'*
Police warning to investigator Larry Hutchinson, 1980

Larry Hutchinson took the call from a Memphis police officer one
Sunday afternoon as he was nearing the end of a long stint of leg work,
pulling together his evidence for the trial of Dr Nichopoulos. Later he
went to the 'Crime Stoppers' unit to listen to a recording of the
woman's voice, detailing the possible threat on his life. He now had
sufficient knowledge of all that was going on in the background of the
Elvis case to know that he could not dismiss it as one more crank.
Hutchinson took it seriously enough to ensure all the necessary
precautions were undertaken, like examining his car every morning,
keeping a close watch on his family, and always checking his gun.

The investigations had been wide ranging, but always within the
brief of formulating evidence against the doctor. This meant, by and
large, that his questioning should be restricted to the drugs aspects.
No other areas of Elvis's life would be considered relevant or
admissible at the trial.

When I contacted him in 1992, Larry Hutchinson was retired from
his job as chief investigator for the state attorney's office in Memphis.
He remembers the Nichopoulos investigation as if it were yesterday,
but he said he had absolutely no knowledge of any other enquiries
being conducted in and around Memphis by the FBI, either then or in
the preceding years. Not a word of it had crossed over to his

department. He remembered there was a court case involving Elvis's Jetstar, but he was unaware of the background of the greater investigative activity being conducted by FBI agents all over the country. I read out a few pages of documents retrieved from the FBI under the Freedom of Information Act. It came as a complete surprise to him.

Wasn't it curious, I asked, that the chief investigator for the attorney-general, who was then in charge of a multiple force of federal and local police probing the supply of drugs to Elvis, among others, should not be appraised of this FBI background? Hutchinson was not enormously surprised by the secrecy; the federal and local police worked totally independently.

There was only a crossover of information when both were involved and clearly, in this case, they were not. And so the link between Elvis and the international securities fraud was kept from the most senior man at local level charged with a grassroots enquiry. In spite of that, there could well have been connections, particularly in unearthing possible motives for Elvis's death if foul play was ever suspected.

Foul play did not officially come within Hutchinson's area of enquiry. He was charged solely with discovering the facts on Nichopoulos and his prescriptions. His combined team of detectives had a daunting task, for the enquiries related not only to Presley, but to nine other patients of Nichopoulos, including Jerry Lee Lewis. A simple statistic puts their project into perspective: they were faced with checking the details of 6,570,175 prescriptions written and filled in the Memphis area during the past three years. It took more than 1000 man hours alone to complete this section of the investigation. There would be thousands of other sheets of documentary evidence, including bank accounts, cancelled cheques, medical notes from hospital records, and literally any other avenue of recorded data that might throw up information.

From this mass of documents, Hutchinson and his team were able to ascertain exactly what Dr Nichopoulos had prescribed to Elvis in a year-by-year breakdown, which provided a general list of the number of pills issued:

1975: 1296 amphetamines; 1891 sedatives; 910 narcotics.

1976: 2372 amphetamines; 2680 sedatives; 1059 narcotics.

1977: (to 17 August) 1790 amphetamines; 4996 sedatives; 2019 narcotics.

This did not include drugs which came from other sources, since the investigators had no authority outside the state of Tennessee; therefore it was impossible to check what supplies came in from Las Vegas, Los Angeles and elsewhere. Nor could it reflect the fact that, as Hutchinson discovered when he began his interviews, several members of the entourage were aware that drugs had been prescribed in their names – even, on one case, one of their children's names – which were in truth destined for Elvis himself.

Hutchinson and his deputy, David McGriff, armed with this inventory and the authority to issue subpoenas to force witnesses into court if necessary, roamed through the recollections of their inter- viewees with the incisive questioning of psychologists; everything they said was recorded on tape.

In my effort to establish the chronological development of events, as they occurred in the years immediately after Elvis's death, Hutchinson agreed to assist with my research. At my request, he personally went into the old files relating to the investigation he began into the activities of Dr Nichopoulos in 1980, after the doctor had been suspended from practice by the medical board. The material he selected had lain in the archives gathering dust for almost twelve years, and along with his documentation and files compiled at the time were many tape-recordings of subjects he interviewed as potential witnesses.

They included several who held vital information regarding the life and times of Elvis, but who have been invariably inaccessible to the media and have seldom made any public statements. These were specially valid because they were made to a determined questioner, a man appointed by the state to conduct the enquiry, backed up by the binding powers of the legal machinery.

Hutchinson, by interviewing one after the other, was also able to assess the reliability of their stories. However, because of the number of witnesses in the case – which did not, it must be remembered, concentrate solely on Presley's case – many of those interviewed by Hutchinson were never called to give evidence to either the grand jury or the district court at Nichopoulos's eventual trial. Thus the contents of the tapes never came into public hearing.

With permission from the current attorney-general for Memphis, Hutchinson copied all of the tapes relevant to this story and these are now in my possession. They constitute a historic record of events in the last five years of Elvis's life and I have filtered much of the information contained within them as background into previous chapters. However, there were some specific points remaining which are worthy of record, and especially poignant is the reaction Hutchinson received from some of Elvis's most long-standing employees.

He quickly discovered that unlike some of Elvis's so-called friends and relatives who had told and sold all in the media for a quick buck, some were perhaps understandably reluctant to say a word against him, or even against Dr Nick, for that matter. Even more importantly, not all of them were even prepared to admit that Elvis was addicted to chemicals.

Joe Esposito, for example, told Hutchinson quite bluntly, 'He had a problem, we knew that. I still can't say he was addicted. I've seen addicts and they can't go a day without it. The stuff that was prescribed for him when we were on the road, other members of the entourage were taking. The Stanley boys took a lot. Most people needed sleeping pills.'

Hutchinson did not accept that explanation. 'Elvis wasn't addicted? Hey, Joe, even the coroner has testified that he was addicted to drugs.'

Esposito weakened, 'OK, OK, I know what you're saying. OK, I knew Elvis had a drug problem. I knew it in the last year of his life . . . but there was nothing I could do about it.'

Hutchinson pressed him further. Why hadn't he spoken out?

Esposito answered quietly, 'I don't like to talk about Elvis. It's a personal thing. When he died I made a statement to myself that I would never talk about him, I would never ever say anything about Elvis. I have never talked to anyone about Elvis, never said anything bad about him for any reason. It's a personal thing. This is the first time anyone has got anything out of me about Elvis and no one will again.'

Hutchinson questioned Esposito about his friendship with Nichopoulos. Hadn't they been good friends?

'Sure,' recalled Esposito. ' I was pretty close to Dr Nick at one time. We entered a partnership together in the racquet club with Elvis and Jim McMahon. We'd all been interested in it and there was no facility in Memphis so that's how it all started. We raised the money to build two courts. Then, Beecher Smith, Elvis's lawyer, told Elvis it was a bad deal. Elvis backed out and it all went wrong. I lost about thirty thousand dollars. Dr Nick put up about fifty thousand dollars. McMahon, he didn't put much in. I learned a lesson there, not to trust people.'

Hutchinson wanted more details about the relationship between himself and Elvis.

Hutchinson: 'You're a lawyer, friend of Elvis Presley, and you cared a lot about Elvis Presley, right?'

Esposito: 'Yes.'

Elvis, he said, had looked after him well and he had reciprocated. When Elvis died, Joe was earning 45,000 dollars a year and received bonuses of around 60,000 dollars. Elvis bought him cars and jewellery. He had always been very generous.

Hutchinson: 'So your concern was Elvis Presley? And you were more or less in charge of finances? Did you ever know or did you ever take the opportunity to look at the bills that were coming to the mansion from pharmacies?'

'No, I was never allowed to.'

'Did you ever hear of a concern being expressed that the medical bills were getting out of hand?'

'They never told me about it. Any bills like that went straight to the office and Vernon handled all those. He never discussed them with me.'

'You knew that Dr George C. Nichopoulos had borrowed 200,000 dollars from Elvis for his house, to be repaid over a period of years?'

'Yes, I knew that.'

'Did you also know that Dr George Nichopoulos borrowed 75,000 dollars in personal loans from Elvis Presley?'

'No, I didn't know.'

'Did you also know that Elvis Presley paid for the services of Dr Nichopoulos while he was on tour with Elvis a salary of 76,108 dollars, paid to him personally by cheque, in his name?'

'Personally, to him? No, I didn't.'

'Or that also for professional services, the [Nichopoulos's] medical group was paid 147,319.17 dollars for professional services? Did you know that, sir?'

'No, I didn't.'

Hutchinson closed the tape on Esposito and the way in which it ended suggested he had, at the end of the day, been dissatisfied with

Esposito's responses. There was a feeling coming across that he expected more, because he knew of Esposito's closeness to Elvis from previous taped interviews, and was aware that no aide knew Elvis better.

Similarly Charlie Hodge refused to state that effectively Elvis was a junkie:

Elvis often needed painkillers after his act. As everyone knows, he could be very physical in his performance, with his karate stunts and so on, and he genuinely used to pull a muscle or damage himself. Actually, Elvis had a high pain tolerance. When they discovered he had an eye condition called glaucoma I went with him to see the doctor. He said it was so bad that he needed to give him a shot right there, but there was no anaesthetist available. So Elvis said 'Do it'. He grabbed the side of the chair and the doctor just gave him a shot right in the white of the eye. It came up like a tennis ball.

Hutchinson wanted to know about the drugs available on tours. Who took them?

Hodge recalls:

David [Stanley] would take some things and become violent. Sonny West took painkillers. Red West used to take uppers when he was writing songs. None of the rest of the guys had a drug problem to the best of my knowledge, although any of us could go to Dr Nick if we needed treatment for an ailment, such as flu or whatever. Dr Nick carried a variety of medication to treat everyone. Elvis told him to put them all in his name and send the bill to his daddy. There were between eighty and 100 people on tour. If someone came to him and they had a legitimate reason, he would give them something, like me – I had back problems and he gave me some shots.

Hutchinson: 'You were close to Elvis?'
Hodge: 'He was my best friend.'
'And he bestowed a great deal of gifts and presents upon you?'
'Yes, he did. And to everyone else.'
'He gave you jewellery, cars, a good salary. A pretty good salary?'
'Yes, I was making 750 dollars a week, plus bonuses. Forty thousand dollars a year.'

'Also the fringe benefits of lodgings and meals.'
'Yes.'
'Did he give you money?'
'The largest amount was 7500 dollars.'
'You loved Elvis?'
'Yes.'
'You wouldn't do anything to hurt his image?'
'No, I don't want to see anyone hurt.'
'And you wouldn't say anything that was degrading?'
'No, and I also wouldn't lie.'
'You were in partnership with Dick Grob?'
'Yes.'
'He was the security chief, what kind of partnership?'

Hodge hesitated before answering. 'After his death I was doing Elvis conventions and they'd want me to appear. And they would want me to supply photographs. So Dick copyrighted some photographs which we sold to the fans. I would walk around and meet fans. I got paid for making an appearance.'

★ ★ ★ ★ ★

Of the remaining members of the entourage, James Caughley was among the most explicit in his observations. But he was a little too eager for Hutchinson's liking. During the interview, he was racing on ahead, and relating stories that really were not relevant to the case under investigation. He wanted to tell about the time in Palm Springs, in 1972, when they almost lost a poor girl who was in bed with Elvis, drinking narcotic cough syrup. The girl was in a coma but they managed to slap Elvis back from oblivion. When everyone finally agreed that they would have to call an ambulance and have her removed to hospital, she was carried into Charlie Hodge's bedroom. He had agreed to take the blame if the girl died. Each member of the entourage present agreed that they would swear, if trouble arose, that the girl was Charlie Hodge's date and that he had provided the cough medicine on which they both got stoned. Every precaution was taken. All present were sworn to secrecy. Colonel Tom Parker who lived in Palm Springs was told of the situation in case it got out of hand.

Police Sergeant Richard Grob, of the Palm Springs police department, handled the investigation of the overdosed girl. But the file was closed the following day when the girl recovered. She had her stomach pumped at Palm Springs hospital and was given injections to counter-act the effects of the narcotic drug in the cough medicine. She was unconscious for seventeen hours, but then woke up and walked away. Caughley said it was a very close call. Richard Grob later joined Elvis's payroll, as head of security.

*   *   *   *   *

Sam Thompson, who became a Memphis judge, and Jerry Schilling, later to become a member of the team that took on the management of Elvis's estate, steering it from the brink of disaster, were the two men who Hutchinson found most useful in his conversations.

Schilling honestly related how Elvis's immunities to medication built up over the years, and it was not surprising considering the intensity of the workload, the constant pressure of the tours – turning on and turning off. He eventually had to seek more and stronger medication. Schilling believed that Nichopoulos tried desperately to control the situation.

When Schilling personally intercepted some medication which had arrived by courier from Las Vegas, he took it to Nichopoulos and asked what he should do. Nichopoulos said he wasn't getting any help from other doctors and was very disappointed. Between them, they devised a plan to see if Elvis was still trying to hide these shipments, even after promising to stick to the drug regime devised for him by Dr Nick. He told him to take the medication back and give it to Elvis. Two days later, Dr Nick told him that Elvis never reported receiving the drugs shipment, although they knew very well that he had. Nichopoulos had searched the Elvis's medicine chest and found the pills.

Sam Thompson, who went on all the tours with Elvis, was less inclined to find any justification for Nichopoulos, but he also agreed that if Nichopoulos refused Elvis any request for medication, Elvis would simply call up his pilot on the intercom and tell him to get out the plane, and fly off to another city in order to find some.

*   *   *   *   *

With dozens of witnesses interviewed, others were brought by subpoena to a series of grand jury hearings which were convened in Memphis. These included the testimony of Ginger Alden, David Stanley, his mother, Dee Stanley, and nurse, Tish Henley. Their evidence – because it related to grand jury testimony – remains secret. Under state law, the statement given by any witness in a grand jury hearing may not be revealed.

On 16 May 1980, the grand jury indicted Dr Nichopoulos on ten counts of over-prescribing drugs to patients, and one of over-prescribing to himself. Two of those named were Elvis Presley and Jerry Lee Lewis. Two others were former members of Elvis's entourage, Marty Lacker and Alan Fortas.

The trial itself was twice delayed for technical reasons and did not come to court until late September 1981. Dr Nichopoulos had lined up an impressive defence, led by the famed Watergate prosecutor James Neal, a tough and skilled attorney. Witness after witness was brought forward to verify that the doctor had prescribed all the drugs that were needed to support habits. And Neal took the most advantage from a situation where medical experts were ranged against each other from both sides to debate the possibility that Nichopoulos was following a programme of attempted reduction of his patients' reliance on prescription medication. The jury found themselves faced with an almost impossible task of attempting to distinguish between the conflicting medical evidence.

A very similar situation existed with Jerry Lee Lewis, who was also a regular patient of Dr Nick. Medical experts were brought on to the stand who would testify that in their opinion the doctor was trying to help his patients by continuing to prescribe the drugs to which they were addicted, only on lesser and weaker quantities, hoping eventually to wean them off them altogether.

Much still rested upon the evidence of one crucial witness for the prosecution – Dr Eric Muirhead, who had led the autopsy team at Baptist Memorial Hospital. But if the state prosecutor had placed great reliance on his testimony swaying the jury towards the view that Nichopoulos had helped cause Elvis's death by the continued prescription of such vast quantities of drugs, he would be sorely disappointed.

Once again, the secrecy of the autopsy report was protected, even though a man's livelihood and possible freedom were at stake.

The autopsy report would not be allowed into evidence because it remained a confidential document. The cause of Elvis's death could not be touched upon by Muirhead. He could not speculate on possible causes, or even challenge or support the official autopsy verdict that Elvis had died from natural causes.

From that moment, the case began to slip away from the prosecution. With great agility, Nichopoulos's lawyers repeated the defence – which had been produced at the disciplinary hearing against Nichopoulos – that he was a good and caring practitioner. Elvis Presley was a fine young man, said defender Neal, but one with many problems. If all that Nichopoulos did was with good intent, then he was not guilty of a crime. This the jury seemed to accept.

He was cleared of all charges.

★   ★   ★   ★   ★

The wheels of justice had turned slowly. Hutchinson was not alone in believing that the spectre of Elvis Presley remained a great influence in Memphis. The fame of the man still counted for a lot. And perhaps this was further confirmed by another fact – that autumn, when Nichopoulos was acquitted, the five men still awaiting trial on the various counts of defrauding Elvis Presley over his Jetstar, had still not been given a date for their hearing.

While their two former associates, Philip Kitzer and Frederick Pro, had already completed part of the sentences they were likely to serve for the Presley fraud and other matters, their five co-defendants were still on bail, reporting weekly to their bail office, almost *five years* after they were first arrested, following the federal grand jury hearings in October 1977.

Though the two prime witnesses in the case, Elvis and Vernon Presley, were now dead, the FBI documents show that all work on the case had long ago been concluded; no new evidence had been trawled, no new charges laid, no further documentation added.

The final chapter of the case involving Elvis's Jetstar was written in the official records in July 1982, when four men were each found guilty on one count of 'Violation of Title 18, United States Code Section 2314', interstate transportation of fraudulent devices. The twenty-one counts originally filed to the federal grand jury had evaporated. On 9 October 1982 they were sentenced: Raymond W.

244

Baszner was given an in-jail sentence of two years and six months, a suspended sentence of two years, placed on probation for two years and fined 2500 dollars. J. Laurence Wolfson was sentenced to two years, and fined 10,000 dollars. Nigel Winfield was given an in-jail term of three years, with two years and six months suspended sentence, placed on probation for two years and six months, and fined 10,000 dollars. Gabriel Robert Caggiano was given one year and six months in-jail term, with a one year and three month suspended sentence, and placed on probation.

In this way, the case of Elvis Presley's Jetstar and the fraud that cost him so dear sank quietly and unnoticed into the record books of the state legislature.

17

The Money-Go-Round

'In 1973, Elvis was only thirty-seven years old, and it was illogical for him to consider selling a lifetime's annuity from his catalogue of over 700 chart songs. The tax implications alone should have prohibited such an agreement or at least prohibited it without further tax investigation . . . thus I must state that Colonel Parker and RCA [Elvis's record company] were probably guilty of collusion, conspiracy, fraud, misrepresentation, bad faith and over-reaching . . .'

Blanchard E. Tual, lawyer for the Presley estate, 1980

By 1980, the Elvis Presley estate had virtually collapsed into a morass of problems, litigation and liabilities. Elvis's inheritance to Lisa Marie appeared to be on the brink of liquidation. It was an unholy mess. Vernon himself had begun some actions before his death, trying to recover money and property from people who he considered should return it, in view of the perilous state of Lisa Marie's fund. Those with no formal agreements found themselves in difficulty. Linda Thompson's parents, for example, lived in a house owned by Elvis, and now the estate wanted it back. Ginger Alden's mother, Jo LaVern, had filed suit in Tennessee, claiming that Elvis had promised to pay her mortgage. Dr Nichopoulos himself had to formalise his loan agreement so that repayments were made to the estate. The racquetball venture also came to the estate looking for an arrangement to stave off liquidation and was eventually accommodated for fear of losing all the investment.

Other more serious matters were building, which dated back to the week after Elvis's death when Vernon was granted 'absolute discretion' as executor of the estate. The will, dated 3 March 1977, was declared true and valid by the probate judge, Joseph Evans, although one or two of the close entourage who had apparently anticipated being among the beneficiaries, made dark allegations about it being a fake. There was much talk around of the validity of the will. Charlie Hodge, Lamar Fike and Billy Smith made no secret of the fact that Elvis had told them he had left them some money. Billy Smith was apparently expecting something like 50,000 dollars. Charlie Hodge was questioned by Larry Hutchinson about the will.

'You were the closest to him, weren't you?' asked the investigator.

'He was my best friend.'

'Didn't it hurt you that you were in the will and then you weren't? There was a lot of talk around about people being upset.'

'No. I know I was supposed to be in the will, Billy Smith, Joe Esposito and myself were in. But I don't know whether Elvis and his daddy had come to another agreement.'

'Did you know there was another will?'

'I understood there were three wills. Elvis had made the first one out when he was dating Linda Thompson. That's the will I was in, along with Billy Smith, Joe Esposito and Lamar Fike. And Elvis came in one day and said, "I've taken Linda out of my will and I've taken Lamar out because he'd blow the money, anyway, but you and Billy and Joe are still in it." That was around the early part of 1977.'

'There is a lot of talk around that you and others were upset when you learned about the third will?'

'No. I was in the will and then I was taken out. It's OK, I get by.'

★　　★　　★　　★　　★

After Vernon's death, the new panel of executors, consisting of Priscilla Presley, Joe Hanks, who was Elvis's accountant, and the National Bank of Commerce, presented a petition to the Memphis court of probate to formalise their administration and to seek court approval of their financial transactions, including on-going payments to Colonel Parker.

Priscilla – who had recently re-adopted the surname of Presley – was herself said to be 'frankly shocked' at the lack of funds in the estate, and all avenues were being pursued to build up reserves. These included special licensing deals with marketing companies who would have exclusive rights to the manufacture and sale of Elvis memorabilia; Colonel Parker, who had been involved in the negotiations for a number of these contracts, would, under the terms of the arrangements he had made with Vernon, continue to take a percentage of the income.

However, matters would not be resolved as easily as he might have anticipated. There had already been a good deal of worry about the amount of commission Colonel Parker had taken from Elvis's earnings, both before and after his death. Some of the income was subject to a fifty-fifty split, and this was apparent to the judge as he read a fifty-page document detailing the estate's earnings since Elvis's death. Far from rubber-stamping the probate arrangements when the petition was presented, Judge Evans expressed his concern over the handling of the estate and ordered that Lisa Marie and all her interests should temporarily be protected by a guardian *ad litem*.

A court-appointed lawyer, Blanchard E. Tual, was given the task of preparing a full report on the finances of the estate, with special reference to the financial transactions involving Colonel Parker. He was instructed that the search should be retrospective, and should as far as possible include a statement setting out the whole structure and consequence of Parker's contracts with Elvis, dating to the earliest days of their association.

The judge wanted to know the basis for the proposals under which Parker would continue to receive a percentage of the estate's income, an enquiry which, said the judge, was particularly valid in view of the pressure on the financial standing of the estate, which might affect the fund that would eventually be available for Lisa Marie.

Until that report had been prepared and considered, the judge ruled that no further commissions should be paid to the colonel and that no outgoings could be allowed without the approval of the court guardian.

And so, while Larry Hutchinson was engaged in his mammoth task of gathering evidence to be presented at the trial of Dr Nick, another inquiry was underway, concerning the remaining funds in Elvis's estate – or, more precisely, the lack of them. Tual's task was complex and wide-ranging and, ten months later, on 23 July 1981, he went back to the probate court armed with an eighty-five-page report which, on the face of it, was a damning indictment of the way Presley's affairs had been handled by Colonel Parker and his record company, RCA, both of whom immediately and strenuously denied impropriety.

Tual first confirmed that the estate was indeed faced with a cash-flow problem, which he correctly revealed was a devastating disappointment, considering the money that Presley had generated during his lifetime. New estimates of his personal earnings were thought to have been in the region of 200 million dollars, and a conservative estimate of the business he had generated through films, records and merchandise was a staggering 3.5 billion dollars. Comparatively little remained, and what was left was in danger of being drained away by fees and running expenses. The Graceland mansion alone now cost 500,000 dollars a year to run (at that point it had not been opened to the public).

Tual acknowledged that Elvis himself had been a reckless spender during his lifetime and that tales of his extravagance and almost inexplicable generosity were easy to come by in Memphis. Furthermore, in the three years since Elvis's death, there had been an income of less than five million dollars, mostly in royalties from the sale of merchandise. But this asset was offset by Graceland's running costs, legal fees, promissory notes that Elvis left with the National Bank of Commerce, and the commitments elsewhere. Colonel Parker was also claiming his shares of the proceeds which went to the estate, and the Internal Revenue Service (IRS) had upgraded its original estimate of death duties; that year it slapped a demand on Priscilla, as chief executor, for 14.6 million dollars.

In the main, the Tual report argued that as sole inheritor of her father's estate, his name and his image entitled Lisa Marie – or the estate, on her behalf – to receive the lion's share of all merchandising royalties. Tual pointed out that this had been virtually impossible under arrangements inherited through agreements Elvis had signed with Colonel Parker during his lifetime. They dated back, he said, to 1956, when the first contract between them gave Parker twenty-five per cent of Presley's earnings. In 1963, when the merchandising side of the income had boomed during Elvis's years in Hollywood, a further deal was agreed, giving Parker fifty per cent of the net income from this source. Both of these agreements were to be superseded by a later arrangement under which Elvis agreed to a fifty-fifty split with Parker on all his net earnings. Tual described this arrangement as 'excessive, imprudent and beyond all reasonable bounds of record industry standards'.

He backtracked through the arrangement made in 1973, when Parker negotiated with RCA to sell them back the master tapes for every one of Elvis's records; it was a deal which, it will be recalled, meant that RCA bought Elvis's interest for 5.4 million dollars. In a nutshell, this meant that Elvis no longer received royalties from those recordings which included 'Hound Dog', 'Jailhouse Rock', 'Return to Sender' and many top hits from Elvis's collection. Tual noted that, of this figure, Elvis's share after taxes was a mere 1.25 million dollars, and he suggested that under these circumstances Parker would have found it difficult to deal with RCA 'at arm's length'.

The lawyer listed other deals from which Parker had benefited in grander terms than Presley. He noted that in 1974, Elvis netted 4.65 million dollars from variation deals for concerts, merchandising and the like, whereas Colonel Parker received 6.2 million dollars. He was also critical about the exclusive contracts Parker had signed with the Las Vegas International Hotel which, year after year, presented Elvis in concert. Parker, said Tual, had failed to seek higher fees elsewhere for Elvis's services in the gambling mecca, and he noted that Parker had a heavy line of credit available to him at the International casino, which he used regularly. Interestingly, Parker had been paid separately by the hotel for 'promotional services'.

There was one other curious aspect of the relationship between Parker and Presley that Tual commented upon. He noted that the colonel had always refused to allow Elvis to tour outside of the United States, in spite of the very lucrative markets that lay waiting to be tapped all around the world, especially in Europe and the Far East. Untold income could have been generated. Tual concluded that this was due to personal reasons in the secret history of Parker himself. Although his well-publicised biographical notes recorded him as being of American stock, born to a West Virginia couple while they were on tour with a carnival, other records showed that his name was Andreas Cornelius van Kuijk, born in Holland, who came to America when he was twenty.

To accompany Elvis overseas, Parker would have needed a passport, and Tual suggested that Parker did not in fact possess one. It had never been determined, he said, whether Parker had ever become a naturalised American, or if indeed his entry into the country was legal. For this reason, Tual concluded, the enormous potential exploitation of overseas markets for Elvis was never pursued and in the latter years Elvis had been confined to circling the United States of America where, eventually, the opportunities for appearances at major venues would begin to subside. Instead, he could have been touring the international stage where audiences were literally crying out for an appearance by the world's greatest entertainer.

Tual pointed out that the post-death merchandising agreements were also controlled by an agreement, set up by Parker and signed by Elvis, with a company named Boxcar Inc., in which Parker, his right-hand man, Tom Diskin, and Elvis shared the equity. In 1976, Parker took a salary from the company of 21,500 dollars, Diskin 27,000 dollars, and Elvis 6000 dollars. And the real benefits came flooding in *after* Elvis's death.

Before he had even been buried, Boxcar – under its permitted licence to control all merchandising – authorised a new company, Factors Inc., to exploit these rights. Factors tried to establish total exclusivity to everything concerning Presley's name and image, even going as far as suing a charitable organisation, the Memphis Development Foundation, in 1979, when it began selling statuettes of the star for twenty-five dollars, to help fund a permanent Elvis Presley memorial statue. The US district court granted the order prohibiting the sale of the statues, although the ruling was overturned on appeal.

All of this was totted up by lawyer Tual. 'Colonel Parker had to have been aware of Elvis's mental and physical deterioration at the time the agreements were made. He made a conscious decision to make as much money from Elvis before his inevitable premature death.'

Finally, Tual vented his feelings about Colonel Parker by calling upon a list of damning adjectives to describe his verdict on the situation; he accused Parker and RCA of 'collusion, conspiracy, fraud, misrepresentation, bad faith and over-reaching' and recommended that the court order the Presley estate to file an immediate suit against Elvis's former manager and record company, cancelling the past arrangements and calling for the return of an unspecified amount of money to which he said the estate was due. 'Lisa is entitled to the benefits of her father's talents and should not be deprived of them due to the self-dealing of her father's manager and record company.'

Judge Evans agreed and ordered the estate to begin actions against the two named parties not later than 12 November 1981, and Priscilla, acting on behalf of the estate, issued a writ soon afterwards, claiming five million dollars in damages from Parker, and the return of some of the copyrights on Elvis's life's work from RCA. Lawsuits began to accumulate. RCA defended its position and Parker began a counter-action, demanding half of all the estate's current income, assessed and backdated to the time of Elvis's death – a claim which was valued at some six million dollars.

Parker argued that his relationship with Elvis was not a normal manager–client relationship. He and Elvis had agreed between themselves that it was a business partnership and that they would share the proceeds equally. Parker would take care of all the arrangements for films, records and tours, and Elvis would turn up and perform. Parker said there were often huge logistical and administrative problems to be solved during the tours, ranging from the overseeing of up to 200 people, arranging transport, hotels, sound, etc., and on occasions the tours did not make a profit. When that happened he and Elvis also shared the losses.

This was the arrangement which lasted for the larger portion of Elvis's career. Neither the star nor his father had ever complained about the relationship or the financial arrangements, and had never suggested that it should be altered in any way. Furthermore, Vernon Presley had agreed after his son's death that the arrangement should continue – and that Parker should retain half of the net income.

Parker did not accept that anything had changed – except for the fact that his client was no longer alive. His argument had certain merits, sufficient to provide his lawyers with ammunition to fire back at Priscilla, who was a somewhat reluctant litigant in the first place. Mounting legal bills meant a further drain on the estate funds, which were already perilously close to vanishing.

And so, while the lawyers continued their battle, Priscilla, almost single-handedly, decided it was time for action. All around Grace-land, the pirates and the traders were making a fortune out of the image of her former husband. There was every imaginable item on sale, from phials of Graceland earth to copies of the press release issued by Dr Jerry Francisco recording death by heart trouble.

When Factors Inc. lost their appeal to stop the statues being sold by Memphis Development Foundation, the ruling stated that there was no copyright on the image of a dead person. This adjudication in itself had very considerable repercussions, not just for the Elvis estate, but for sales of merchandise relating to many other deceased stars in the state of Tennessee.

Almost in desperation, Priscilla began to fight back, to discover what she could salvage from the wreckage. In 1982, she formed Elvis Presley Enterprises, a foundation whose income would ultimately be transferred to a trust fund for her daughter. Among her first acts was to invest 500,000 dollars in the refurbishment of Graceland, which she then opened to the public. It was criticised in some quarters, but was certainly a sensible move, considering the simple fact that never a day passed without there being huge numbers of pilgrims travelling down Elvis Presley Boulevard. Most did no more than stand around, look at the house from the outside, and buy the tacky trinkets and souvenirs from a row of shops that had opened up across the road. Why not invite them in?

The investment paid off. The money was recouped within forty days of opening the house to the public. It became an immediate target for tourists and the tour buses and, within two years, more than 500,000 visitors were passing through the gates annually. By the end of the decade, the figure had reached 650,000 a year and Graceland became second only to the White House for the number of visitors received by any American home in a year.

The main source of income, however, was to come from the licensing of merchandise, and this was continuing to run away from the estate like water from burst pipe. They had absolutely no control over the Elvis industry. Next, then, Priscilla sought the advice of a young, high-flying Los Angeles lawyer, Roger Richman, who specialised in such matters. He decided that the only way the estate could regain control was by persuading the Tennessee legislature to pass a new law which would retrospectively grant that the rights and image of any star, sportsman or other celebrity would automatically pass to that person's heirs and estate. He had already promoted similar legislation in the state of California, where the descendability rights laws were passed to protect the exploitation of dead stars.

Richman was formally hired by the Presley estate to draw up a bill of rights, entitled the Personal Rights Protection Act, which was then submitted to the Tennessee state offices. Richman explained, 'When the estate approached me, I became collaterally involved as a basis for assisting them. I drew up the suggested bill and they found the legislators to promote it.' His bill became known as the Tennessee

253

Celebrity Rights Law, and was passed in 1983. It became the model to end all unlicensed souvenir and posters sales throughout the United States, and, indeed, the Western world, where copyrights were adhered to. 'It was a logical step,' said Richman:

Firms like Coca-Cola go to the end of the earth to protect their name, so why shouldn't a person, or the estate of a dead person, have similar rights? It had all gotten out of hand and it was not just a matter of money, of securing the royalties on manufactured goods. When pirates were making products like dildos with facial images on the end, or were manufacturing birthday cards showing Marilyn Monroe snorting cocaine, they were quite obviously overstepping the mark with horrendous bad taste. It was designed to stop this kind of thing as much as anything.

Richman, incidentally, went on to become adviser to the estates of more than forty celebrities, including James Dean and Sigmund Freud.

Priscilla and her advisers then sought to take complete control of all Elvis merchandise. The estate subsequently regained control of the exclusive rights granted to Factors Inc. by Tom Parker's Boxcar company, and once the new law had passed into the Tennessee statute book, the rights were handed over to Curtis Management, a company specialising in licensing rights. A subsidiary company, Curtis Publishing, then employed a bank of legal eagles led by lawyer Mark Roesler to police all merchandise sales and to take action against any company producing unlicensed material.

Slowly, but surely, Priscilla and her team had tackled the problems that had beset the estate. The legal tussle between the estate, Tom Parker and RCA records was quietly resolved. They reached an out-of-court settlement, in which Parker relinquished claims on the estate, and eventually the estate agreed to purchase from him a very large stock of Elvis memorabilia. This included, it was rumoured, a batch of love letters written by Priscilla to Elvis. The figure was never revealed, but was rumoured to be in the region of ten million dollars.

The estate also reclaimed certain royalty rights from RCA and within four years of facing the gloomy possibility of Lisa Marie's inheritance running towards bankruptcy, Priscilla had turned the whole Elvis remembrance business into a highly profitable organisation.

Control of merchandise is strict and unwavering. Several lawsuits have been filed over the years against unlicensed producers, and one British firm, run by Sid Shaw from Shoreditch, discovered to its great cost (in legal fees) that it was virtually impossible to break the monopoly.

When the ensuing action came to court, the estate lawyers held with great derision one of the firm's products, a pair of 'Elvisly Yours' girl's knickers, which they said was a desecration of the memory of Elvis. Shaw submitted that Elvis had never had any scruples about wiping his perspiring face with fans' knickers at his concerts, so why should the estate object now? He lost his case and was barred from selling any of his products in the United States.

By the start of the Nineties, such rigorous policing of the Elvis image had paid handsome dividends. In 1991, the estate was valued at an estimated 75 million dollars – a far greater wealth than Presley had ever accumulated in his lifetime – and the estate's net annual income had risen from a million dollars a year in 1979, to in excess of fifteen million dollars. The estate's business manager, Jack Soden, meanwhile, continues to marshal the guards and to maintain quality control over the merchandising, even down to keeping check – as far as they can – on the activities of the worldwide brotherhood of Elvis impersonators. It permits the Elvis impersonation contest to be held annually in Graceland, and the work of some of the more successful mimics. Those who are making a decent living at it are eventually contacted, auditioned and, if they pass the test, licensed. Television programmes and documentary producers have to apply to the estate for any use of songs and archive material, which the estate now controls.

Soden says that the estate continually tries to raise their standards and are willing to help those who wish to use the Elvis image, as long as these standards are met. So, in death, Elvis is being portrayed within the bounds of a far greater vision of morality than ever existed at Graceland and its surrounds when he was alive.

★   ★   ★   ★   ★

Meanwhile, the young beneficiary whose estate now keeps a management team and a bank of lawyers in constant employment, has been largely shielded from the tackiness of the battles over her father's memory and finances, as well as being protected by Priscilla from public glare during her teenage years. In 1992, Lisa Marie, twenty-four, lived in Beverly Hills with her husband Danny Keough, a musician who she married in 1989, and their two-year-old daughter. She wants to become an actress. She will assume control of her inheritance when she is thirty.

But there has been speculation that the replenished fortunes of the Elvis Presley estate might yet be diverted in part to other quarters. This follows Lisa Marie's association with the Church of Scientology, the cult religion founded by L. Ron Hubbard. She attended the Celebrity Centre International, which is known locally as a spiritual detoxification centre, run by scientologists. Those who attend the centre are encouraged to confess past sins and remain loyal to the beliefs of the religion.

18

Who Killed Elvis?

Slowly but surely the loose ends that remained after Elvis's death were dealt with, though many questions lay unanswered. The entourage had scattered. Relatives and some members of Elvis's inner circle remained in Memphis, attempting to build new lives and new careers. Others took off to pastures new, mostly in Los Angeles. Some, like Sam and Linda Thompson, Joe Esposito and Jerry Schilling successfully moved on and forged new and successful lives for themselves.

Several others picked away at the carcass for as long as they were able and finally had to settle for a much reduced lifestyle compared to the glamorous but pressurised existence that had come with their respective jobs. Gone were the expensive gifts, the ever-ready generosity of the man who supported them for all of his working life – the new cars at Christmas, the jewellery and cash hand-outs.

Several of the lesser members of the group are today sad cases, burned out by life with Elvis and the excesses that mirrored his own. Most, whatever their circumstances, are unable to shake off the spectre of the man.

Dr Nichopoulos resumed his practice in Memphis and continued to pay off the loan he had from Elvis. He reckoned it had cost him 300,000 dollars in legal fees to fight the charges of over-prescribing, though some of his regular patients in the Memphis Greek community took a collection and raised a substantial sum towards that. Today, he talks slowly and methodically about the past, thinking out his answers to questions about Elvis, as if he were still on trial.

Colonel Parker retired to his home in Palm Springs to write a book which will probably not be published in his lifetime. He is the man with the secrets. According to Todd Slaughter, director of the official Elvis Presley fan club, who knows Parker well, he is not the ogre he is made out to be. Slaughter is virtually lynched by fans whenever he makes that statement at conventions.

Beneath this heavy layer of former associates of Elvis who had to come to terms with life after he had gone, there remains a fermentation among the dregs of the whole murky business. Somehow the story of Elvis, either in life or death, does not make sense, just does not ring true. As I said at the beginning of this work, there have been plenty of theories.

Albert Goldman in his biography, *Elvis*, published in 1981, concluded that Elvis had died from drug abuse. He based this conclusion on the scientific analysis which said there were traces of up to eleven separate drugs in Elvis's body when he died. Ten years later, in a smaller volume, *Elvis: The Last Twenty-four Hours*, he admitted he had placed too much reliance on some of his informants for the biography. For his new book, he chose to go on the evidence of David Stanley, who had recently concluded that Elvis had committed suicide by consuming a cocktail of drugs that he knew would put him to sleep forever. Goldman wrote a thesis on this proposition which became the cover story for *Life* magazine.

He used Stanley's testimony, which had already been expounded in Britain, in the *Sunday Mirror*, that when Elvis took his last pill he knew he was going to die. Stanley claimed that the last time he'd seen Elvis, three days earlier, Elvis had said to him, 'David, take care of yourself. I'll never see you again on earth . . .' Based upon this and his own re-examination, Goldman argued that everything that Presley's life stood for had ended. The fun had gone, his talent was shot, he was bloated and impotent, his love life was a shambles and in the cold light of day, he knew he was totally addicted to drugs. He could not face it any longer, and ended his life the day before he was due to go back on tour. Goldman said he believed death had become an obsession, and that Elvis meant to take his own life; that for this end he had built up a cache of drugs in the previous twenty-four hours.

This expansion of David Stanley's theory was unsurprisingly supported by David's mother Dee Stanley who, at the time, was preparing her own new book, the fourth written by a member of the Stanley family. She claimed to have seen a suicide note which Elvis left for Vernon, but was unable to produce it because it had been destroyed. It was one of the many claims that she made and some were clearly aimed at lurid sensationalism. Her book, *The Intimate Life and Death of Elvis*, trawled up all the bad stories about Elvis and rolled them into one horrific package that provided the *National Enquirer*, who serialised it, several weeks of headlines, beginning with: ELVIS AND HIS MOM WERE LOVERS and following up with HIS BRUTAL RAPE OF PRISCILLA. All of these 'new' facts were emerging in the Nineties, ten years after Dee Stanley had written her first book with her sons, called *Elvis: We Love You Tender*.

The suicide theory was never mentioned in her earlier book. Nor does Rick Stanley support this view. He denounced it as unlikely and admitted that in the mid–Eighties, when he had discussed the prospect as an idea for another book with his brother David, he had been thinking of the dollar signs and not the ethics of the situation. He now says suicide was unlikely.

Very few people who were truly in touch with the situation could support the theory, either. Joe Esposito and others at the sharp end of life with Elvis said it was a ridiculous idea. I have been unable to find anyone who seriously believes it was a possibility.

Another reasoned assessment of Elvis's death was presented by Charles Thompson and James Cole, the two Memphis journalists who worked on the Elvis story for ABC's '20/20' programme. In their 1991 book, *The Death of Elvis*, a parochial account of their own investigation of the story, they submitted that Elvis died from multiple drug ingestion. Their final conclusion was that Elvis was allergic to codeine, which he had taken hours before his death, and that was the key factor which activated his lapse into a coma induced by polypharmacy. The basic flaw in that argument, as Goldman later pointed out, was that Elvis had consumed codeine medication in very considerable quantities for years.

And this brings us back to Dr Jerry T. Francisco, the county medical examiner, who first pronounced death by natural causes at eight p.m. on the night of 16 August, and continues to reiterate that to this day. His assessment of the cause of death solicits agreement among many of those who have written on the subject – that natural causes was least likely. Francisco denies that there could be any basis for believing any of the above theories. As far as he is concerned they are just as far-fetched as the 'Elvis Lives' brigade. Death was by natural causes, heart problems unrelated to drugs. Death was natural, and death was not by foul play, or an intentional administration of a drugs cocktail either by Presley himself or by any other person.

That was Francisco's view even before the autopsy was actually completed and he has not deterred from it in twenty-five years. He refutes the Goldman suicide theory, he rejects the Thompson-Cole suggestion, as he did the '20/20' television programme, which they researched. Meanwhile, the autopsy report remains locked away from public view and he refuses – or is unable – to reveal the contents.

It remains one of the most controversial documents in existence in the Elvis story, if only for the fact that no one outside the Baptist Memorial medical team and Vernon Presley have seen the full text. The single most crucial issue is what killed Elvis Presley. Francisco has repeated and repeated that there were insufficient amounts of any drug to kill him. Others have disagreed, making assessments based on the leaked contents of the chemical analysis of his body tissues and blood, which showed what would normally be a fatal concentration of at least three dangerous drugs, and traces of numerous others. It is also, however, a fact that Elvis had become very used to these drugs. It would not be difficult, either, to come up with several case histories from the entertainment profession who were known users of prescription and hard street drugs at equal, if not higher, amounts than those taken by Elvis on the night he died.

Put to a jury, as indeed it was, when George Nichopoulos was charged and cleared, it would be hard for any prosecution case to prove that Elvis died of drugs. A mass of medical experts could be brought to the witness stand for both sides, each armed with sufficient data to prove or disprove any point at issue.

It would be equally difficult, as has also been shown by similarly conflicting medical opinion, to prove that he died from natural causes, and especially the heart problems suggested by the medical examiner. That issue was in dispute before Elvis was even buried.

★   ★   ★   ★   ★

There came another theory, bred by Dr Nichopoulos, which surfaced a decade after his own trial – at which his lawyers conceded he was all but being accused of murdering Presley by implication, and was cleared. In 1990, he came out with the startling claim in the synopsis for a book he was preparing, entitled *Who Killed Elvis Presley?* in which he stated that Elvis did not die of drugs or natural causes, but that he was murdered by a blow to the back of the head, probably a karate chop which broke his neck. He reiterated his own qualifications for making such an assessment – that he was in the ambulance that took Elvis to hospital, and that he was present at the autopsy. He said that in his view, Elvis had been dead for at least three hours, probably longer. There was no hope of saving him.

He stated that he had finally revealed this information after thirteen years of keeping silent because he was fed up with being blamed for Elvis's death. He would not say whether or not he had volunteered this theory to Vernon, and explained that it had not been possible to do so at his own trial. The question of what killed Elvis Presley had been ruled by the presiding judge as inadmissible speculation in the absence of the production of the autopsy report as evidence. Nichopoulos believed it would have been easy for the autopsy technicians to have missed the injury to the neck, because their major concern was with the organs of the body.

Needless to say, Dr Francisco denied the possibility of murder, or a broken neck, or any other cause of violent death with the same vehemence that he denied the possibility of death by drugs or suicide. Even Nichopolous, in an interview from his office in Memphis on 26 October 1992, backed away from his earlier claim. He now wanted to say that the murder theory was just one of a number that he had discussed with his ghost writer.

And so, for the past dozen years or more, the pundits have been arguing amongst themselves. Let us now go a little deeper and try to discover an underlying cause for this division of opinion.

Consideration of all the background activity that surrounded Elvis at the time of his death has never been given a serious airing. Television programmes and books have used rumours about FBI documents to either support or ridicule the silly claim that Elvis is alive. But there is good reason to consider these facts.

The sheer volume of the FBI documents I have seen relating to the securities fraud demonstrates with supreme clarity that the bureau must have been worried sick when it became known Elvis was dead. There can have been no other reaction. The shock waves that ran through the entire investigative operation were confirmed to me from three separate FBI sources.

Knowing what was going on at the time, knowing that there were undercover agents still in the field and knowing some of the names who were said to be involved, even the most slender link with Elvis ought to have been sufficient to merit a closer investigation of his death. The very big link which actually existed was even more reason why someone, somewhere, should have said: What really happened?

Vernon Presley himself persisted with his enquiries to ascertain whether or not foul play was involved. He obviously believed it was a possibility – quite understandable in the light of his knowledge of the background activity.

He voiced his suspicions to members of the Elvis entourage on separate occasions; they in turn have repeated his suspicions publicly. And from the various versions of the story, it is possible to conclude that literally anyone could have walked into Graceland that morning, perhaps as early as nine a.m., when the house would be peaceful, and most of those who had been up with Elvis during the night were sleeping. While Elvis's minder, Rick Stanley, was himself – and by his own description – knocked out on Demerol, the intruder could have padded quietly upstairs and along the corridors to Elvis's bedroom. There, he would have found Ginger Alden sound asleep. Elvis was in the bathroom, drowsy from the medication he had already taken and ready to consume his last batch of pills that would make him sleep. The intruder could have been someone he knew.

Vernon himself had believed there was evidence of some kind of struggle, which would account for the disarray in the bathroom reported by the paramedics; a mess which was cleared away by the time they came back to pick up their gear. It is within the realms of possibility that Elvis was knocked to the ground or even injected with multiple drugs. David Stanley says he picked up four syringes that day and threw them away.

It is easy to speculate on possibilities, and to theorise on reasons. No one, not even the advocates of a natural death, has been able to put forward a fully convincing or provable case, and perhaps no one ever will because of the haste in which the death of Elvis was disposed of by public officials.

The question is, Why?

Larry Hutchinson, the district attorney's investigator, believed that in part Memphis wanted to bury its famous, wealthy son – someone who was highly regarded, and was known for his kindness and generosity – with the minimum of fuss. But, as Vernon knew, there werc several situations that could have been the motive for foul play, and collectively, the FBI knew far more about the circumstances abounding at the time.

One other key element in the equation, which has, perhaps, been overlooked, is Elvis's money – or, rather, lack of it. He earned millions of dollars in his lifetime. We have already discussed the figures. They are astronomical, as was the cash he generated throughout the many sidelines that fed off his career; merchandising, for example. Yet, in 1967, when he was at the peak of his movie career, he had to borrow what ought to have been a paltry 500,000 dollars to buy his ranch. In 1968, when his movie carccr had ended, he had to go straight out on the road again to get a quick cash injection. In 1977, after eight years of continuous touring around America, earning many, many more millions (7.4 million dollars in 1974 alone) he died broke. His liabilities, debts and pledges outweighed his assets and cash at the bank. He would have to have gone on earning for another two or three years without spending another penny just to pay off what he owed.

Where had all the money gone? Not just the money from recent income, but all the way down the years of such massive earnings? We know he gave away millions, bought cars for everyone from his shoeshine boy to his dentists. His living expenses were enormous. His wider family group and his cntourage cost plenty to keep up. But surely there should have been something left?

One way or another, surplus money, after paying his commissions to Tom Parker and his tax dues to the IRS, was siphoned away to some other source. In reviewing the material for this book with Elvis 'experts', all agreed that murder was a feasible proposition. One suggested there were rumours of a long-standing blackmail, or some element in his past which brought him into contact with organised crime, long before the fraud case ever appeared on the horizon, dating back perhaps to army days.

In hindsight, that curious journey to Washington to see President Nixon and J. Edgar Hoover might, as we look back, easily be interpreted as a cry for help. He invented his ideas for drug prevention and his views on the Beatles as a cover for deeper personal worries which he wanted to discuss. His letter to the president, for instance, was suggested by the US senator he happened to be travelling with. Could it really have been a silly effort on his part to get a federal narc's badge? Or was there some ulterior motive that remains undiscovered? Even Priscilla Presley could not explain this strange episode.

The darker scenario, then, is this: Elements of organised crime had been in the background of his life for many years and were being paid off by a slice of his income. Lately, he had become tiresome, worryingly temperamental and unreliable. In 1977, it became known on the criminal grapevine that Elvis and his father were to be key witnesses in the fraud case, which had wider implications leading ultimately to some known personalities of La Cosa Nostra. Suddenly, Elvis became expendable. His career was precariously balanced. Anyone close to him knew that he could not continue his career and lifestyle much longer. The drugs, as John O'Grady testified, had taken a massive toll on his ability to perform. He was a physical and financial wreck.

Outside in the real world into which he seldom ventured, criminals were floating worthless paper, purported to have a face value worth billions of dollars, into banks around the world. There was talk of gambling links in the Caribbean and drugs cartels on the periphery. The whole operation was under threat. And as the FBI's undercover operation came to the ears of Mafia network, along with the news that Elvis was flashing his federal badge around once again, one of those ghosts from the star's past gave the order: neither Elvis or Vernon must ever go to court.

And neither of them ever did.

Index